Searching For Elsewhere

Graeme Johanson

Searching For Elsewhere

To any who are lost, who struggle to find their way.

Searching For Elsewhere
ISBN 978 1 76109 559 7
Copyright © text Graeme Johanson 2023

First published 2023 by
Ginninderra Press
PO Box 3461 Port Adelaide 5015
www.ginninderrapress.com.au

Contents

One: Bruises, Brethren and Bibles	7
Two: The Inside Track	21
Three: Others	53
Four: Mother in the Mix	80
Five: Father and his Nemesis	111
Six: Can't buy love	139
Seven: Eccentricity	169
Eight: Learning	198
Nine: Ruptures	228
Ten: Mould-breaking	259
Eleven: Arrival	279

One

Bruises, Brethren and Bibles

My back garden was a crucible for experimentation with my two older brothers. They acquired an air rifle, and they used my ankles for target practice.

For weeks, they had tried to shoot down sparrows and myna birds from the edges of spoutings around the eaves of our Canterbury house. Whoosh smack. I went bird spotting with them, but I do not recall them ever succeeding in a killing with the air rifle.

Together they asked me to act as a decoy. At the age of eight, I was naïve and unaware of danger. They were old enough to know better – David was fifteen and Peter was eleven – but were driven by the boredom of Plymouth Brethren requirements that we never play with non-Brethren friends, at home or elsewhere in groups, and by their growing belief that Brethren were grossly deficient when it came to providing exuberant excitement or entertainment. They needed to let off steam.

So I became the sacrificial lamb. I was conscripted to prance backwards and forwards within a confined section of the garden near the woodshed, while they took potshots with lead pellets from a distance. I never had ballet lessons, but this experiment was an assured incentive to leap high.

Complying with target practice, I put on my thickest long, woollen school socks, with the green and red bands at the top folded over my elastic garters on both calves. I never reported the victimisation to an adult in the family. I tenderly rubbed the deep bruises, not cuts, which resulted, and requested the brothers that they limit practice to some days apart, so that my bruises had time to heal. Using me did not improve their accuracy in any way, because (to my relief) most shots missed entirely.

After weeks of cooperation, I realised that acting as a living target required minimal skills, and I told my parents of my boredom with the trial, not that I had any sense of risks. The ankle-shooting ceased instantly.

Near the same woodshed, occasionally Father chopped the head off one of our home chooks, in the interests of initiating an unusual treat of roast chicken. I watched the chosen bird run madly from the chopping block around the lawn headless for a few seconds. Smelling the removal of the lurid gizzards and gazing at the plucking of its warm feathers were much less interesting. They turned me off.

The beheaded chook gave David and Peter a fresh idea. One of them grabbed a tardy hen from its pen while the other tied it by the legs, upside down, to a wire on the rotary clothes hoist. Then they spun the hoist madly with the chook squawking wildly as it veered around in tight circles. When it was untied and released onto *terra firma* again, it rushed crazily in all directions, bumping into obstacles and collapsing in a heap from exhaustion and vertigo. Usually, full of mirth, we retrieved the sad bird from the garden and returned it to the pen – for another whirl another time. But when one hen died from the stress, the dejected brothers were banned (again) from persecution permanently.

Until just after my twenty-first birthday – from 1946 to 1968 – I belonged to the strict religious community known as the Plymouth Brethren. Among Brethren, I often felt like my long-suffering ankles, or the disoriented chook, enduring unwarranted physical, emotional, and mental brutality beyond my control.

Quite early at primary school I was asked if I was a Christian. I had hardly heard the word Christian and knew little about it.

'No,' I tried to explain. 'I am one of the saints who gather in the name of the Lord Jesus Christ' (based on Hebrews 10:10).

Reciting that elongated title of our minor religion had been drilled into me by my parents. Explaining conundrums by means of biblical bits we regarded as completely sufficient, simply because they came from the Bible, however obscure their meaning.

'Who are the saints?' asked my playtime inquisitor in the schoolyard. 'Do you belong to the footy club?' The Saint Kilda Football Club was known as the Saints.

'No way. Instead of going to church, I go to meetings.' I tried hard to explain, but it only confused.

'Crikey.' The bewildered boy looked dumbfounded, threw up his hands and walked away.

No doubt before long, I was marked out as an oddball across the playground.

It is said that there were about forty thousand Plymouth Brethren worldwide at that time, and about the same number still now, although how it is estimated and how accurate it is, cannot be determined. The membership sizes cited by Brethren themselves are bound to be inflated. It is stated (by insiders and outcasts alike) that Brethren are more numerous in total (perhaps twenty thousand?) in Australia than in any other country, but again statistical proof is impossible to find. They refuse to contribute to government censuses and belong to a confusing array of hybrid subdivisions anyway.

The Faroe Islands in the north Atlantic Ocean have the honour of hosting the most Brethren per capita (at 13%). Thanks are due to a Plymouth Brethren missionary who arrived from Scotland on a fishing trawler in 1865, and was sufficiently astute to realise that using the vernacular for worship was the best means to attract converts. But before then, the populace had been fully softened up for conversions of one sort or another, anyway, if not in their own tongue – first by Celtic priests, then by Viking deities, followed by Catholic bishops blessed by the Pope, and lastly by Danish Lutherans who beheaded the last bishop in 1540.

The USA always had far fewer Brethren, although evangelical sects there have borrowed Brethren ideas (for example, dispensationalism) and in the 1950s Scientology in the US imitated the Brethren practice of auditing newcomers. The wide spread of Brethren is a testimony to the influence of early imperial missionaries of British origin on European expatriates in the colonies. Plymouth Brethren actually began in Dublin in the 1820s in spite of the use of Plymouth in their name. They were in Western Australia as early as 1839.

The founder, John Nelson Darby (1800–1882), anxiously took control of Brethren in Plymouth in a bold coup and consolidated them under his wing in 1845. He was forceful and very familiar with politics: his godfather was Admiral Lord Nelson, and he himself had just escaped a religious revolution in Switzerland. His ambit claims in Plymouth caused the first major Brethren split, creating a branch called 'Open Brethren', who disagreed with Darby and the Plymouth Brethren over the proper timing of baptism, and the role of the Holy Spirit in the holy Trinity (God the Father, Jesus the Son, and the Holy Ghost). These disagreements seem inconsequential today. Because of their enthusiasm for embracing any self-professed Christian, at present Open Brethren disown Plymouth/Exclusive Brethren, and as a result have grown far larger than any other brand of Brethren.

Australia's ex-prime minister, Scott Morrison, spent time at university researching the successful recruitment efforts of Open Brethren. He was laissez faire about Christian differences, saying in 2022, 'I've never been that fussed about denominations. I just like a community, Bible-based church.'

Many early Plymouth Brethren were like him, dipping into various Christian creeds ad lib. A founder of Pentecostalism (the plumber Smith Wigglesworth) belonged to Brethren for years.

Very little is understood publicly about the Plymouth Brethren currently, let alone in the past, and mostly their reputation is negative. They have only themselves to blame for bad publicity, which is due to their shyness, secrecy, and antisocial customs. It is impossible to understand them properly without referring briefly to their evolution.

The long moniker of 'the saints who gather in the name of the Lord

Jesus Christ' proved far too much of a mouthful for most outsiders, let alone as a descriptor for distinguishing religious concepts, so for simplicity they were just dubbed Plymouth Brethren by other religious denominations in the UK and, as a series of British colonies, Australia followed suit. Denomination mattered a lot more to adherents in the past than it does today.

At every election time – state, federal and municipal – the adults in my family had to account for their deliberate refusal to vote. The Electoral Commission regularly sent a 'show cause' form with a threat to fine Father, Mother, and my aunt for non-compliance.

I asked my father why he did not vote.

'Because the Bible says that we should render unto Caesar the things which are Caesar's, and unto God the things that are God's.' He paraphrased Matthew 22:21.

'What is Caesar?' I asked. Why did he have a role?

'It's government,' he replied curtly.

'What do you give to him?' I wanted to know.

'What the law says that I have to.'

'What do you write on the government form?' I persisted, not easily thrown off the trail. I suspected a twist.

'Just "Plymouth Brethren",' he confessed.

I felt a real let-down that I had to profess to belong to 'the saints who gather in the name of the Lord Jesus Christ' at school, while the government allowed Father to get away with just two words. In any case, not participating in elections hardly seemed necessary when I realised that our local member of parliament was the prime minister of Australia, Robert Menzies, who remained in continuous control of our electorate for seventeen years (until 1966). I once shook his chubby hand and was congratulated in his deep bass voice at my graduation.

It took me years to learn what was included in Caesar's orbit, and what not, because the difference seemed arbitrary. For instance, Plymouth Brethren did not vote because God alone decided election results, but they paid taxes and parking fines. Elections looked very like Caesar to me, as much as did any taxes, so I found it impossible to unravel the theological contortions.

For my first fourteen years, Brethren moved with the pace and the predictable direction of a glacier. God hijacked the never-never: eternal life was guaranteed in heaven only if I asked sincerely to be saved from hell by Jesus while I was on earth. Faith alone was viable, no other dreams being permitted. Faith trumped all logic. Brethren alone controlled what was in store for the chosen few, and any hope. Having any other vision for a prosperous or fulfilling life was unheard of. They trimmed my sails.

The Bible, as translated by none other than John Nelson Darby, was treated as the font of all truth. Interpretation of the Bible posed many problems, a fact that this memoir explores, but the irrefutable sanctity of the black book itself attracted myths and supernatural powers which were retold with fearful reverence. More than once, I was told solemnly of the religious soldier in World War II who kept a Bible in his haversack. When he was shot by the Nazis, the bullet went almost right through the Bible, but stopped at a place in the text that God meant the soldier to note. Fortuitously, the bullet did not reach his body, stopping at Psalm 91. The moral: God 'will command His angels concerning you to guard you in all your ways' (Psalm 91.11). I was awestruck by the miracle, lost for words – as much at the second retelling of the miracle as at the first. My mouth fell wide open.

The vital role of the Bible in our lives was described lucidly by another Brethren escapee (and poet) in Vancouver, Roy Daniells:

> Having no creed, no priesthood, no sacred edifices or holy days, no Book of Common Prayer or Order of the Mass, [Brethren] were committed to the Bible, those square black letters bitten into the white page. We learnt it by heart...the words were more firm and immediate in our minds than our own names and addresses...

Then an eruption hit: a major global split in 1960–1961 led to well-recalled bedlam. Reference to any Biblical mystery or wonder was jettisoned. The Bible became a book of punishment solely. To insiders, it was really the end of everything 'Plymouth'. Open Brethren went out of their way to dissociate from the Exclusive branch. The mainstream – ruled by a new dictator – were labelled 'Exclusive Brethren' by the mass media, and many of the two thousand or so who were ejected in protest in Australia called themselves the 'Outs'.

The Exclusive Brethren 'withdrew from' my family in 1962 when they classed us as 'iniquity' (2 Timothy 2:19). We were pushed out because we supported my older brother David to go to Oxford University for a postgraduate degree.

But my family were not done with Brethren. In 1962, we were still fearful and gutless. We gravitated to a remnant rump of 'Outs' in Melbourne for a short period, my parents deeply hurt and insulted by the ejection from the Exclusive Brethren and fuming at the self-appointed dictator who caused the mayhem.

Once again, a name became problematical. The rejects had no name other than 'Outs', defined solely by what they left behind. I invent the name 'rump' for them, trying to clarify the confusion of hybrids. They believed that soon thousands of others would flock to join them. They did not. They tried desperately, with about three hundred wounded in Melbourne, to return to the old habits of the 1950s. The tiny group fired up, licked its wounds but dissipated and faded away altogether within eight years because the old formula was unsustainable. It appeared spent, desiccated and lifeless. I finally left this rump of 'Out' Brethren in 1968 before its final disintegration, and Open Brethren absorbed most of the handful of rump survivors.

Meanwhile, the hardline Exclusive Brethren regrouped under the tyrant, Bruce Hales Senior, described later, and made an ambit claim by registering their logo as 'The Plymouth Brethren Christian Church', with the primary aim of collecting handouts in the form of Australian government funds, and in an effort to re-create reputational continuity with the 1840s. In fact, after 1960 they broke with all old Brethren traditions radically. Open Brethren no longer allowed themselves to be labelled 'Plymouth', as they had often done in the past. Now, the Exclusives hide behind a lucrative law firm which defends them against threats of defamation, and a public relations company which tries to concoct a positive image. For ample evidence of self-promotion, just peruse their website.

Beginning on a large scale in 1960, Brethren acquired all the features of an introverted cult, and invited opprobrium from government and the media for arrogant over-control of members, breaking up families and cutting off ex-members cruelly from relations and heritage. Suicides and mental breakdowns proliferated. Their self-appointed boss became as omnipotent as the pope, but without even the moderating pantomime of cardinals or priests to advise. During other historical periods, they had gloried in names associated with strict behaviours and exclusive beliefs, but within social standards of some decency for their times, and only in the past decade have they felt it necessary to emerge nervously from their tight-lipped seclusion and silence to lock horns reluctantly with mass media.

Innumerable divisions and subdivisions of Brethren over the past hundred and eighty years resulted in offshoots and variations around the globe, with concomitant name variations that are impossible to track consistently. They split like the variants of a bad virus. An upshot of the many ructions and separations over generations is a plethora of group names that causes any attempt at tracing lineage or origins to become impossibly entangled and meaningless; I have never known anyone to create a successful chart with all dates and locations of changes. The causes of divisions were doctrinal and political, internal and external, local and international, and emanated from strong individuals or single-minded cadres.

Divisions were usually the result of prolonged internal squabbles over petty points of doctrine, such as the timing of baptism (baby or adult?) or whether a convert should be just sprinkled with water or completely immersed at baptism. Any group that was caused by division required another name to differentiate it from the other parts of the segmentation, which may be more than one part, even though the resultant segments might create meetings consisting of only two families or individuals. Thus a false impression of immense profusion was created by dispersal. Some reminiscences, such as those by the well-known radio personality, Garrison Keillor in Minnesota, gave the impression that Brethren groups like those of his childhood were monolithic. They were not. On the whole, they were fragile, scattered and isolated, like dying species in a dry desert.

This memoir merges my personal development with my experiences of a stable life in my family and a community of Plymouth Brethren and (for a couple of years) with the pandemonium that destroyed the Plymouth culture in the turmoil that was Exclusive Brethren. It deals very little with my adult life.

My parents already had two sons before I came along and they were expecting a baby girl. They had no name ready for me, so for weeks I was Robert, then John and finally Graeme – just in time for official registration of my birth. The parents of another Brethren baby (Max Maynard) forgot to register him altogether, so that he was never sure of his birth date. The reason: 'they were so occupied with the Lord that they forgot'. Both my parents were born into Plymouth Brethren families, Father in Adelaide in 1909 and Mother in Kyneton in 1912. About twenty years from the end of their lives – in the 1970s – they left all Brethren and joined the Church of Christ, clinging to the familiar security of fundamentalism.

The timespan of this memoir extends roughly to a century, but my story does not follow strict chronological order. Rather, it favours themes over a sequence of dated events. It is to be expected that an early childhood such as mine that was strictly controlled by oppressive religious ideas and practices should embed anxiety and guilt in me, but at the same time my family and immediate community provided welcomed reassurance, self-respect, stimulation and predictability as I grew.

Born in 1946 in Melbourne as a post-war baby boomer, I was heir to relative political peace, economic prosperity and shared conservative social values. Most families in my suburb paused on Sundays for church and a roast.

Although my own emotional life felt disordered, in my childhood Brethren habits could be relied on not to change while much transformed around them. Susan Swingler's description of staying at her grandparents' home in Kent, England, at the same age as me was familiar although it occurred on the other side of the globe. Her old folk were strict Plymouth Brethren.

> I embraced the ways of my grandmother's house unquestioningly. When staying…at night, after hot milk and malt, I knelt by the side of the bed and said my prayers. I was allowed to have one story… What was comforting was to know that things were always the same there. The same people at the Meeting Room, the same food on the table, the same hymns sung around the piano at night-time.

The regular domestic decorum reassured Susan in the face of abandonment by her father. Susan's mother was forced to leave Plymouth Brethren when she chose to study at university. There she met and married Leonard Jolley, a fellow student, who abandoned her with new baby Susan soon after. The mother was forced back on her parents in Kent for support. Leonard then married Elizabeth Jolley, the Australian fiction writer, and moved to Perth as a university librarian. The first child of Elizabeth and Leonard was born in the same year as Susan and me.

At home, my life was very predictable day by day. Before long, I learnt to become a chameleon, changing colours at home, at school and in Brethren meetings. The steadily influential members of my family were my mother and oldest brother, David, enriching my maturation.

By the time that I finally left Brethren in 1968, I was self-conscious about subscribing – as I was – to Brethren dogma in the form of lip service only, decrying them and having absorbed all of the worthwhile life skills that they offered. I stretched the limited resources of Brethren to breaking point and held them in contempt. My cynicism built methodically until I abandoned the rump permanently in 1968, stopped all religious practice and went on to drop all belief in divinity entirely.

My memoir recounts my struggles with religion as a child as well as my ultimate disaffection with exclusive dogma in my teenage years. The account focuses on the interactions between my personal growth and the cult. It is not intended as a comprehensive autobiography, but rather as my story of early struggle between personality and unwarranted constraints, a contest of wills and outlooks, and the reasons for forging a path to liberation. When I was young, personal faith was not a topic for public discussion – just as political preferences were avoided in polite society – so one of my aims is to reveal my cult experiences fully. My emergence to adulthood compares with the coming-of-age of anyone who has been constrained against their will by fanatics. I outline my struggle, with escape hatches and preferred routes to personal freedom.

Some advisers and mentors guided my path to a few rescue options, and to a few lasting attitudes and habits which acted as effective weapons for my unavoidable battle with blind beliefs. But ultimately I was forced to grasp the nettle alone, and to find my own inner strength in order to forge a unique path to freedom and to break away from secure (but misguided) Brethren safeguards.

Once reborn on the outside, avoiding the stifling smog of sanctity, new challenges confronted me, including deeper exploration of identity, unfamiliar environments (such as romantic relationships and popular entertainment) and unexplored moral dilemmas. By the late 1970s, their resolution proved more pleasurable than the old ones, and ultimately they yielded richer rewards, creating my own close loving family, a satisfying career, intimate friendships and a breadth of bounties that are not dusted off here for extended display. They belong in another time.

To achieve my aims for this account, I have relied heavily on my own memory, which has expanded in capability since I first began to write about the themes of my early life and Brethren. Fortunately, flexing the brain cells added more and more memory layers, like the opening up of Babushka dolls. I have consulted friends whom I have known for up to seventy years, about my storyline of oppression, escape and liberation, and they have contributed frank memories of their own as well as adding further stimuli for me to absorb; in this way, there is communal interaction.

A basic question is: how much control did I have over my young life? Some of my memories of my reactions to events or authorities are a little vague simply because I was so young emotionally and mentally. In places, it is hard to distinguish between adult and child emotional reactions at all, maybe because they are unchanged over time, and in others, the old and fresh are enmeshed because my emotions about a situation changed very gradually as a result of reflection over long periods. Where I am able to separate my child from my adult responses, I make it clear in the memoir.

Without being presumptuous, this memoir and Geoffrey Chaucer's in *The Canterbury Tales* of 1400 present amusements in common. Chaucer used poetry to convey individuals' stories within an overarching story of their travels as a group of pilgrims trekking from London to Canterbury. I have no intention to compare literary quality, but interesting features of social customs and habits abound in both stories. Obviously, descriptions of Canterbury in Melbourne, Australia, in my time come across now as dated geographical and sociological arenas. In this memoir, there are cherished and sensitive stories of several participants in my pilgrimage from saintliness to rebel, even as secular aspirations overwhelm the religious in both my characterisations and Chaucer's.

The few fictional accounts of Plymouth Brethren that exist are far from true – but it is not surprising in that they did not intend to be accurate. Brethren did not have to make any effort to attract caricature and satire. Close examination of the novel *Oscar and Lucinda* by Peter Carey, and of the film *Son of Rambow*, for instance, show them to be incomplete fantasies which have little resonance with my experiences. They used Brethren as devices for character and plot development but they rely entirely on parody and not realism.

My family nominated me as family historian long ago, so conveniently I have inherited cardboard boxes full of curled letters, musty diaries, partly covered notebooks, sepia photos and motley publications as memory jolters. For fifty years, I have collected and read accounts of Plymouth Brethren from various perspectives, including more sympathetic argument than cynical critiques, as well as academic research publications and published memoirs.

Very little is known of the origins of Brethren in the antipodes. From archival records, it is clear that a handful of adherents migrated from the UK to the Swan River Colony (Perth) and Adelaide by the 1830s, but never in large numbers. The trickle grew to a surge in the 1870s when British Brethren missionaries swept into urban centres, stealing members from other congregations. One Australian Congregational minister complained,

> Our decrease of members is owing to the influence of…Plymouth Brethren [who] hold services regularly in…the city and country… [The missionary] preaches much against all other sects… The wife of one of the judges, a Wesleyan local preacher, and a manager of one of the banks, six church workers from the English church and members from other churches including our own [have joined Brethren]. Wealth, and position, give this party a powerful influence – which is employed in getting members from other churches.

None of the recent published commentaries on Brethren seem to adopt the approach of asking the dual questions which I regard as vital: how and why did the reverse process – escape – happen? The answers are driven not only from inside me, inside my family, and inside Plymouth and Exclusive Brethren, but also from external attractants; the 'pull' factor was essential. The world held out powerful inducements to a fuller life that Brethren never knew. I am attracted by the power of the myth of the 'butterfly effect', when minor disturbances, like a flutter of wings, can eventually set off bigger developments that lead to massive disruptions, such as a hurricane. As an adult, I have gained much serenity and reconciliation from arriving at the calm beyond the storm, from the sweetness of liberation, from appreciating how and why I orchestrated my emancipation, and who and what assisted me along the way.

Among Brethren I was a bonsai tree – forever pruned, contained, manipulated and deprived of external nutrition. I was taught to remain passively on display, in spite of the fact that I lacked all desire to be miniaturised or inhibited by Brethren.

On the whole, Brethren were quietly obsessive, as much as my brothers with the air rifle, never allowing their religious zealotry to falter, never apologising for beliefs. They were focused and committed, alert to any chink in their moral armour or external threat. They excelled at business and their careers because they entertained none of the distractions of personal indulgence or escapist leisure of the majority. In their single-mindedness, they were doggedly disruptive, even revolutionary in theology. Faith and ambition marched hand in hand. Their singular desire to order their own lives and futures clashed with traditional orders, and they courted self-deprivation, professing that all their rewards lay in a future heaven. They were dangerous motivations.

Two

The Inside Track

Wriggle room

A good friend once observed that I was expert at exiting from social events unnoticed. It seemed an odd attribute. From a young age, I developed the habit of inconspicuous disappearance – from the shadow of Plymouth Brethren pressures. My temporary withdrawals gave me wriggle room – emotional and physical – from stress and unwelcome coercion. When young, meetings, outings, birthday parties or dinners meant little more to me than tense audits. Expectations for good behaviour and moral conformity were overwhelming, rarely allowing for relaxation or a chance for self-expression. Socially, I lacked finesse.

Dodging my origins became ingrained. I used two methods. I shall never forget dinner at the home of the state librarian, Ken Horn, in 1972 soon after he employed me. He 'took an interest in me', colleagues said, teasing me. He had a reputation for bonhomie. At his retirement, it was noted that 'Ken's many friends appreciated above all his ability as an after-dinner raconteur and his splendid appreciation of fine wines and convivial discussion.' His highly polished dinner table was distancing, with diminutive Mrs Horn at the kitchen end while gangling Ken held forth at a distance at the head. She tutored in philosophy at the University of Melbourne, but none of our chatter connected with her special interest; he tended to hold the floor. The dinner smelt of well-baked potatoes covered in gravy.

Ken had a reputation for striking up conversations with total strangers and as a result, the young couple sitting opposite he had met on a city tram stop. I had left Brethren four years before, and was petrified that my past might pop up in roaming conversation and stigmatise me. It became my serious super-sensitive secret, avoiding the spotlight.

In complete contrast, on other occasions in casual conversation I had an urge to pre-empt criticism by rushing to explain my religious background as lucidly as I could. Witness this party:

'Hi, I don't think that we've met before. I'm Graeme,' extending my hand.

'I'm Joseph. How do you know Ron?'

'Oh, we were at university together. Ron was researching Moravians in England in the eighteenth century.'

'He tutored me last year,' said Joseph.

'I understand Ron's focus well, because I was brought up in a religious sect myself.' I felt tense and defensive already.

'What sect was that?'

'Plymouth Brethren.'

'Don't know anything about it. Do you still belong?'

'No – left them long ago. They had some weird practices, though.'

Joseph scratched his chin and suddenly needed to go to the kitchen on a pretext.

My confessions like this one failed invariably. I was disillusioned on both fronts. It took me a decade to realise that no one really cared about my exceptional cult upbringing with any of the intensity or paranoia that I did. They brushed it aside, as not integral to my being.

Nevertheless, I became like the nuclear briefcase with the bomb code in it, the result of centralised controls. Controls ranged from rigid principles of domestic worship prescribed by the cult, to hours and hours of sitting under silent scrutiny in endless Brethren meetings, to circular explications of senseless doctrine, to being refused daily interactions with kids of my age, to unimaginative rules about strict limits on non-Brethren activities inside or outside the home, and to deprivation of all popular culture and team sport. I carried enormous moral responsibility for a kid. It was stressed that my demeanour at all times should be a testimony to the World of my glowing holiness. There were occasions when I did not want to 'shine like a little candle burning in the night', as suggested by the child's hymn that I was required to sing. God's perpetual surveillance scared me. Every now and again, I tried to trick God by suddenly thinking of something quite outlandish, out of the blue, but I could not determine if He was thrown off my trail or not. Unwanted attention led to the circumvention noted by my friend, and ultimately to permanent avoidance of anything that had a whiff of Brethren on it.

Around the moment of my escape, if I was destined for a nuclear explosion, I wanted to control it myself. I was not alone in enduring Houdini-like urges and finding them hard to suppress.

This memoir aims to describe why and how I escaped from the grip of Brethren at the age of twenty-one, as part of my early development, not only explaining the reasons for leaving but also how it affected me during the struggle and after freedom was achieved. Most chapters deal with the reasons for my rebellion from my unusual cult, and later chapters focus on how I – as a black sheep – progressed after moving out of the home paddock.

Each chapter deals with different escape themes, incorporating the important role of my close family, and using original source materials along with my current reflections. It seems important to review the influence of family members on me before considering broader Brethren effects. Others' voices are inserted alongside my own, some from the distant past, some from recent times, to add authenticity. The focus of this chapter is on my three siblings, to describe how the experience of Brethren faith was filtered within the household, and how my siblings planned their escapes, which contrasted with mine. How different were our paths to freedom?

Intense boredom

It is hard to convey the depth of the boredom that I experienced at Plymouth Brethren meetings. As a child, the monotony seemed never-ending; I estimate that I spent about ten thousand hours, or one and a half years of my life, in meetings. The sensory deprivation was like being buried alive.

Little reward for patient compliance was to be found in endless hours spent in 'halls' sitting with family members. There was no stimulation. Halls were spartan shells, with no adornments inside or out, so nothing decorative could be enjoyed there. Any form of art was shunned as a Worldly excrescence and I was robbed of aesthetic appreciation. I can still visualise every detail of our rectangular brick hall on a corner of Maling Road, Canterbury – a gaunt design, bleak in shape, layout and decor. It offered no visual cues except faded post-war blackout paper slowly peeling off high windows to the north with their frosted glass, and cobwebs cluttering green lampshades. It smelt stale. Any farm shed was more stimulating.

My family always arrived early at the hall on Sunday because my father had a key to the room and set the time on the main home clocks early, to deceive the rest of us into getting ready before any other Brethren. With thirty-two clocks in the house, he had sufficient time to alter the main ones before eleven a.m. in order to hurry us up. Any family member with a watch argued volubly with his predictable time-fiddling.

Once in the hall, we waited silently for the large clock on the wall to click over to eleven a.m., adding to the boredom. The roar of the engine of Lena Allen's diesel Mercedes sputtered to a stop outside; we heard her pull the handbrake on. In winter, the heavy vehicle squelched in deep ruts in the muddy grass. Lena had a healthy crop of brown hair and generously avuncular manner. She was among the first female pharmacists in Melbourne and usually the last to arrive at the meeting. All senses were heightened by our stillness. Any stray fly caught our attention as it buzzed by.

Another noisy car arrived soon, driven by the owners of the hall, who also owned a bread and flour company, Reg and Jack McAlpin and family, of McAlpin's Flour. Both were thin and jumpy. In haste, they brought a fresh loaf of bread from their factory for breaking as part of our communion. I could hear the pretentious throb of the engine as they cruised onto the back grass in their massive silver Chev, with ostentatious tail fins and cat's-eye tail lights.

Revealing our status, we owned a modest FJ Holden, yet we were proud of it. In those days (1957), boys were expected to know the name of every car on the road (or the grass). Actually, I walked usually to the meeting with my brother David – because we preferred it – via back lanes and circuitous streets most times, leaving the family car to others. We kept our compulsory hats at the ready in our hands until within coo-ee of the hall, when they were transferred reluctantly to our heads.

The wearing lasted a very short time because at the front of the hall was a small foyer for hanging hats and coats. At the back of the hall in the corner of the yard were tiny corrugated-iron toilets. I patronised them as often as I could, without wanting to attract attention, to enjoy the jolly, musical tinkle of the stream of urine on the corrugations and to escape surveillance.

Indoors, a rectangular space remained open in the centre of the hall. At the sacrosanct Sunday morning meeting, a simple table in the space was covered in a pristine, starched tablecloth (by a volunteer Sister) for the bread, wine and (at slight remove) the wooden collection box. We continued to wait in silent expectation. The McAlpin bread smelt sweet. Everyone sat solemnly on hard bentwood chairs in rows around the bread, anticipating its transmogrification into the flesh of Jesus. The glass mug of maroon Marsala wine with two handles was on the verge of becoming his blood. Yuck. Transubstantiation was asking too much of my imagination.

Old members were permitted a footstool resembling a dumpy, furry fungus. As children, we swung our little legs vigorously until whacked in admonition on the knee by a parent. Brothers swung one trousered leg over the other, then the other way around, sequentially, but were never punished with whacking. Sisters never swung anything, not even their handbags. They were sedate and still.

I tried hard but could not manage to do the leg swing-over until I was about fourteen. Jumpy Brothers with lanky legs might do it twenty times. It was an indication that the Spirit was stirring them into action – soon we could expect that they would announce an ancient hymn to sing or launch a lofty prayer heavenwards. Much swinging and thought preceded any vocal outpouring.

There was no heating or cooling inside the hall. Physical comfort belonged to the World. In winter, God warmed our hearts, and the surroundings were designed to keep our minds focused on God alone. In summer, I sat as close as I could to my mother with her handwaving fan and borrowed it often; the female congregation resembled a sea of colourful fluttering butterflies. Sweat trickled from the tie at my collar to my navel.

A slight element of unpredictability created a perfunctory order of service in meetings. Every time was slightly different while remaining much the same. In prolonged silences, I tried to guess who would speak next. The slightest variation was worthy of note. My brothers kept the score at the same time as me – we discussed it at length afterwards, to see who achieved the correct number of guesses. The World whizzed by outside the hall. As we sat, we heard a motor mower roar, the wind blowing the old gum tree on the corner, dogs barking. The World corralled us.

We waited for the Holy Spirit to inspire, pushing back at the evil World. The wall clock seemed to tick more and more slowly, but we were the Olympic champions of endurance anyway. The meeting could not end until at least sixty minutes passed. With no minister to manage proceedings, Brethren contributions happened in fits and starts, generously interspersed with deep quiescence.

It was an event when the Spirit moved Brothers to speak. Always did, such was the power of the Spirit. Sometimes, I could almost smell the Sunday roast cooking two miles away while we waited for the Spirit, on tenterhooks. Was it God or a Brother who hesitated to contribute a spontaneous prayer? Extemporising took too long a time. Among Brethren, only a male could act as God's mouthpiece. But any male could. Some were painfully slow to pray and then forgot to stop. We learnt everything there was to learn about patience.

Writing of Brethren in the 1920s in Torquay, in Devon, England, another child of Brethren (Patricia Beer) noted the consequences of the absence of spiritual depth in meetings:

> No sophisticated brain was present to tamper with whatever slippery underwater ideas might evolve and prosper in the Brethren's minds, no trained intelligence to inform their confident piety.

Demonstrative piety outdid imagination every time.

As four siblings in the family, we each escaped from meetings eventually, and all covert forms of control, in our own special ways. I am the only one of the four who will tell of the omnipresent ducking and weaving that it involved. My two brothers have died. My sister, Bettina, has not abandoned Christianity and will not talk about herself. Brethren affected my two brothers, sister and me in different ways, but none of us stayed in the fold. The strain of growing up and breaking out was a most dramatic part of our lives, played out against the tedium of meetings.

Origins

A prevailing myth in my family was derived from the protected community created by the Plymouth Brethren way of life. It implied that my ancestors were committed to Brethren as far back in time as was possible. Brethren emerged as an identifiable sect in the mid-1840s, in fact! The premises of the myth were that the effulgent light of heavenly beneficence was bestowed on all of my ancestors, and that my grandparents were fully immersed in Brethren at the first possible opportunity. Both were false.

Father professed deep admiration for two Brethren missionaries, Arthur Lee Mallalieu and Hugh Wasson, who migrated from England to hold tent meetings, to poach adherents from other religious denominations all around Australia in the 1880s and 1890s. Established churches were angry at the leakage of adherents. Take the example of a cabinetmaker and piano-maker Joseph Hamblin, who migrated to Perth from England and made much church furniture in the new colonies. He had skills. He crafted a fancy chair for the Queen of Spain, commissioned by the Benedictine monks of New Norcia. He taught singing, violin and flute. Joseph migrated to Kyneton, to die of influenza there in 1899. During his life, he progressed from the Church of England to the Methodists to the Baptists to the Salvation Army, then settled with Plymouth Brethren for his final resting place in Kyneton. In addition to pianos built of English oak, his shop sold concertinas, Bibles and fishing tackle. His legacy of twelve children added to the small Kyneton assembly of Brethren, with the extra value of the flourishing business, continued by sons John, Arthur and Henry. Joseph's handicrafts are prized by collectors to this day.

The mellifluous names of Mallalieu and Wasson rolled off Father's tongue, and fascinated me. I practised saying their names to myself. My paternal grandfather was supposed to have been influenced by them, but my interpretation is that it is more likely that Oscar Johanson, my gaunt grandfather born in 1882, fell in love with Catherine Dover (born in 1883), who already belonged to Plymouth Brethren in Adelaide, and Oscar escaped the Church of Sweden in order to marry her in 1908, aged twenty-six. Grandfather was not the first church-hopper in our family, nor the last. He was like Hamblin and others. Brethren were only allowed to marry Brethren.

Similarly, my maternal grandmother (Frances Wright) was the first of her family to leave the Anglican Church for the Plymouth Brethren, influenced by nomadic missionaries. Her mother advised against it, but she took the leap anyway. William Airey (my grandfather on my mother's side of the family) already belonged to Brethren; in fact, he probably escaped himself from the Anglican Church in his early twenties in Limerick, Ireland, where he knew John Nelson Darby, the Brethren founder. Frances married William (eleven years older) in 1911 and enlisted with the Kyneton Brethren of Hamblin acclaim.

My parents never spoke of some dark secrets that lurked beneath the lives of both of the exemplary Plymouth Brothers, William Airey and Hugh Wasson. I have only discovered them recently with the assistance of both my son, Tim, who has researched our family tree, and with help from an English descendent of the missionaries Mallalieu and Wasson, the author Rebecca Stott, who has written some of her own story in *In the days of rain* (2017).

Wasson and his wife, Ada-Louise, had two daughters in England before they migrated to Australia. Unfortunately, Ada-Louise developed severe epilepsy, for which no treatment was known at the time, and because she had a reputation for being wilful, she was incarcerated in the Ballarat Mental Asylum from 1914. Forty years later – which time Wasson spent scouring the new nation of Australia for converts and making sure that Brethren communities were on the right path – helpful drugs were found for epilepsy and Ada-Louise was released. The reunited couple returned to England in old age in 1953. Wasson continued to rampage with Exclusive Brethren, declaring that his grandson (Robert Stott) would be the last Brother to attend a university (in his case, Cambridge). Robert – soon to be father of Elizabeth Stott, who wrote so much about him – had acquired irreligious ideas on campus. The ruminant brains of Brethren were chewing sluggishly over anti-education dogma around the globe.

On Mother's side of the family, Tim found that my thick-bearded grandfather William had married before Frances, a Brethren widow named Harriet Rathbone, who was eleven years his senior, in Melbourne in 1903. She already had a son from a previous marriage, whom William respected, but disaster descended with force, and just one year after the new marriage, Harriet was admitted to the Sunbury Mental Asylum with severe melancholia. No more despondent a woman could have sat for her official asylum photo – which I have seen. In the photo in the archive, she resembled a deranged criminal. She could not be helped, would not stop self-inflicted wounding, and died six years later in the asylum. William married Frances the following year, but then he died suddenly himself three years later in 1914 from nephritis of the kidney. My mother was aged only two and my aunt aged one. Tragedy followed disaster followed catastrophe in a cascade.

Neither of my parents were involved directly in the fates of Ada-Louise or Harriet, but keeping the backgrounds completely secret from us as children and adults suggests an excess of devotion to propriety, and a hint that these shrouded histories and secrets caused the forebears high anxiety at times. They did not experience only joyful peace by any means under God's umbrella, troubling thunder rolling in the distance.

David

My oldest brother, David, had an experience with Oxford University that replicated that of Robert Stott, the Exclusive Brother who was the father of the contemporary author Rebecca Stott.

As a child, David suffered five years of indoctrination alone, before the arrival of my other brother, Peter, who was three years ahead of me. I was born in 1946 and my younger sister three years after me. Her exposure to Plymouth Brethren was diluted partly because they became purely 'Exclusive' in 1960–1962 and the family left much extreme dogma behind. As a girl, much less public obeisance to God was expected of her than it was of boys anyway. In spite of leaving the Exclusive Brethren, our parents continued their dependence on Biblical fundamentalism with about three hundred idealistic stalwarts who also left Exclusive Brethren in Melbourne around the same time, forming a small rump of survivors. But beneath the surface loyalty to family, different paths of resistance were developing with each sibling. Each of us chose our own escape route individually at separate times. No family lifeboat was provided.

Often the centre of family melodrama, David was the immediate trigger for our exit from Exclusive Brethren as a group. As a history tutor at the University of Melbourne, he accepted a scholarship for postgraduate study at Oxford University in 1962. Normally, a bunch of friends would be full of congratulations, but instead a Brethren hubbub of disapproving mutterings and murmurings bubbled up and quickly clung to us, smothering us.

David was not told categorically not to attend Oxford, because no doctrine on university attendance had been promulgated as yet. Brethren accepted or rejected new rules in an unpredictable fashion – a bit like windsocks swaying in the breeze. Mostly, new rules were slowly formulated and poorly communicated. Commonly, one congregation of Brethren was not aware of what the neighbouring congregation decided. The absence of a doctrinal chain reaction is not hard to imagine.

With restrained delight, David sniffed the chance of a pitched battle. He felt that the wind favoured his direction – which was Oxford, come what may. He loved a hullabaloo and did not seem in the least perturbed by the ruckus that he was initiating. He escaped on the sparkly white *Oriana* into a spring sunset across the ocean in 1961. Wind gusts off the 'Rip' buffeted me as we waved him goodbye from the base of the lighthouse at Point Lonsdale. I must have looked diminutive. I certainly felt it. I missed him a lot; he was my frequent companion and mentor, a flawed hero whom I loved dearly.

For weeks, the rest of the family in Melbourne mulled over David's contrived predicament, exchanging letters and telegrams and expensive telephone calls with Oxford. The frenzied communications reminded me of the messages flurrying around inside a busy air traffic control tower. Control became the key success factor in this crisis. Unbeknown to us, sleuthing Exclusive Brethren were using just the same communications with their Oxford counterparts as us. From them, the Melbourne Exclusives discovered that David was comfortably ensconced in Balliol College, itself an evil association to their way of thinking. David enjoyed eating meals with dozens of sinners in the College Hall and living with them cheek by jowl. It was no surprise when Exclusive Brethren dumped him in 1962. He was a thorn in their side.

In fact, David's expulsion marked the end of tertiary education for Brethren children in Australia. As an elder in England, Wasson (the former missionary to Australia) was doing his darndest to achieve agreement on the same edict there. If students were enrolled, they were instructed to stop attending university. Up to then, my family had

Brethren friends who were dentists, doctors, pharmacists, psychiatrists, surgeons, teachers, bankers, architects, engineers, kindergarten administrators, horticulturalists, and all manner of educated managers. One Plymouth Brother (Maurice Koechlin) was famous as an engineer who designed the Eiffel Tower in Paris. Another – Frederick Baedeker – began life as a Plymouth Brother and finished as co-publisher (with his brothers) in Germany of the famous nineteenth-century European guidebooks, Baedeker's. About six thousand editions were published over a hundred and eighty years.

Ironically, John Nelson Darby, the illustrious founder of Brethren, in 1819 attended Dublin University for two degrees and spent all of his life reading theology and law widely, managing to convert other educated professionals. But that was not remembered in 1962.

Having left the Exclusive Brethren, my family continued to defy their education prohibition: Peter continued with his medical degrees, and (in 1965) I would soon begin my Arts (Honours)-Law degree at the University of Melbourne. Bettina was halfway through secondary school.

In Melbourne, Exclusives meticulously prepared a case for removing my family from their lair for supporting David's educational expansion. It is hard to believe now that as a family we resisted them, but we plotted to challenge their confusion with enthusiasm, to tangle the disordered implementation of their rules, courting a showdown. We were subversives, attracting unsolicited support. We knew that we were bound to fail to deflect the massive Exclusive putsch but aimed to cause as much of a conflagration as we could as we crashed out. To me, acting as saboteurs was enervating. We believed that many thousands would abandon Exclusives around the same time. Ours was a just cause. To an outsider, our public trial resembled the manic courtroom of the Queen of Hearts in *Alice's Adventures in Wonderland*, where it was impossible for any accused to win a case or avoid a sentence of execution. 'Off with his head!' David drew the powerful analogy with Napoleon's rule-bending in *Animal Farm*.

After Oxford, David married Turid in Norway and for a short time pretended to pursue the Brethren portal. He achieved first-class honours at Oxford and returned to work at the Australian National University in Canberra in 1965, where no Brethren lived. In a job interview with Professor Manning Clark, also a Balliol graduate, David chatted only about the experience of his Brethren upbringing, ensuring that no workplace trivia intruded. Manning – who resembled my impression of an Old Testament prophet – was the fretful son of an Anglican priest.

As work colleagues for some years, he and David seemed to share empathy, intellectual restlessness, political intensity and a fascination with the disorder of human nature. In David's mind, life was full of gambits and contests well before he shared his rash ideas with Manning – who faced his own emotional perplexities. Regardless of their potential compatibility, or shared soul-searching, my cautious father spoke of Manning as a terrifying influence.

I did not know Manning by means of any face-to-face encounters myself, so could not verify Father's prognosis. I did attend a lecture at the University of Melbourne that he gave in 1967 about the political leader, Robert Menzies, and at that time Manning believed that Menzies was well-intentioned, but a backward 'Edwardian, a destroyer of civilisation'. I was beginning to learn more of the broad sweep of politics and the sociology of power. In my diary, I wrote that Manning was 'absent-minded, witty, and nervous'. Through his many publications – often with biblical overtones – it was clear that Manning's 'punishers, straighteners and enlargers', from his themes about history, could all be found in my old Brethren community. Many of Manning's thoughts were embellished with religious gravitas.

Manning told David an anecdote about the visit of two Jehovah's Witnesses to his home.

'Can we pray with you?' they asked Manning as he opened his door to them.

'I don't need you to,' replied Manning.

'Then tell us if you believe in the power of salvation?'

'No,' said Manning, 'I believe in the power of osmosis.'

The evangelists left unrewarded. I knew their dejected feeling well.

Having migrated outside his comfort zone of well-known Brethren guidelines and doctrines, David found his new world unsettling. He was most stimulated when solving a crisis, usually of his making. To soothe his nerves and bolster his self-confidence, he drank alcohol excessively. He believed that grog and fifty cigarettes a day would steady his trek. While he still professed to believe in Christian values, he conducted extramarital affairs, lied to his closest friends, failed to keep commitments and never completed his grandiose projects.

Any sincere religious pretence was wiped out by his deceptions, but he managed to keep his job as a very popular university lecturer. I worked with one of his ex-students, Barbara, who praised him as the best teacher she ever had. In her professional career, she was well-placed to understand the needs of learners and researchers herself. She oversaw the transformation from paper-based access to government data by its conversion to online formats. She was responsible for transforming land titles, certificates of births, deaths and marriages, and other records.

David's physical and mental health went into steep decline. Family members rescued him from his office floor, where he slept drunk and prostrate. His eldest son had to hide David's rifle well out of reach, above his wardrobe. It was sad to observe. His hands trembled nonstop. More than once he knocked on my front door in Brunswick in the 1970s, with another addict, seeking shelter for the night.

With the encouragement of his wife and five children, he subjected himself to detox live-ins and counselling, but he turned those efforts at rehabilitation into mind games that no one else cared to share. His deterioration was too awful for game-playing. He became an emotional opportunist and his drunkenness led to violence and abuse of his family. He was utterly miserable, and one night in 1985 near his country home he died during a solitary walk in a paddock.

Father and Mother believed that ploughing through all life's drudgery would make the afterlife worthwhile, because no satisfaction was ever to be found on earth. In their view, because David had been baptised into

Brethren as a child, he was predestined for heavenly bliss regardless of any hurt caused by his midlife devilry. Brethren baptism was their insurance policy – guaranteeing long-term benefits out of this world. Although understandable, coming from bereaved parents, this attitude dodged their own responsibility and glossed over serious flaws in Brethren misinterpretations of a damaged person. They helped create a fiend. Throughout later life, my parents avoided acknowledgement of any of the effects of their inhumane views on their children individually.

Peter

My other brother, Peter, took a very different route out of Brethren. The three remaining siblings learnt somewhat from witnessing David's stellar ascent and chaotic self-immolation. Peter's primary means of coping was multilateral disengagement which began at a very early age. His own adage was 'Just avert your gaze'. This was applied to any perplexity.

For a start, Peter did not like people. A family story had it that he befriended a white chook at the bottom of the yard when he was four years old and squatted by its cage to talk to it. He always found pets (usually dogs) easier to build relationships with than humans. For a while, he toyed with the idea of becoming a veterinary surgeon.

At the age of nine, Peter avoided surgery himself when Mother commissioned the family doctor, amiable Dr Roy Bartram, to check Peter's tonsils and mine to see if they needed removing. The moment Peter saw the doctor at our front door, he disappeared over the back fence for a couple of hours. Typically obliging, I hung around for an examination and inevitably lost my tonsils and adenoids on a Friday afternoon at Bryson Hospital, a block away from the back gate. Next night, I was wrapped in a blanket and carried home, slung under the arms of David and Father. I can still feel the bumps of the footpath, and the grumps of Father disagreeing with David about the best distribution of my body weight. By running away, Peter managed to keep his tonsils for ever; I convalesced for a week, believing that I had only just escaped permanent entry into the pearly gates.

The difference between Peter and me picked up apace. At the start of my first day at Canterbury State School in 1952, Mother asked Peter to accompany me up the hill and show me where to go. She should have known better.

Peter (aged nine) certainly sent me an emphatic message about distancing as soon as we were out of sight of my mother. 'I do not want you to walk with me. Keep ten paces behind always,' he commanded.

I was uncertain about how to measure ten paces when we had to cross a busy road. I just crossed on my own, far behind him.

As we neared the north school gate, he continued, 'I never want you to talk to me at school.'

I was puzzled but agreed to comply. We progressed a few steps.

As a repetitive afterthought, he added, 'In the schoolyard, you will never speak to me unless I ask you to.'

His message was unequivocal. It seemed hard-hearted at the time, but I was powerless to disagree. He studied a supercilious indifference as far back as I can recall. If I had been a pet dog, he would have been more devoted. As it was, I was just a b(r)other.

The same blackout rules were followed rigidly by Peter over the next four years at primary school, when I was left to my own devices, then for four more years at secondary school when we overlapped again. He and I never talked about school at home, in spite of my babbling to the rest of the family about the trivia of my school day. Peter was quite uninterested in my prattle about the content of the first movie that I ever saw in my life in the school hall. It made me excited nevertheless. All the kids squatted on the wooden floor, where at one end a huge projector shone a black-and-white film onto a white sheet at the other end. The Education Department had made the film for the purpose of moral instruction. In case we were slow to pick up the themes, a robber on the screen was dressed in a white lab coat, for easy recognition, while police in dark uniforms chased him through paddocks and murky forests. Although his capture was inevitable, the flickering story completely absorbed me. It was my first experience of moving images after all.

I recall that I thought Peter's silence mighty strange in the presence of such exciting news. I suspected that perhaps he feared that I would want to keep an eye on him. He may have felt like me, always afraid of surveillance – I had been brainwashed into believing that omnipotent God watched my every step. Imagine someone else knowing what I was about to do, even before I did it! It was very frightening, so much so, that the memory still makes the hairs on the back of my neck stand on end. The idea of the unconscious – not knowing why I thought, what I thought – added another worry to my worries.

The separation of school life from home life, and from the Brethren community, was assisted by Peter's unwavering isolation. In the long run, I benefitted from it because Peter never bothered to pry on me, his little brother, and in parallel, I witnessed him crafting his own inconspicuous steps for his incremental separation from Brethren. As my older brother, he was always ahead of me and he taught me something of a lesson about wriggling, subtly but effectively, out of the cult constraints.

Peter was shy and reserved. He shared opinions reluctantly. He evaded discussions. He avoided human contact. Peter was but he wasn't. I could make whatever I liked of his remoteness – Peter did not care to know what I thought. Even when trauma hit him when he was fifteen, he never talked to me about the experience. I witnessed it second-hand.

A balding paedophile (George Cunningham) came to Melbourne from Tasmania with a Brethren testimonial commending his good character. He had a simpering smile and deferential handshake. George proceeded to hold bawdy weekend sex romps with vulnerable under-age local boys at his home in Belgrave. Peter was entrapped, at the age of sixteen, but I escaped. What I recall most vividly about Belgrave is feeding kookaburras on George's veranda and how uncomfortable I felt in a cold bed on winter nights in his flimsy weatherboard home in the forest. Moisture dripped non-stop. Everything about him was craven, cold and calculating.

Brethren took homosexuality to be an abomination. It was the offence they charged George with: 'You shall not lie with a male as with a woman…' (Leviticus 18.22). Brethren adduced Old Testament parts of the Bible whenever the New Testament was considered insufficiently explicit. Either would do. The principle of cross-fertilisation was applied inconsistently, just for convenience, to mine prohibitions from either section of the Bible opportunistically.

Months passed after Belgrave before Father, acting awkwardly, cross-examined me in his bedroom about my awareness of adult sex with children. The sensuous scent of Mother's perfume filled the air.

Father was lost for words, could not bring himself to say 'sex', and began with a surprising image. 'Have you behaved like a dog with George Cunningham?'

I realised what he meant immediately, and without further elaboration, because various sexual behaviours had been discussed at length in schoolyard gossip. Kids are curious.

I said, 'No, I never have.'

His face showed instant relief. I was answering correctly.

He went on, 'You'd better be sure, because others have confessed.' He could not wait to finish the conversation, conducted entirely with averted eyes. 'Peter has got caught up in it,' he muttered nervously.

I assured him that I had not, and sidled out of a prolonged silence slowly, unsure whether we had finished. This strange conversation took one minute perhaps but felt to me like a drawn-out cross-examination. It felt like the sort of event where one sees an accident about to occur in slow motion, understanding the consequences well before they happen.

Peter's abuse as a subject was wiped from the family slate for ever afterwards. Like a meteorite, it departed as fast as it came. Any allusion to the event was muzzled craftily, never discussed openly.

In 1960, after Belgrave, Brethren introduced regular group confessions to shame transgressors like George Cunningham publicly. The new Brethren leader, Bruce Hales, decided that Brethren needed cleansing. Hales was a tyrant, champing at the bit to become world leader of Brethren. His cruel techniques aimed to unsettle peaceful practitioners, to shame as many individuals as possible, to enable his increased control over daily lives.

It was time for seventeen-year-old Peter to be humiliated publicly, two years before David's expulsion from Exclusive Brethren. Peter was required to tell the assembly (of about a thousand people) about his wicked behaviour in Belgrave in veiled language. We were spared the details. A series of confessions about sexual sin – excruciatingly sensitive – by George's victims and others ensued in so-called care meetings at the hall in Prospect Hill Road, Camberwell. Forgiveness was dished out instantly to Peter, but it did not reduce the guilt or lessen the pain of the shame. My thirteen-year-old ears burnt with dishonour.

George was withdrawn from, as Brethren excommunication was known, and as he bowed his head, he screamed loud and long on exit from the judgement hall. He was all alone. He took off to another state, as sex abusers do still, and probably abused others elsewhere. He was neither the first nor last Brethren sex abuser, but the first to touch on my life.

Some Brethren confessions at care meetings were mild, just about bad thoughts or eating with a sinful relative, others much more serious, about premarital sex or extramarital affairs, for example. The unnecessary public trial and judgement was more traumatising than the requirement to self-identify sinning itself. Everyone was made to feel glum, disgraced and guilty.

An author who abandoned Brethren soon after my family, Joy Nason, in *Joy and Sorrow* recalled an incident in a care meeting in Sydney that was both amusing and indicative of prevailing ignorance about sexual interactions. As was common, when confessions from Brothers lagged at meetings, they were invited to come to the centre of the hall and be cleansed of all sins. An old Brother shuffled to the centre. What was his sin?

'Sodomy,' he said.

'When did the sin take place?'

He answered and was admonished.

Where had it occurred, he was asked. How many times had it happened?

With whom had he sinned, asked the elder inquisitor finally.

'No one,' said the Brother. 'I was alone in the paddock behind my house.' He meant that he had masturbated alone, but he did not know the right word for it.

Ngaire Thomas, author of *Behind Closed Doors,* submitted to a similar experience in Auckland when she kissed and cuddled a boy at the age of fifteen and was convicted (in ignorance) of fornication at a Brethren show trial in 1958. She had no idea what fornication was when cross-examined, but agreed that she must have indulged.

After Peter's trial by ordeal, light peeped at the end of the tunnel. My parents were delighted, after our family's group extrusion from Exclusive Brethren, that Peter for a short time befriended a woman among our rump of Brethren, named Marianne, seemingly with engagement prospects. She was petite and blonde.

'He couldn't have chosen anyone better,' wrote my aunt to David in 1962. 'If she had been somebody outside [Brethren] it would be dreadful.'

Aunt paid for an engagement ring.

Even though aged nineteen, Peter and Marianne were set a curfew of ten thirty p.m. It was whispered that Marianne's sister (Elspeth) had rushed to marry because of an early pregnancy. Adults in our family lacked basic trust. Sexual knowledge (if any) was withheld – as secret as Vladimir Putin's mobile number.

Further parental enthusiasm was derived from Peter taking on the role of interpreting for deaf members of the three hundred or so stalwarts in the rump. Our parents grossly underestimated his scheming ability.

A disproportionate number of the entire deaf and dumb population of Melbourne joined Plymouth Brethren decades before, probably because communities like theirs are always close-knit and supportive of each other. About fifteen deaf folk followed us out of Exclusive Brethren into the rump of leftovers around 1962–1963. If you were a hearing member, it was a high honour to translate into sign language during meetings. Signing was very animated. I had never seen Peter so expressive.

Peter readily helped by translating in a back corner of the hall as a means to avoid oral participation, which all hearing Brothers were pressured to provide in the central space. He never confessed to me of aiming at long-term avoidance by his apparent altruism, but from close observation I am certain of his ulterior motives. I was never proficient enough myself in signing to attempt simultaneous translation, so was stuck in the centre in the panopticon of elderly Brothers. Pressure on me to perform increased but fortunately I had no stage fright. After eighteen years of observation of the circus, compliant professing was a cinch. Pretending deep faith and dissembling became a way of life.

Peter attended meetings less and less, becoming too busy with study to participate, and ignored my parents' pleas. They wanted him to succeed as a doctor, but they also expected him to mirror their beliefs. They were too late – Peter refused to discuss his departure with anyone. He left without fuss or bother by simply refusing to speak about it. He just averted his gaze. Monica and Gracie, an inseparable pair of older deaf women, were distraught about Peter's slip-sliding, because they loved him and had delighted in his recent twenty-first birthday celebrations. The couple had lived together for so long in Northcote that they looked like identical twins. My aunt protected Peter by helping him to avoid any scrutiny. He played a clever exit card: he would not talk to anybody. I could never have been so shifty. I admired his determination but could not envisage imitating his stonewalling strategy.

Whatever impacts Brethren may have had on Peter long-term were carried to his grave when he was killed instantly in a car accident on his way to work in Vevey, Switzerland, in late 1995. His car skidded on black ice and smashed into a tree. He never shared any religious thoughts with me, his wife or his four children. His thoughts were almost certainly secular as an adult.

With his mourning family, I crunched through a thick blanket of fresh snow to the village cemetery in Le Vesinet, sad and shocked. Our sombre funeral cortège processed slowly along back lanes, complete with the ministering priest from the small Lutheran church nearby who had never met Peter. He managed to wear a suitably mournful expression. Roses on top of the coffin left a sweet scent in their wake. Four huge white geese in a field honked at us noisily. We were a long way – about fifty years and 16,480 kilometres —from the friendly white chook in the home garden.

Bettina

My sister Bettina experienced less pressure from Brethren because she was younger (aged eleven) when my family departed from Exclusive Brethren due to the tightening of their dogma and behaviours, and their disgust with David. She was too young to belong officially. She was also less exposed because girls and women (Sisters) were not required to participate in Brethren meetings, that is, to make an oral contribution – other than to sing hymns. Only men (Brothers) were obliged to be involved. The apostle Paul 1,950 years before had told women to keep quiet in meetings, the command echoing down the millennia:

> If they desire to learn anything, let them ask their own husbands at home; for it is improper for a woman to speak in church (1 Corinthians 14:34).

Paul omitted to mention unpartnered women, of whom there were many. His misogyny trickled down to our cult. I always imagined Paul as hyperactive, intolerant and florid.

An even older rule was regurgitated to control the dressing of men and women:

> A woman shall not wear a man's garment, nor shall a man put on a woman's cloak, for whoever does these things is an abomination to the Lord your God (Deuteronomy 22:5).

Much argument among Brethren revolved around whether this should prevent women from wearing slacks or pantsuits. I doubt that the putative author of the text, Moses, had slacks in mind at the time of writing (about a thousand years before Paul). In a similar vein, kaftans, kilts or kimonos for men were unlikely to have been readily available in the Egyptian wilderness in Moses's time.

Nevertheless, Bettina was required to conform more or less to demure Brethren constraints as monitored by Mother – when she chose to monitor. Bettina wore a squat hat or scrap of a scarf on her head outside the house, skirts or dresses below the knee, short white frilly socks, her blonde hair in plaits, and she used no make-up or jewellery. I had the calming pleasure of plaiting her hair when Mother was not available.

A crisis erupted when as a teenager Bettina requested that the split ends of her long hair be trimmed a little at the tips. Long before this request, Mother and Aunt had secretly hired a hairdresser to visit home to do their hair. The hairdresser, Josie, was Italian, and on each visit she regaled Mother with stories of her drug-addled adult son who lived at her home. Mother loved to pass the gossip on to the rest of the family.

Because Saint Paul declared that 'it is disgraceful for a wife to cut off her hair or shave her head' (1 Corinthians 11:6), Mother determined to find the way to dodge – to get the hairdresser to visit the home, so that she and Aunt were not sighted at a salon. Over time, the two adult women allowed trimming to increase little by little by little. A chignon was used to disguise hair volume. The adults' cover was blown because Bettina was simply requesting that her hair be treated similarly. She was permitted a modicum of pruning under an oath of strict secrecy. Keeping up appearances was a well-developed custom in our home.

As the life of a Brethren girl differed from that of a boy, by the time of Bettina's teenage years, a veneer of compliance was sufficient for both genders. Policing of rules was hit and miss. Mother's hair could be taken as a barometer of her warmth for Brethren. As she distanced herself slowly from Brethren, the home hairdresser dyed Mother's hair bluer and bluer in accordance with prevailing fashion – eventually as blue as an emu egg in the 1970s – and her hairsprayed bouffant took on the shape of a large egg as well. The split ends and chignon disappeared altogether.

I was never close to Bettina and spent less leisure time with her than with my brothers. She had little interest in me, except when she needed help with her studies. My 1967 diary records that I gave her a goodnight kiss, to which she responded, 'Quick! Ugh! Bring me a tissue.' She was kept away from the boys and somewhat mollycoddled. The gender gap was expanded by girl events for her arranged separately from the boys.

A fanciful fable developed in the family, blown out of proportion, based on a minor interaction between Bettina and me when I was almost four. It involved an escaping cat. It illustrates how my perceptions differed from the rest, even at that tender age, how I was not believed, and how stereotyping happened hurriedly. As a young child, I could not avoid the opprobrium dumped on me; it added to my load of collected theological anxieties.

My family celebrated school holidays in 1950 by renting a house in Rosebud. It was squeezed into the weekdays between weekends, so that we did not miss Lord's Day worship back home. Holidays far from a meeting were sinful.

As we unloaded the family Austin car, I was entrusted to look after the cream plywood pram (containing the precious new baby, Bettina) on the front path beneath ominous black cypresses. Cypresses smelt distinctively of sap. It gave me great pride to be asked to perform the task. Mother went to the back of the run-down house to find the planted door key. I was distracted and let the pram roll forward a little on a sloping path and onto a hungry, curious cat, which squealed and spurted off, never to return. As the pram half tipped towards the yowling cat, my mother rushed back to rescue the baby, concerned that the squealing was Bettina in distress. I grabbed the handle to prevent complete toppling. The baby was asleep and content, oblivious and intact, not having fallen out.

Yet forever afterwards, the myth was told that I tipped Bettina out of the pram in a rage because she had displaced me as youngest in the family. It was a story that I tired of hearing, because it assumed a false intent. It suited a narrative of family drama and base instincts, deliberate malice. I was not angry with nor jealous of Bettina at all, just absent-minded. I simply did not notice the slight slope on the path. No purposeful intent was involved. The cat did not hang around to present essential testimony on my behalf. In any case I felt no guilt about it at all but was expected to bear the ongoing burden of family judgement passively. It grated as time went by.

The edict by Moses about women – already mentioned – led to Brothers acting with extreme chauvinism. Domestic tyranny and controlling terror in our home could have been a lot harsher than they were. Some homes were more extreme, as the case reported in the *Brisbane Courier-Mail* in 1950 that highlighted male domination. Tryphon Theoharris, a hairdresser, lorded it over his family after leaving the Greek Orthodox Church. In his newspaper photo, he resembles Socrates in glasses with thick plastic frames. He stopped his son playing Satan's music on the saxophone, turfed him out of home, took his children's bank money, required breakfast Bible discussion, and forced his wife Annie to grovel. She divorced him and demanded maintenance.

The court heard about 'a long course of tyrannical behaviour by her husband, apparently due to his religious fervour'. He placed a sign (beside a threatening razor strop) on his kitchen wall as follows:

> WARNING. The Master of this house is the Lord Jesus, and I am His acting master. Therefore, I warn you! Take heed! Pervert not the ways of the Lord. Be not ignorant, but be wise. Help to promote love, peace, and unity with me. Do not provoke me to wrath. Don't insist playing the fool. Fools die for want of wisdom. Please discontinue practising against me – to scoff, and mock, and scorn, and disobey and rebel against me… Now I command you to stop, and take warning and advice, given in love. Written this day, January 6, 1950. — Signed on behalf of my Master. The Acting Master Of This House.

I am compelled to compare our own house to this one. My father adored his only daughter, Bettina, and never punished her physically as Tryphon threatened to do to Annie. Mother was not manhandled. Yet Father's razor strop was always to hand for use on the boys, but not on Bettina.

Father did believe strongly that Mother should be subject to him. His Bible (Ephesians 5:22-24) was unequivocal:

> Wives, submit to your own husbands… For the husband is the head of the wife… Now as the church submits to Christ, so also wives should submit in everything to their husbands.

Mother resisted such nonsense as vehemently as any free spirit, and said so, making Father very red in the face, to the extent that he avoided mentioning subjection altogether. He wielded ample domestic power in any case. He led our lengthy Bible exegesis for up to thirty minutes after dinner (rather than at breakfast). Home Bible reading – totalling about a hundred and four hours per annum – was usually followed by prayer on our knees. The boundary between conforming pressure and tyranny was wafer thin, and put me on edge.

As in the Brisbane home, our music was censored; no instruments marred our barren meetings. Brethren associated music automatically with libidinous wildness, and only carefully vetted hymns and pianos were acceptable. Pianolas were wicked because they could play non-religious music. Saxophones or guitars were beyond the pale, belonging to popular pubs and clubs.

When Bettina was only six, in our Canterbury home a modest piano graced the sitting room, as it did in most homes at the time. My siblings and I all had music lessons with arthritic Miss Crump in Balwyn Road. By the time my age allowed for lessons, her swollen finger joints hardly fitted onto a single white note on the keyboard. With my sister, she was even more crippled. For no logical reason, I used to associate her name with the cow with the crumpled horn: 'This is the maiden all forlorn.'

This maiden was commanded by parents to use only the tune collection titled *Hymns for the Little Flock* bound in eggshell blue. The cover of our copy was very worn and contained many pencilled marginalia – mostly added over years by Miss Crump herself. The book had been closely vetted for religious propriety, and it only contained tunes sung in meetings.

Where the Brethren heritage of piano-playing began we shall never know. It was a fixed tradition. A new convert to Brethren in Ireland (an uncle of J.M. Synge, the playwright) deliberately broke his fiddle bow and abandoned Irish music in the 1830s, accepting the tyranny of the piano. To vary our musical input, and extend our musical pleasure, David and Peter bought a maroon piano accordion with bright red strips, thus doubling the number of our musical props. It was an attempt to break the mould. The new accordion was as smart as a sporty roadster and they relished the risk.

I found the thin wheezy sound exciting. It could be made to sound like a husky whine. Being a busybody, Father orchestrated discussions with other Brothers about whether it was a piano, whether it should be allowed in a Brethren home, and indeed whether 'the boys' had strayed into the evil World with this purchase. The real reason why Father raised doubts was that Aunt had paid for it; he was jealous.

I eavesdropped and reported on confabulations secretly to my brothers. The accordion had a piano-like keyboard but relied on air to make sound. After close examination, Brothers in conference concluded that if it was used for God's praise alone, then the accordion was an acceptable hybrid and no moral principle was violated. I made sure that the word was passed back to my brothers before they were officially exonerated. It suited them to have me as conduit for confidential news; when little, I found that eavesdropping could be extremely exciting when parental shutters were pulled down. Our Brother discussants were ignorant of the popularity of the accordion in vaudeville, theatres, dancing, and on radio – out in the normal World. I felt proud to make a small contribution to expanding horizons.

Bettina loved singing as much as I did, and when she was about eighteen, she expanded her own horizons by using non-Brethren hymns as her means of final escape. By sampling the Church of Christ, where a cappella was practically an article of faith, Bettina discovered a gospel choir called FindingEmotion. Who dared question its honourable purpose? After a couple of years of fertile musical immersion in her new community, she also found her husband, the son of the conductor, and married him in 1971. He sported enormous black sideburns, as was fashionable. The conductor's two daughters also married choir members (also with bushranger sideburns).

Bettina left Brethren with no fanfare, or plotting, because the small Brethren rump disintegrated as an entity, and my parents made no protest at the time of her slip sideways, their three boys having already left, and eventually they followed her into the Church of Christ themselves. Its emphasis on strict adherence to the New Testament fitted roughly with their old beliefs.

I felt angry that her move was so smooth, when mine, and my brothers', had required extreme struggles. The small rump of Brethren – that had peaked at about three hundred members in about 1963 – dissolved altogether as Bettina made her cushy transfer. The boys were not presented with such an obliging option. One of my children made the observation that Bettina never abandoned dour rigidity, in fact – never really being liberated. She was always controlled and uptight.

Open Brethren offered another alternative. There were few partnering prospects in the shrinking huddle of our ageing saints of the rump and entertainment elsewhere was marketed seductively. The spectre of much more popular Open Brethren always loomed large over our narrower Brethren group. I had several ex-Exclusive peers who found Open Brethren more appealing; they stayed with their gospel for life.

Leapfrogging to another Christian group was seen as much more acceptable in the eyes of my parents – even if undesirable – than abandoning belief altogether. Unlike Bettina, I took departure to its extreme; I lost all Christian faith, as I recount later. Such a degree of distancing was unusual; most felt less anger and disgust than me. My repulsion was my own. Neither brothers nor my sister provided any long-lasting guidance to help me find my way into a new World. David went off the rails altogether, Peter silently slipped out of Brethren without a whimper or a bang, and Bettina never really connected with Brethren at all.

Late in the escape race, believers shuffling around the Christian chessboard were easier for my parents to tolerate than total abandonment. Most of the few extant printed accounts of departures from Brethren reassure the reader that the author has not lost all faith in God. In contrast, I agreed with the poet T.S. Eliot that 'you have to risk going too far to discover just how far you can really go'. Bettina was still proud to stay within broader fundamentalism, demonstrating traditional loyalty to Mother, Father, and Jesus. They were old mates.

Internecine strife

To an outsider, Brethren groups were so similar to each other that utter confusion prevails about the slight differences. International variations over time added to the confusion. Yet the bonds of tribal loyalties within groups were so strong that cross-over was marked out as desperate and dangerous wavering by insiders. A basic mistake of Exclusive Brethren was that adherence was regarded as all or nothing; it left waverers with Hobson's choice – only one option. Brethren were experts at Separation – from splinter Brethren groups, from the bulk of errant Christians, from recalcitrants, from the World, and certainly from other religions. We grew up fenced in (by choice) by outsiders – including heretical Micks, churches with clergy, believers in half-truths, whacko evangelical upstarts, deviants, pagans, idol-worshippers, and heathens. They were all as evil as each other.

An American writer, Theo Maynard, whose parents were Brethren, was told by his mother in the 1910s, 'I would rather see you lying in your coffin than see you a Catholic.' It did not restrain his inclination to Catholicism.

Brethren were rabid. The author Arthur Conan-Doyle was a Spiritualist who complained in 1921 that one of the most persistent disruptors of his global lectures and public demonstrations of spiritualism were Plymouth Brethren.

Leaving the protection of Plymouth Brethren was regarded as self-destructive by the faithful; backsliders would not go to heaven, because they had witnessed the Truth as revealed to them alone, and chosen to ignore it. It was impossible to reconcile this conceited belief with the theory of the permanent power of baptism and predestination. In advanced age, even my conflicted parents finally abandoned the attitude of purist exclusivity.

Over the decades since the 1840s, Brethren formed groups, separated, seceded, rebelled, re-formed, rejoined, hived off again, began anew, and faded away. They were like bees or ants, setting up new hives and nests regularly. Every single member was convinced of the veracity of their interpretation of the Truth. All groups were experienced at leaving others behind, because in a welter of self-destruction, they perpetuated the cycles over and over again. The finer details of theology were hotly debated as schisms churned. Everyone agreed in the fundamentals of Christian doctrine – such as belief in the death and resurrection of the Son of God, Jesus, and his gift to provide believers with their eternal salvation in heaven – but beyond those tenets there was ample room for bitter argument about the rest. It raged.

A list of a few names of Brethren resulting from vituperation and dismemberment convey an impression of the profusion of types of Brethren. It is surprising that the options for names were not exhausted: Sanctified Brethren, Newtonites, Irvingites, Kellyites, Ravenites, Bethesda-ites, Bowes Brethren, Grant Brethren, Stuart Brethren, Lowe Brethren, Open Brethren, Cox Brethren, Tunbridge Wells Brethren, Glanton Brethren, Johnson Brethren, Dennis Brethren, Bird Brethren, Beale Brethren, and Taylorites. There were many others – whom I was warned to avoid altogether.

From the perspective of an insider, major differences between Plymouth or Exclusive Brethren, and Open Brethren, caused dispute. They had separated in 1845, but each party still felt the sting. Finer points of different beliefs were identified. The primary point of dispute was the acceptance by Open Brethren of any self-professed Christian into their fold, whereas Plymouth and Exclusive Brethren were more strict and carefully vetted newcomers, who were expected to demonstrate conformity to a very narrow set of values over a long period of probation. Paedophile George Cunningham slipped through the net.

Another dispute raged over the Open lot baptising adults only, whereas Plymouth Brethren baptised babies. I was fully immersed – the Plymouth requirement – at seven months and Mother recorded that fifty-four approving onlookers stayed afterwards for supper in our home. Whenever the opportunity arose, she lavished food on top of religious ceremony.

To give an impression of the strength of anger between Brethren groups, consider the advertisement placed by Open Brethren in the *Sun* newspaper in Melbourne sixty years back (1962) at a turning point in my own attitudes to Brethren. The ad aimed to deflect media disapproval thrust on the Open Brethren by the behaviour of Exclusive Brethren. Open Brethren were afraid of being seen in the public mind as allied with the age-old enemy:

> Not for more than 100 years have 'Open Brethren' had any association whatsoever with 'Exclusive Brethren'… This disclaimer is regretfully necessary because of the publicity given to the continued…teachings of Exclusive Brethren which have been a cause of grief to all right-thinking people.

My family cringed at every new media revelation of scandal and cruelty among Exclusive Brethren at that time. I filled a scrapbook to overflowing with sensational news cuttings. For a period of about five years, Father scanned his favourite Melbourne *Herald* for hot scoops, while David kept a close eye on *Truth*, a newspaper that focused on any gossip, taking up the cause of ejected Brethren. It was a tits-and-bum rag which specialised in unearthing putrid scandals of any sort – political, sporting, social, business, financial. In 1962, it reported a typical scoop – that Bruce Hales compiled a list of seventy husbands who should be abandoned by their Brethren wives and children for sinning.

From a simmer to a boil

Long periods of tranquillity were rare in my childhood. There were tensions of one sort or another right, left and centre – between members of my family, between my family and other Brethren, between us and enemies outside (most of them imaginary). Tensions among us as a family were due to clashing personal preferences and punishing controls imposed on us. The next few chapters try to sort out which influences on my alienation from Brethren were due to family members and which to other causes. My yearning to exercise discretion was perpetual. Any inclination towards a desire for genuine freedom was squashed dramatically. Any sign of personal gratification was deflated instantly. Seeking elbow room or feeling pride were horrible sins. The exercise of free will was as elusive as choosing your own birth parents.

Historically and in my time, Brethren courted disagreement and disunity. It kept them pure (in their own eyes) and provided a modicum of excitement where the humdrum was in danger of dominating daily life. So long as Brethren managed to maintain the illusion of evil terror in the World beyond our boundaries, they kept petrified adherents fearful and captive. They wallowed in fear, unresolved argument, suppression, keeping watch, backbiting and bitterness.

I had never heard of the word trauma in the 1960s but witnessed a bombora of it regardless. My solution was to swim free of the causes of it altogether, but it took time, practice, strength and courage. This memoir will describe further reasons for my departure from the maelstrom, how I engineered it, and how it affected me. For comparison with mine, the stories of my siblings' escapes have been outlined, and in the next chapter the religious encounters of others are commingled.

Three

Others

Remnants

According to my mother's account written in an old exercise book, on 17 September 1954, one week after my eighth birthday, I was

> asked to Peter Hammet's birthday party today, but of course, he was not allowed to go. Poor darling had a weep, as Tony Goss and Gregory Roland were going, but we went down the street, and Graeme had a peppermint ice cream, which helped to compensate.

'But of course'! I felt anger for years about not being allowed to mix amicably with others, with my peers. Many times I played 'Keepings-Off' at school with Peter Hammet and knew him well as an expert dodger who ran very fast. I have no memory of what I told him about not going to his party. Resentment still glows in me, because I cannot resist correcting my mother posthumously: the flavour of the ice cream was not peppermint, which I disliked, but vanilla.

Mother would have concocted a lame excuse on my behalf to avoid Peter's party. She was expert at making excuses for not fraternising: I recall her making excuses about not attending a Tupperware party, even though she desperately wanted Tupperware products. That brand was only sold at social events, not in shops. She found a non-Brethren relation to buy containers for her at a party so that she could keep up with the latest plastics. She coveted a hoard.

In addition to using food as bribery – her passion for food is in the next chapter – another of Mother's fascinations was observing people.

This enthusiasm may have instilled a sense of the value of history and biography in her. Each of her children inherited one of her memorial exercise books when they 'reached maturity' (her specification).

'Now, you are not look in them. Promise?' she admonished me as a ten-year-old.

'All right then,' was my vague reply. The promise had a use-by date on it. I would bide my time.

The conversation was an invitation to check on what was so very confidential about the contents. Mother's brief longhand entries reveal few instances of her fears of my contamination by the World. The bulk of them recount the food and presents at every one of my birthdays. The pages bulge with my baby teeth which were taped into it – the tooth fairy had been a keen recycler. If ever anyone needs a sample of my DNA, there is enough raw material for many decades to come.

Turning points that Mother heralded as indicative of my growth feature in the book, such as achieving at school, contributing to Brethren activities, or dealing with small medical emergencies. The book was lovingly covered in 1946 with leftover wallpaper and given to me when I turned twenty-one. Although my house fire singed it badly in 1980 and charred many of my other books, the innards of the old exercise book survived miraculously. Thereafter, it became part of what middle-aged friends spoke of as my collection of dirty books. It did not contain a full diary in that entries were irregular, sometimes more than a year apart, but in the absence of profuse records, they plug gaps in my memory.

My bronze medallion for swimming and lifesaving was also taped into the book with care. I loved swimming; it was one of the few sports that I was permitted to enjoy fully, it being assumed that I swam alone. I dutifully parked my bike in the backyard of a Plymouth Sister who lived near the public swimming pool. Although I belonged to no official team, in order to comply with the Brethren principle of Separation, in fact I spent most summer afternoons in the Camberwell baths, with self-appointed competitors who were as keen as me. Peter Gronn –

mentioned later – was one of them. Effectively, I joined team competitions, informally and secretly joining in with the local water polo club in their training games, for example. Chasing and challenging in deep water was fantastic exercise, a healthy strain on the muscles and lungs.

I always loved the sense of swirling through water and peering into depths below. And the glorious vision of a bright sky from beneath – looking up through the water to the surface above – never leaves my mind. In water, all cares were left behind in my wake; swimming acted as an emotional and mental purgative whether in a pool or the ocean. It was a relaxing opportunity to jettison a bundle of moral burdens. And after a workout at the baths, if I had the cash, I indulged in a large lime sundae (with half a banana and a scoop of vanilla ice cream) covered in malt, served on an elongated glass dish at the humble pool canteen. What luxury. My mouth salivates at the memory of that indulgent intake of sugar.

Difference

The aim of this chapter is to determine – as far as possible – how different my upbringing was from that of any other white, middle-class boy in Melbourne's eastern suburbs, born in 1946 or thereabouts. How different were my family from families of neighbouring children of the time, such as Peter Hammet or fellow-swimmers? Often I am asked these sorts of questions:

'Was your personal development similar to mine in any ways?'

'To what extent did Plymouth Brethren influence your personal growth and shape your thinking and behaviours?'

'Were regular releases from any stresses caused by religion available to you?'

'Did your experiences of Brethren leave you with any lasting benefits?'

These big questions do not have simple answers, for a range of unusual reasons.

For me, it is almost as hard as trying to explain the evolutionary function of the horn on a unicorn. But I attempt to answer them here and a little more in subsequent chapters.

In my cult, Great Brothers wrote hagiographies of other Great Brothers after they had gone to heaven; they alone were glorified. De facto canonisation only occurred at a respectable period of about a generation after a death. Mostly, Brethren sought obscurity, regarding it as a high virtue, and kept no records of their activities. Members believed that their time on earth was finite and insignificant, not worth noting, especially if they were women. They had no church organisation that automatically generated archives, and they resented intrusive inquiry. They preferred to be nonentities.

Thus in the 1870s, the great-grandfather of Jane Campion, the filmmaker, worked for Her Majesty's Customs and Excise Service all his life and (according to his son)

> he was impressed by a [Brethren] preacher who taught that it was wrong for a Christian to seek promotion [in any job], so my father did not take the next step, which was to sit an examination [for the Customs Service].

My father espoused similar attitudes, never putting his competencies forwards at his workplaces nor pushing for promotion.

Unobtrusiveness continued one hundred years later. Rosemary Stanton was just as self-effacing as any other member of a Plymouth Brethren family. She lived at home in Sydney until she turned twenty, and could never bring herself to look in the mirror, even twenty years after she left Brethren. Looking was tantamount to self-admiration, which was a sin. Rosemary left to follow her yearning to study nutrition, and by dint of skill and hard work and a PhD became world-famous, modifying her reflexive reticence in order to share her knowledge, to achieve accolades and publicity in magazines, on radio and television. Two years older than me, she escaped one year before, with her family, causing her father a mental breakdown.

The humble life of anonymous ants, noted in the Bible text from

Proverbs 6:6–7, fascinated me when I discovered it as a child. Some modesty had rubbed off. I felt that the ant in me sought no recognition but was determined to get on with the job efficiently, mostly by helping others in the nest. The nameless ant needed no direction either; it was completely free of oppressors and quietly enjoyed its productive roles. The simple sound of the Biblical words rolled off my tongue:

> Go to the ant, you sluggard;
> consider its ways and be wise!
> It has no commander,
> no overseer or ruler,
> yet it stores its provisions in summer
> and gathers its food at harvest.

Father was impressed by my ability to recite the lines, not noticing the footloose rebel that I identified with in the tiny ant.

Two researchers who undertook a statistical survey of religion in Scotland, ending in 1950, were told by a Plymouth Brother that

> we shun everything that would draw attention to ourselves in an outward way... The path of obscurity, unknown to the World, is ours.

Permanent distancing from the World made the work of researchers very hard; isolation was absolute – past, present and future. Thus any form of extant reminiscence – other than displaying testimony to the World – is exceptionally valuable today as a memorial. Frank and unemotional assessments of Brethren events and life stories are as rare as hens' teeth.

It is a privilege for me to be able to describe some of my inside stories of Brethren, most of whom lived guileless and unexceptional lives in comfortable – and more or less socialist – communities worldwide before 1960. Homogeneity inhibited change for them in Australia over seventy or eighty years, but within a short period of two to three years (my teenage years) the tranquillity was shattered by self-appointed tyrants whose only interest was their own self-aggrandisement. The effects on me and my family were dramatic. The surprise takeover of old traditions paralleled the rise by political despots in post-imperial countries of the world generally. Few victims of the Brethren tyranny have spoken up, but the handful of extant accounts of Brethren life that exist focus a lot on the Exclusive revolution of the 1960s. Before that time, inconspicuous Brethren clung to each other cautiously, fearfully and anonymously. The World threatened their furtive muteness, hermetic seclusion, and the very odd practices that I note. Their entire cosmos was confronted by inside and outside assaults together in the early 1960s. Events of the revolution of that decade reverberate in this memoir.

It is necessary but not easy to differentiate my family's lives from our immersion in Plymouth Brethren. One way to attempt answers to the differences, and to questions about similarity and difference between Brethren and others, and between the many Brethren groups, is to interrogate those who migrated from Exclusive Brethren to another Brethren group, or migrants from Plymouth Brethren and away from all religion, around the time of my departure in 1968. Such people are hard to find unless I kept in touch with them over a long period, but most of them I have lost track of. One ex-Brethren friend, Percy, has emailed me and left me in no doubt about

> the strange (often downright mediaeval) beliefs, ideas, ideologies and behaviours inflicted upon so many of us as naïve kids. I often wonder at the innate resilience which prevented us from being completely fucked over and allowed us to survive and even thrive as free-spirited, free-thinking…adults… I found reading [your memories] to be a liberating, cathartic experience.

In his twenties, friend Percy followed a path very like my own – out of all faith completely. He has led a full and satisfying life since as a forester and as an ambulance paramedic. He told me that he relied somewhat on boating for wriggling free of his youthful Brethren burdens. His father loved boats too – he taught me to water-ski on Port Phillip Bay. The rest of Percy's family – his parents and three brothers – joined Open Brethren in the late 1960s.

I have the impression that the traffic from Plymouth and Exclusive over towards Open Brethren was always greater than in the other direction, but there are no statistics to prove it. The greater freedom and less exclusivity among the Open lot appealed to many ex-Plymouth and ex-Exclusive Brethren. The Open group were welcoming of any self-professed Christians, in contrast to the other two branches which scrutinised newcomers suspiciously for long periods. According to research by an Australian ex-prime minister, when he was twenty-five and at university in Sydney, Open Brethren were focused on promoting the church in the broad community, humanising their image, in order to rustle up more followers. Scott Morrison wrote a thesis about them. My lot never entertained such crude strategies. Mingling could taint us.

My own great-uncle Jim (Johansen) took the very sinful route into Open Brethren in the 1920s. As well as working as a bank manager, he declared himself a missionary on the Eyre Peninsula in South Australia, among Aborigines and whites. He was the milder, older brother of my forbidding grandfather and spoke with a gentler voice. Did he taint us?

We did not mingle often, and in my tight family enclave he was not warmly welcomed. We were taught to disapprove of him because he was Open, but also because he had no children (presumably through no fault of his own), and in addition he made up for the deficiency in offspring by marrying four times – to Millie, Annie, Esther and Amie. Separately.

James spent all his working life as a bank manager at Cowell, Cleve, and Kapunda in country South Australia. At the age of fifty-five, he was required to leave work because the Australia and New Zealand Bank objected that he handed out religious tracts to customers during business hours. He married his second wife, Annie, after he was sacked. Annie Lock was a very determined woman who had worked solo for thirty-four years as a Christian missionary with Aborigines across many desert regions of Australia – before James. She knew Daisy Bates, the eccentric white anthropologist (who herself almost equalled James by marrying three times).

Annie lived (for six years) with James in the back of a Model T Ford truck, while travelling to nurture the souls of indigenous and settler South Australians on the Eyre Peninsula. James was extremely tall (about two hundred centimetres) and would have had great trouble fitting horizontally onto the tray of the truck with a length of only a hundred and forty-three centimetres. Annie looked about half Jim's height in photos but I never knew her myself. They must have curled up tightly in the tray. She died well before my arrival, in 1943 at the age of sixty-six. James survived until 1970, then aged ninety.

James's liking for wives caused his behaviour to be judged as licentious and unforgivable in Mother's eyes, propped up by Aunt's open inhibitions about any kind of male partner. His manifest sins only made me all the more curious about him. Face-to-face, I could not put my finger on any problem whatsoever. He just seemed a jolly giant when he visited our home occasionally. Father, his nephew, only feigned innocence; James's lifestyle was not Father's fault. But a final problem with visits by James (as reported by Mother) was that he outwore his welcome on more than one occasion. He apparently did much the same in Cleve, South Australia, where as a long-term bank manager, Brethren locals complained that he was in the habit of dropping in to visit them only at mealtimes.

I made recent contact with a few others of those who crossed over to the Open Brethren lot, seeking reminiscences, including from another relation – my cautious cousin. They are very reluctant to discuss their beliefs or experiences for fear of offending their surviving relatives or God himself. Or, they find my queries a threat. Or, they feel a need to forget their exposure because they are embarrassed by the Brethren or tired of them. Many old wounds are sealed, but maybe not yet healed.

A clear example of such a person – who wanted to, but who could not let Brethren go – was the Irish playwright J.M. Synge, born in 1871 in Dublin, dying young (at thirty-seven) of cancer. His grandparents lived next door to the first Brethren meeting in Dublin, where they became committed to the new faith. Into his twenties, Synge depended on his mother, more devoted to Brethren than his father, who had died of smallpox when Synge was one year old.

At the age of fourteen, Synge's ideas were influenced by Charles Darwin, Karl Marx and William Morris (socialist and designer), with the result that he lost all faith. His mother and seven siblings despaired, believing that writing plays was a waste of his life. His mother's neighbouring household included a beautiful woman called Cherrie Matheson, another Brethren devotee, with green eyes and red hair. Synge visited often on numerous holidays. He asked Cherrie twice to marry him, and she twice refused, on the grounds that their beliefs were too incongruent. Literary critics claim that four of his most famous plays contain pained characters that can be sheeted back to his traumas with Brethren.

Publications

A scan of published literature about Plymouth and Exclusive Brethren yields sparse biographical pickings. A handful of research theses focus narrowly. Journal articles typically adopt an academic methodology – in sociology, psychology, theology or local history – and generate narrow generalisations.

In contrast, recent activity on the Internet provides lots of subjective, short accounts of escape from the clutches of the Exclusives, as they came to be known. Extroverts use YouTube to recycle sensational snippets of news footage from TV about Brethren abuses. Shock impact has a high priority in headlines:

> An Extremist Cult.
> Sect's secretive leader tells followers to drink rat poison.
> Doctrine that divides.
> Potential witness in Exclusive Brethren sex abuse case paid to remain silent.
> Ex-Exclusive Brethren accuse church of tearing families apart.
> My escape from the Exclusive Brethren.

And so on.

In-depth memoirs are harder to come by. One reason is that the current Exclusive Brethren Christian Church employs lawyers to shoot off threatening letters to any critic pronto, in order to suppress defamation. In parallel, an alert public relations company pumps out online propaganda to impress mass media with Brethren good works today, especially near election times.

With justification, accounts by ex-Brethren of trauma and ostracisation tend towards self-pity and a focus on the horror and pain of cruel escapes. Partly because most online accounts are so personal and heartfelt, they rehash accounts of repulsive punishment in the here and now. They hardly ever contain reflection over time on how freedom was achieved or why. Recent victims are overwhelmed with anger, indignation and resentment.

Many online stories tell of sadness and deprivation. For example, as a child in Invercargill, New Zealand, in the 1990s, Craig Hoyle relates how his Brethren grandmother told him that, when the rule was introduced (in the 1960s) that sect members should not have pets – because they represented an emotional bond that might come between the Brethren member and God – the family cat was drowned in a river. Goldfish went down toilet bowls. Craig was rebellious and would not confess to wicked thoughts; he was subjected to physical abuse and emotional manipulation, and advised in Sydney to take a hormonal suppressant when he outed himself as gay. He felt catastrophic heartbreak and anguish when forced to leave his entire family behind with the Exclusives.

The fullest personal account of gradual escape that I know was published in 1907 as *Father and Son* by Edmund Gosse. It was a pioneering landmark that is hard to surpass. It has to be acknowledged that the Gosse Meeting was Open rather than original Plymouth Brethren, but little distinction between the two groups was discernible in 1846 when Henry Gosse, Edmund's father, joined. The split between the groups had only occurred one year earlier and is unlikely to have affected Edmund's life greatly.

The most remarkable feature of the experience of the escape of Edmund is that it is so similar to the pressures on me and on contemporary children of Brethren. Although lacking any literary pretension, ninety years later, David Tchappat's book titled *Breakout; how I escaped from the Exclusive Brethren* in 1994 in Gosford, New South Wales, is eerily similar to Gosse's in its recounting of types and degrees of suffering.

Father and Son has the subtitle *A study of two temperaments*, which warrants closer examination because the author implies that personality differences were the main cause of their clashing points of view. In my opinion, Edmund tries too hard to treat his father gently by asserting that their disagreements were an inevitable outcome of innate antagonisms. Much beyond character was at play; the systemic cult pressures on Edmund continue on others to this day. The fact that Edmund revealed late in life to friends – and not in his memoir – that he was secretly gay would have added to the feelings described in the book of hesitancy, otherness and alienation as a youth.

Edmund regrets that his father, Henry, mistook fear for love; intimidation was his weapon for curtailing independent thinking. In his shyness as a child, Edmund suffered shocking nightmares which Henry could not explain. Henry was a keen naturalist, obsessed with the detail of marine biology. In photos, his downturned mouth even made him look like a fish. He collected marine specimens all his life, inventing the indoors aquarium, and earnestly published in order to support anti-evolutionary theories. He was vehemently opposed to the mega-theories of his contemporary, the evolutionist Charles Darwin.

Edmund was able to expand his repertoire when he was allowed to enjoy poetry and fiction-writing with the help of his stepmother. Opening windows onto worlds was part of my own liberation; my mother was the means of access to literature outside the Brethren straitjacket. In my late teenage years, the Bible outlived its purpose, and I engorged my imagination with as much fiction as I could feast on. Comics were banned, but I loved anything cartoon-like; *The Incredible Adventures of Professor Branestawm* with illustrations by Heath Robinson were an example of my taste in perfect entertainment.

When Edmund Gosse was about fourteen, Henry could only view morals as absolutely black or white. He realised that he could no longer force Edmund to devote his life to God. As a child, Edmund tells that he

> carried…such a confused throng of immature impressions and contradictory hopes. [He] was at one moment devoutly pious, at the next haunted by visions of material beauty and longing for sensuous impressions.

When Edmund left for work in London at the age of seventeen, his mind was full of apprehension. Henry sent letters daily about Edmund's spiritual failings, which the son finally refused to answer after years of harassment. Yet until Henry died, when Edmund was thirty-nine with a family of his own, a high-flying career and a list of publications, Henry continued to harangue Edmund violently about his sins, about his fleshly lusts, insidious infidelity to God, and dreadful conduct. To his father's immense shock, the normal literary world embraced Edmund; his friends included Henry James, Thomas Hardy, Aubrey Beardsley, Rudyard Kipling, Arthur Conan Doyle, Robert Louis Stevenson, Henrik Ibsen and many other prominent creatives.

Like my own parents, Henry Gosse could not admit to any wrong perspectives, nor to having even the slightest doubts about his own beliefs. Dogma was an impenetrable security blanket. Their worlds would collapse around them if they entertained any reservations.

Every now and again, I wrote a spasmodic diary, and it happens that on 28 June 1967 – when I was on the cusp of leaving Brethren – I read *Father and Son* for the first time. I found the book confronting because I was put off by the fanaticism of Gosse's parents, who were (in habit, thought and speech) the product of their age. I tried to fool myself that they were an anachronism. I was blinded then to any similarities between the parents of Edmund and my own, not having yet thought through the issues. In fact, the two sets of parents were not far removed from each other in attitudes at all.

I explored other British books which cover the same frightening territory as Gosse. I had an urge to know what happened to other disaffected Brethren. Were their adventures comparable to mine? Did they use similar escape methods? Chief among them were Christine Wood, *Exclusive by-path; the autobiography of a pilgrim* in 1976, and Rebecca Stott, *In the days of the rain; A daughter. A father. A cult* in 2017.

When in her twenties, Wood dipped into Exclusive Brethren in the 1940s en route from Catholicism to Anglicanism. A naturally devout person, she was deeply shocked by what she encountered – the strictest control and surveillance at every turn. Her aim in publishing the book was to explain to enquiring Christians (primarily) how Brethren treated those who fell into their clutches. She claimed never to have surrendered her inner being to them, in the way that Gosse also said that he kept a secret part to himself. I suppose that they meant they were knocked down by Brethren, but not out. I was never aware of having an inner self as a child; the Brethren concept of a soul was a total mystery to me, so I felt no need to protect it.

Rebecca Stott focused on her father. She was also a victim, although she left Exclusive Brethren herself in 1971 at the age of seven with her family. It is her father's long immersion in and diversion from the Exclusive creed that fascinates her most. It can but be dramatic. I have special interest in her account, because her father Robert was born in the same year (1938) as my brother, David, thus encountering the cult in a comparable period to my family. Further, Rebecca's grandfathers (Mallelieu and Wasson) persuaded my forebears to join Brethren in Adelaide and Kyneton early in the last century. She agrees with me in email correspondence that her own childhood overlaps with my experience.

Too distressed by his pro-Brethren behaviour in the decade of the 1960s, Robert Stott could not bring himself to rationalise it in print by himself, and leant on his daughter to do the job for him. In a BBC TV interview in 1976, he appeared stiff and depressed, as he said

I deplore the waste of 12 years of my life really… I hate the fact that I had that out of my life and so much I could have done with it.

In his worst Brethren moments, he harassed vulnerable followers, made them confess concocted sins, dragged them through public humiliation and judgement, and administered rites of exclusion. After departure, effectively he broke down, then became besotted by whisky and gambling, was imprisoned for embezzlement, and pursued a BBC career in production, and a fascination with live theatre. His bizarre behaviour over this time led his daughter, Rebecca, to suffer double stressors – by immersion in Brethren culture as a young girl and by her father's deep shame and incapacity to come to terms with it later on. Robert fell terminally ill while Rebecca strove to recount their joint heritage. All the while, as she tried to get him to recollect, her dying father was befuddled by terror and painkillers.

There is one more category of books about Brethren breakouts worth mentioning. As a group, it includes full autobiographies with a section (often small) about leaving Brethren before the age of about twenty-five. Usually, the full reasons for the flights to freedom are not explored, just the drama of the flights themselves. An energetic example is Joy Nason, *Joy and Sorrow; the story of an Exclusive Brethren survivor* in Sydney in 2015. Most of the book deals with her migration from the UK to Australia as a child, and her very active life after release from Exclusive Brethren – much more than mere survival. Others are Ngaire Thomas *Behind Closed Doors* from 2004, and Noel Virtue, *Once a Brethren Boy; an autobiography* from 1995. They contain familiar stories of strict controls as children, minor misdemeanours in their teenage years, followed by tragic separation from extended families when the pressure on them for conformity became unbearable. Virtue suffered a mental breakdown and persecution by his family for being gay. Typically, these authors assert that their motivations for writing were catharsis and to assist to shepherd existing Brethren slaves to emancipation, although it is hard to imagine how that might occur when inmates have no access to such accounts. Many old escapees are hopeful of being able to assist new escapees who are confused and disoriented, not acknowledging that everyone's path is different. The need to rescue souls had become ingrained.

If I analyse all these publications of first-hand experiences and make a crude matrix to summarise the causes for leaving Brethren as described in the books, some preconditions are common to most accounts. Robert and Rebecca Stott can be treated as individuals for this exercise rather than as one. In every case, abnormal levels of guilt, fear, panic and nightmares afflicted children during their Brethren lives and gripped them with terror. In Joy Nason's case, she did not rid herself of nightmares until thirty-three years after she left the cause of them. In five of the six cases, parental love towards children was intermittent, to say the least, and clinical breakdowns were reported. In two out of six cases, parents were forced to seek medical assistance to try to cope with children's hallucinations. All the details are harrowingly miserable. They tormented me as I researched them and as a result, in one of my own recent nightmares, a faceless Brother threatened to stab me to death with a knife.

Many less severe reactions to Brethren were reported in all six instances – such as the boredom of attending too-numerous meetings, or instances of supposed Brethren friends dobbing others in for errant behaviour. In themselves, these lesser irritants were not a sole cause for departure, but cumulatively they added to ultimate disillusionment. Unfortunately I experienced all these common repellents.

Who else?

Perhaps it would have been ideal to retrieve first-hand evidence from non-Brethren boys in the 1950s, but at the time it was not possible, because as a family we had nothing to do with them in our monastic world. Boys my age were aliens, kept at arm's length always, and I was not permitted to play sport or organised games with them. I was not allowed to muck around with them at home. I did not attend special events with them. I talked to them at school but never at length and never in depth.

People ask me if I was like other children of the time. Did others have deeply religious families? Some did; in biographical writing, there are plenty of examples of family influence on faith. For example, the Australian novelist Tim Winton in *The Boy Behind the Curtain* describes his dry-as-dust upbringing with the Church of Christ in the 1960s, and how badly he was bored out of his mind by attendance at church three times on Sundays. At the risk of upsetting his parents, he moved on to Presbyterians, followed by Catholics, then Anglicans, then Catholics again.

In an effort to try to assess the uniqueness of my self-portrayal, I fell to quizzing my own non-Brethren contemporaries about their exposure to religion as they grew and developed. The four interviewees attended my Canterbury State School in the 1950s and lived fairly close to my home. They led separate lives and did not consult each other before my questioning. In adult life, all four of them showed respect and caring towards others, and achieved leadership roles in their different careers, with or without religion. Each of their stories differ. I am very grateful to them for sharing their memories. They are Maree, Peter, Greg and Philip.

I chatted to them informally. Their exposure to religion did not involve coercion, control or fears as in my own childhood, nor like that described in the published accounts that I have mentioned. At the same time, faith played a part in their development, but was just one of many influences, neither overwhelming nor oppressive. They chose freely, not encountering any threat of a hellish life sentence, nor inner turmoil, nor blinding light. It appears that they slipped gently in, or gently out.

Maree

As a child, Maree moved from a country town to Canterbury, where she conformed to the social norm of attending Sunday school. Across the road from where she and her siblings lived in Camberwell was a Methodist church, which they attended conveniently, even though her mother was Anglican and her father had been brought up a Presbyterian. Mother kept attending an Anglican church and generally within the family there was an attitude of tolerance and acceptance of individual difference and choice in relation to faith.

Maree was not conscious of any obligation or family pressure to attend. As a teenager, her attendance was self-imposed, and she enjoyed friendships, fun activities and groups, picnics, camps and performing musicals.

From attending secondary school at the same time as me, I am aware that she had the (unfortunate) role of head prefect, requiring her to set an example by regularly wearing full regalia outside school grounds and at special events in the school. But she seems to have found it as routine as her approach to faith. The girl's uniform of longish skirt, green blazer, hat with curled-up edges (like spouting around a house) and grey gloves, was monitored at the school gate on arrival in the mornings. To loosen the top button of a blouse or shirt was a serious misdemeanour.

In my case, my thinning old green tie grew to resemble a frayed leash in its dotage. I remember one irate teacher using that thin tie to drag me closer to his rage-red face, to make his anger known up close. To top our uniformity, boys were expected to wear a peaked woollen cap. Mine spent most of its long life in my hip pocket, slowly fading and acquiring deep creases over a period of six years. On ceremonial occasions, it perched on my growing head, looking like the shrivelled crown of a protoceratops.

In her late teenage years, Maree began to drift away from church-going, irritated by narrow-minded attitudes to different sexualities, other faiths and gender roles. Maree never suffered any struggle to escape the influence of church, drifting (like others) in the 1960s, at a time of great social change, of questioning, of broader tertiary education, and of the ability to reside overseas.

She became a social worker, helping many disadvantaged and marginalised groups of various faiths, in outback Australia, South Africa, Kenya and London, and has

continued through life to explore different religions, philosophies, aspects of faith and spirituality, through reading, meditation, seminars, and ongoing groups.

No turbulent emotion or stress afflicted her because of religious adherence, or lack of it. Today she walks against war, for refugees, for social justice, and along the beach.

Peter

Church was something I just did or engaged in, probably unthinkingly until adolescence when I began to…engage in self-questioning as to why… As an adult I am motivated in the sense of a positive commitment to belief, in a way that I wasn't when I was young… Now I desire faith engagement in a worshipping community. The parish is vital in sustaining that…

Neither Peter's parents nor household were religious, except for launching him into Sunday school, so his ongoing habituation was entirely voluntary. From the age of five, the church that he attended was part of the Canterbury Circuit of Methodist Churches. It was the church nearest his home, where Maree also attended. He enthusiastically joined in church activities, like Maree, and more – Sunday school, youth group, cricket, tennis, swimming, holiday camps, church fetes and acting in plays.

At school, I was extremely jealous of three aspects of Peter's life. With his scout troop, he went on exotic adventures which I could never hope to experience. He understood much more about politics than me – I remember that he heard of the assassination of J.F. Kennedy on the radio at home, an informed me of its possible implications. I knew nothing of US domestic affairs, and had to wait to wade through newspaper reports. Thirdly, when we studied the Victorian gold rushes in history, a subject that we both enjoyed, I learnt that Peter's Danish grandfather – named Claus – had kept a handwritten journal of his experiences as a gold digger. They provided an enthralling read in book form. Later in life Claus had the best possible job in the city – he became chief gas lamplighter in the streets of Melbourne in the 1880s.

As well as the proud heritage of a diary, Peter inherited the shape of Claus's nose and forehead.

In the late 1960s, Peter and I finished our first degrees at the same university. His beliefs were challenged by moving away from home to the country for his new teaching job, and by growing social secularism, but when his children were born, he enjoyed participating in the newfound vibrant community associated with the local Anglican church. It still stimulates him. His social conscience, civic commitments and personal connections are inspired in part by embracing church worship and practice. His final job before retirement was as Professor of Education at Cambridge University.

Greg

I believe that Greg was probably born with a cricket bat in his hand. Greg, bat and ball were inseparable in the schoolyard. Not satisfied with school cricket, he played team cricket with Methodists, has played all his life, and is currently president of Veterans Cricket Victoria.

Greg is a contrast to Maree and Peter. He says that religion 'played little part in [my] development'. But the Church and its activities were the focal point of his early social life. In his home, his extended family of three generations provided plenty of stimulation and guidance. As a child, he attended St Paul's Anglican Church in Canterbury with his parents, where he went to the same church kindergarten as me.

When he turned thirteen, his parents bargained with him that if he was confirmed in the Church, he would not be required to attend regularly. He took up the offer, welcoming the opportunity to have the option. To him, sermons were too unreal. At secondary school, one teacher spent a term dealing with comparative religion, causing Greg to realise that Christians had no monopoly on God. It was the genesis of his belief in an undefined, benevolent supreme power.

His passion was sport, primarily cricket and football. He played football with Camberwell when young. For a long time, he has volunteered to assist at a disability centre. He practises no faith, although he has a sentimental soft spot for St Paul's in Canterbury, where all his family ceremonies (baptisms, marriages, funerals) have been held. To him, it is a retreat of calm and mystery that he visits privately every now and again. Not so long ago, he retired as Victorian State Manager for Medicare Australia, the national health insurance service, having begun work at the tender age of fifteen.

Philip

I once walked along the beach at Ocean Grove, listening to a serious conversation between my brother David and Philip, about the similarities between Karl Marx and Jesus. Philip was a deep thinker and itched to share his thoughts.

But the first time I met him was much earlier. He was on the gravel playground at our primary school, expertly wielding his cricket bat. Then twenty years later, we met again as adults at a little Fitzroy house, where he was practising his beliefs on the floor. This time, he was meditating on a rug with his partner.

Although mystical may not be precisely theological, it describes the thrust of Philip's beliefs. He is different from the others. He has known both Greg and Peter for a long time. He continues to play cricket with Greg. Philip and his family attended the same church as Greg, but he 'never experienced any pressure to belong'. He played sport with the church and joined scouts, like the others.

As a young man, Philip's father farmed in harsh conditions in the Mallee in north-west Victoria, where he belonged to the local Anglican church. He was involved in fearsome battles in Crete in World War II. Afterwards, he recovered in the Heidelberg Repatriation Hospital, a symmetrical arrangement of low ex-army Nissen huts with no summer ventilation. For some relief from his traumas of war, his visitors included Philip's mother, attending as one of a group of volunteers come to help to cheer up the returned soldiers. She belonged to the Malvern Anglican Church. The women of the horticultural society of Canterbury took fresh-cut flowers to the hospital.

In the 1940s, Plymouth Brethren made converts of returned soldiers. No doubt many men had ample reason to explore allegiances at that time. Brethren other-worldliness appealed to veterans who (*ex post facto*) crossed over from soldiering to pacifism. My father and mother both took their old-fashioned biblical injunction to visit the sick and needy (Romans 12:13) very seriously, and one recipient of our many visits was Keith McLeod, a soldier who had been gassed in the war, and converted. I wondered how his red hair glowed. Was it caused by the gas? Before his demise, he spent many coughing months in the repatriation hospital.

Philip's parents had a brighter future. They married in the 1940s and were never strict about his commitment to the church, but Philip was attracted. At the age of seven, his father asked him to caddy for him on the golf course. Philip says at that time father was more devoted to golf than to religion.

One day out on the course, his father – seeking a wholesome relationship – asked casually, 'What do you want to do when you grow up, Philip?'

'I want to be a priest,' Philip replied instantly without hesitating.

His father was shocked. 'Go and sit in the car and wait for me,' he commanded as a form of punishment. It was less than his father could hope for and more than he could cope with.

There was no further discussion. Philip went into academia and the future waned until he went to London at the age of twenty-five. He was drifting and took up serious meditation regularly as a means of clarifying his thoughts, calming his mind and pondering the path ahead. A Catholic nun influenced him in deep conversations. He taught meditation to others. He determined to return to Australia to approach the Anglican Church, and to train as a priest. Philip experienced a very powerful vision of Doubting Thomas when he committed to diligent devotion as a theology student.

For the rest of his career of faith, Philip engaged in life-nurturing humanitarian commitments and advocating for the disadvantaged, as a caring clergyman living in different parts of Australia. His most recent official role was as bishop. Early every morning in his retirement now, Philip swims in the ocean, then returns home to his favoured meditation for an hour in his little shrine in his back garden. He rekindles his credence daily.

For each of the four interviewees, personal needs and free consciences drove their relations with a church. I venture that they contributed to societal welfare in community and in their work, not so much because they were driven by their beliefs directly, but as alongside them. They were not assailed by a clash of cultures as I was. None of their parents or friends applied any pressure. They took their own chances.

Maree found her own path out of Methodism without fuss and into a rewarding career, while keeping her belief in Christian values and her curiosity about faith. Peter was committed to sport and social activities until he became a father in need of greater inner satisfaction, of community succour and of faith-bound support. His father was not religious. Greg followed conventional church habits until he decided to leave at the age of thirteen, to focus on family, cricket and a laudable career in health administration, starting young in the workforce. His inclinations morphed into a fulfilling life without public worship. Philip had a seven-year-old itch which was resisted by his father at the start, but which grew over time, and matured into full and constructive immersion in the Anglican Church. He has a dogged determination to improve the well-being of various disadvantaged minorities.

Eggs and options

It is impossible to determine whether these four, or other individuals, are predisposed to embrace and enjoy a life with faith, or if faith directed their lives in subtle (and direct) ways. Maybe it alienated. Interaction probably occurs in all directions without being flagged at any instant in time. As far as my first exposure to education was concerned – in kindergarten at the age of four – faith acted as a catalyst for several notable influences. Some were good, some bad. It heralded the beginning of my awareness that I was different.

Mrs Tribe, our kindergarten teacher at St Paul's, Greg, Philip and I liked very much. She was gentle and encouraging towards hundreds of Canterbury kids over many years. In spite of the manifest heresies of the Anglican Church, as identified peremptorily by my Plymouth Brethren family, I grew very fond of the kinder at Saint Paul's Anglican Church. I was probably not sent there for its creeds, but simply because it was close to home.

At Easter, Mrs Tribe put on an exciting chocolate egg hunt, such that I had never experienced. Ferreting crazily in grass and among play equipment, pouncing on glittering quail-sized eggs, was a one-off thrill. In my cult of Brethren, Easter was not recognised. Nor was Christmas – yet Mrs Tribe still taught us to sing carols which mentioned neither dour holiness nor theological imponderables. That 'Jingle bells' rhymed with 'Santa smells' was hysterically funny. So were the morose shepherds who 'washed their socks at night, all seated round the tub'.

At home – all seated around our dining table – I was told that Easter and Christmas celebrations were not biblical and therefore they had no place in our sanctified lives, no matter how much devoted exuberance they may attract from the big wide World. It was a harsh lesson. Brethren abstinence from merrymaking stretched back a long way: Edmund Gosse described how in Christmas 1857, his Brethren father Henry defied his cook and threw a fresh plum pudding (uneaten) on the rubbish heap because it represented the evils of Christmas – of the Pope and pagans combined. In my own mind, a vexing awareness of the gap between appealing practices outside and inside home was opening. Kinder raised questions.

It was probably the first institution that allowed me – outside home and Brethren – to be free physically and emotionally. A clear advantage of childhood life in 1950 was the degree of independence that I enjoyed. It has disappeared for suburban children of today. After Mother ushered me over the busy Wattle Valley Road, I walked up the hill to my kindergarten with David Tregellas, a neighbour. He taught me how to deflate the tyres on rows of parked cars and the outrush of air soon became an eruptive addiction.

I had no sense of inconveniencing drivers of the cars – just impulsive fascination with the smelly whooosh of escaping air from the valves. I never mentioned my deflating practices at home. I was not aiming to conceal my behaviour; it simply did not occur to me that it was of sufficient import to mention. If David could wangle whoooshes, why not me?

I am sure that my parents had no inkling of my bold sins. After a few of our kinder walks, an offended car owner complained to David's father, who in turn complained to mine. David's family were long-standing pillars of the established Canterbury community – staunch Methodists whose number included a haberdasher, an ornithologist, wildlife photographer, journalist, returned serviceman, councillor and bowls champion. According to the national census, my part of Melbourne (including Canterbury) was more non-conformist Protestant than any other. Out of respect and a demand for firm tyres, David and I were required to stop our depressurisations, but to this day anticipation tingles inside me whenever I uncap a valve to pump up a car or bicycle tyre.

When you are very young, your mind is impressionable but slow to synthesise information. I had no sense of being naughty, and indeed actually took great delight in this pastime. How many dots are required before they are joined to create a sense of guilt? It takes time. Back in 1950, there were only a few dots for me to work with. The dark blanket of comprehensive guilt was a sensation that awaited me further into the future. My mind was fully occupied with absorbing sensations from kinder – freedom, friendship, excitement, competition, humour, singing, curiosity, boundaries, conformity, difference, risk, and play. It was a heady mix.

If I ask myself the pertinent question, what *effect* did Plymouth Brethren have on my childhood and youth, plenty of experiences and events – such as at those at kindergarten – can be adduced as answers. But if one asks the more difficult questions – what *difference* did Brethren make to my personal growth and character, or adult personality; or which life influences mattered most; or which ones drove my escape – such questions are much more difficult to sort out and sift through. Writing this memoir assists.

I was looking for firm ground during periods of instability; on my twentieth birthday I wrote,

> 20 years represents a long time when you look at it in a detached manner. Think of all the tremendous things that have happened in the world…economic development…world alliances…saturation by mass communications…commodification… All these serve to reduce an aura of mystery that once dominated… I dislike getting older immensely, and wish the whole earth would stand still and give me a few years to catch up with it.

As a fresh adult, I was not coping well with the forces of uncertainty. From inside the cult, everything outside looked menacing.

Some escapees from Brethren, for example Ngaire Thomas, mentioned above, believed that she was an outcast by nature in her family, and destined for exclusion. I cannot attach any such inevitability to myself. Probably some innate personal tendencies were magnified or restrained by my Brethren upbringing, but no single effect alone is easily identifiable as crucial, and there was a build-up over time, leading to an escape. Personality does not explain everything. Not all escapees were as slow to act as me; some were much more impetuous. Character-building attitudes grow at different rates in different people. Undoubtedly, the evidence is unequivocal that Brethren upbringing involved excessive oppression, anger and trauma. They were part only of the whole story.

A question arises as to where Brethren influence might end in its impacts on descendants of fully fledged Brethren? For how many generations after escape can sinister clouds continue to send down emotional bolts of lightning and storms? Genes are in play. My own clouds originated from both my parents and grandparents, and felt threateningly near at hand. Others were affected from a greater familial distance. One was the author Helen Garner, as I relate further on.

Another was Jane Campion, born in Wellington, New Zealand in 1954, a film-maker and director who professed to inherit trauma from grandparents, as well as production skills from her talented father. Commentators on Jane's life and critics of her films assert that her parents experienced a litany of psychic fears in life – partly caused by Brethren – that resonate in Jane's films. Her audiences are drawn to the fears intuitively. For me, the psychological dramas in her films are extremely intense, often glum and visually raw.

Jane's grandfather, John Campion, made a living as a butcher – and butchered his third child (born in 1923) emotionally with his Plymouth Brethren rules. He had eight children. He threw Jane's father, Richard, out of home when he was aged only fourteen. What wicked sins against dogma did young Richard commit to warrant such harsh treatment? They were Richard's love of theatre and, because he had no books at all to read at home, his frequenting the Wellington Public Library in New Zealand secretly. Richard's favourite clandestine reading as a boy was from the Just William series, as was mine. I loved *William Does His Bit*. The English hero in the series, William, aged eleven, always gets into trouble with his parents, although he can never work out why. Nor can the reader, of course. Richard enjoyed the books so much that he made his own friends at school act out the plots of the novels.

Richard lacked loving care when young, as an emotional orphan, and took to acting spontaneously – with an in-built need for self-exploration. It is said that Jane's mother, Edith, was also emotionally deprived, full of fears and uncertainty. Her rich parents died from alcoholism when she was ten. She became an actor. As an adult she suffered from deep sadness and loneliness which she channelled into her poetry and novellas. She became dependent on antidepressants.

As a natural actor, Richard was obsessed with theatre. He said that for him acting was just his way of living. In this compulsion, he reminded me of the behaviour of my eldest brother, David; life for him was in essence an endless game.

Richard reached high status as actor and director, being honoured as Officer of the New Zealand Order of Merit for lifelong services to the theatre. But he alienated himself from Edith by indulging in multiple extramarital affairs and squandering her inheritance. According to Jane, her parents were very much in love, but totally absorbed by their acting, overlooking the children's needs. As a child, Jane fought with her sister for her parents' affection. Richard and Edith divorced when Jane was thirty years old.

When young, Jane had watched Richard direct theatre and ballet, and deeply admired his 'innovative qualities, courage and independent-mindedness in directing'.

They inspired her. Jane lived and breathed storytelling, yet she endured parents who were dysfunctional geniuses. Seeds of trauma were sown; her pent-up needs as a child were not met because her parents themselves had been deprived in a similar way. Fiction in her films functions as a form of psychotherapy. I am not aware of any Brethren characters in them, but the films are powerful – full of foreboding, ferocity and fury.

Accounts of escapes by other children from other faiths (as comparable controls) are hard to find. As previously stated, at the time of involvement, I was not permitted to mix with others, so cannot recall being aware of or able to testify to their feelings. During periods of religious instruction at school – when most kids listened to a volunteer who tried to make Christianity dance – I was sent down to read in the school library. In this chapter, I am lucky to have been able to rely on a handful of published accounts and volunteered reminiscences which reveal some templates for shaping of life, evolving character, and escape from oppression. They embellish mine.

Four

Mother in the Mix

Clash of cures

Loud noises came from behind the locked bathroom door. Bursts of a prolonged gargling were followed by impulsive choking. I heard it for the first time as a six-year-old and it terrified me. I rushed to tell Mother in the kitchen.

She was uninterested: 'Oh, it's probably Father cleansing his throat.'

'Sounds like someone strangling him.'

'Yes, it is disgusting.'

'How does he do it?'

Next time in the green and cream bathroom Father showed me how he controlled a thin bottlebrush with brisk bristles. He dipped it into his bottle of violet iodine, wiggled it above his open mouth, dripped a little liquid into his yawning gullet, then plunged the bottlebrush down, chasing the drops. I anticipated the strangled retching all over again. How he avoided violent vomiting I shall never know.

The iodine was but one treatment that we as a family inherited from my Grandmother Cate, Father's mother born in 1883. Cate was always sick. It was common for Plymouth Brethren to pursue homeopathic healing, including the Bastow family in Harcourt, mentioned below, as did many in the general community of the day. Grandmother's homeopathic remedies survived in the face of challenges from medicine based on the latest science, also advocated at home, and from God's will being 'done'.

God's will could never be known until it was done, that is, reverse engineered, but we subscribed to it wholeheartedly anyway. *Deo volente* was peppered over Brethren conversation with abandon. It meant God willing. Prayer and Providence worked hand in hand, although my fervent prayers to be healed of appendicitis when I was twelve fell on deaf ears. I had to go to hospital for the operation regardless. Beseeching the Almighty at bedtime had very limited leverage and I was admonished to thank Him for allowing me to avoid peritonitis.

We were also world leaders in having family access to the latest lotions and potions, some of them not even yet available in Australia on prescription. My aunt spent most of her working life with medical practitioners whom she had a good deal more faith in than she had in divine perspicacity. We were treated to new sample medicines one after another. My family embraced a bewildering tangle of old and new approaches based on contrasting philosophies.

Providence

Over and above homoeopathy and modern medicine hovered God's will, which prevailed willy-nilly, if ever competition between any of the three nostrums arose. We were indoctrinated to believe that every event was guided by remote control and we respected God as a far-out drone. Mother would never use the word luck, believing that it denied the power of Providence. Occasionally, she uttered the words good fortune, but only in situations of dire distress, as when my brother Peter somersaulted his soft-top sports car on the Geelong freeway near Werribee, and just survived.

This chapter reflects on the influence of Mother on my early life, and her role in mediating faith and practicalities. Our house was her empire, which she bought at auction for £900 in 1940, when Father was at work, supporting the war effort. And her sway reached well beyond the weatherboard house.

The strength of God's influence was demonstrated clearly in the rescue of Kenneth Overton in 2009. Mother befriended his mother and encouraged my friendship with Kenneth. He was my walking mate – agile and strong – in 1965 when we were both still (almost) Plymouth

Brothers. We belonged to the same Brethren rump at the time that Kenneth and I scrambled up Frenchmans Cap (1,445 metres) and down in the dark, gingerly, without a torch, followed by a hike for five snowy days in January through Cradle Mountain National Park in Tasmania. After I left Brethren in 1968, I lost track of him; he went into making plasterboard and property development in Devonport. From news reports, I found that in 2009 he contracted hemorrhagic necrotic pancreatitis and was stuck in hospital for eight months as he battled multiple organ failure which few survive. He had 'a feeling of God walking with' him instead of me:

> God intervened in a series of remarkable and unprecedented events that had even the medical profession using the word 'miracle'.

He was not comfortable calling his recovery a miracle like the doctors, because God intended it always, in Ken's opinion. I could not be so cocksure myself.

The most miraculous rescue that I ever experienced was as a deliverer of pathology specimens for a diagnostic group in 1966. Just the memory of my luck causes my pulse to race. If my awful mistake had become known, I would have incurred punishment much more swift and dire than God's wrath.

The temporary holiday job required me to visit pathology centres at the back of seven Melbourne hospitals twice a day, delivering samples from one centre to another, packed into reused cardboard shoeboxes. Sometimes, small Eskies were used too. Speedy delivery was essential to the job. At the back of Saint Andrews Hospital in East Melbourne was a steep driveway for entering and leaving by car in and out of the hospital car park. On leaving one afternoon, I accidentally left a shoebox of specimens on the roof of the bronze Kingswood as I reversed down the driveway at full tilt. All other samples were packed away securely in the back seat; they included specimens from biopsies and autopsies, bits of bodies from surgery, blood vials, multicoloured fluids, and unidentifiable human detritus in test tubes.

Following my routine, I switched on the car radio, drove fast down the slope, bounced over the deep gutter at the end, and swung around towards Bethesda Hospital. Then suddenly I remembered the box on the roof, sensing an awful catastrophe. How negligent was I? I drove slowly, slowly, slowly to the road edge, and opened my car door very apprehensively, only to find the shoebox still sitting angularly on the car roof. If it had not been full of the mess of human specimens, I would have kissed it. I was overwhelmed with a sense of relief. The rescue was not just a miracle, it was also the most fantastic good luck. I was never brave enough to recount my negligence with the shoebox to anyone for years.

I came to realise at the age of twelve that much personal effort lay behind some achievements, and not just Providence or exceptional luck. A specific competition influenced me towards becoming a young cynic. Although the Coca-Cola company contributed nothing to the health of my juvenile teeth except cavities, it unknowingly assisted in challenging the strict moral regime that I was forced to live under as a child. Coca-Cola, Fanta, Sprite, and Passiona regularly satisfied my lust for sweet fizzy drinks, whenever a milk bar was at hand. Young's, next to my primary school, held a Coca-Cola promotion in 1958.

I was not attracted by the modest prizes so much as by the thought that I might be the best at yo-yos in my school of 1,200 pupils. For a week, I practised day and night, at home, on my way to school, and on my way home from school. I was so obviously obsessed that my relentless enthusiasm alerted my mother to my intensity. She required a theological ruling on the legitimacy of a public contest with other students. The key moral question was whether a competition involved an unholy association, a form of gambling, an evil alliance? Doubt was often concocted to curb visceral impulse, to buy time for God to give a sign.

There were more pragmatic influences. Who else but Brethren would go to the bother of attaching theology to two plastic discs at the end of a cotton string? In retrospect, I note that lack of clear rules on certain activities or events gave Brethren space to chew the cud over many doctrinal dilemmas. It allowed for prolonged cogitation, to avoid commitment, and maybe definitive arbitration, but it failed to deliver any urgent solutions when timely and precise interpretation was demanded for legitimate reasons. Their irresolute vagueness enabled their desperate recourse to hypothetical behaviour like doing the right thing, or plain common sense. Both were touted too often.

After extensive adult consultation in the family – and beyond – I was given the all-clear by Mother. That is, my entry into the competition was approved by God. I was not privy to her discussion, but I am certain that the decision to go ahead was based more on my enthusiasm and expediency (that I would not be discovered) than on any religious requirement. I asked no questions about the reasoning behind the decision, having no intention of hesitating at a green light.

I was ecstatic to be allowed to enter, and even more so to win! However, independent achievement and self-promotion were frowned on in my community, so my yo-yo victory was not broadcast, and certainly not within earshot of Brethren. I was not allowed to show my prizes outside the family. I remember divulging them proudly to my cousin in the privacy of my bedroom. Frivolous fun was regarded as a waste of time. For us all, rewards lay in the afterlife alone. For a young boy bursting with energy – whether from excessive sugar or superfluous testosterone – deferred gratification meant nothing whatsoever.

Outside Young's, the local Coca-Cola rep was businesslike, so impressed by my special moves with the yo-yo, known as 'Walking the dog' and 'Rock the baby' and 'Around the globe', that he did not hesitate to award my prizes – a Coca-Cola logo embroidered on a felt badge (which I treasure to this day), one small bottle of Coca-Cola, and another Coca-Cola yo-yo. My ego inflated in front of all the onlookers outside the milk bar – not just the dozen competitors. I was in heaven when I won. It mattered nothing that Brethren did not know of my yo-yo prowess.

Homoeopathy

To return to the theme of homeopathy and Brethren, as the alternative medicine applied in early Melbourne, the father of Father's handsome friend, the dental surgeon Vernon Sealey, was a Plymouth Brother and the first homeopathic doctor in 1910. My paternal grandmother, Cate, a contemporary of Sealey senior, believed that a sure remedy for the common cold was the chinner. The chinner consisted of a piece of red flannel soaked in a mixture of warm water and methylated spirits. The flannel would not work unless it was red. It smelt overwhelmingly abominable. My older brother David advocated that it should have a layer of mustard also. It was wrapped around my neck several times and became excruciatingly prickly as it cooled. I was not allowed to remove it, even when asleep, in case I interfered with its penetrating efficacy. I assume that the pungent odour was to relieve congestion in the throat – it cleared out all my nasal passages very powerfully as well. I cannot imagine a better incentive to get over a cold as fast as possible than the chinner.

My father, born to Cate in 1909, was mostly healthy. He made further use of homeopathic medicine, which he stored in the form of a secret cache of pills on a lofty shelf in his capacious wardrobe. He handed the pills out very parsimoniously. They were dispensed with the utmost secrecy because Mother disapproved of the procedure and Father was a little embarrassed about his penchant for archaic remediation. She dismissed them as ancient quackery. He never admitted to their existence even though he gave them out secretively to us children at night as required. I required often – to cope with my nightmares. Mother professed to believe only in the remedies of modern medicine, not forgetting the overarching primacy of God's cures, of course.

If I woke with a nightmare and wandered sleepily into the vicinity of my parents' bedroom at the front of the house for reassurance, which I often did, I would benefit from the ministration of a few tiny bitter belladonna pills, tapped from a thin glass vial, followed by the offer of a jellybean from Father. Father always slept much more lightly than Mother. She did not wake. Noting today that belladonna is an hallucinogenic and poison, it is not surprising that it put me back to sleep. The jellybean counteracted the bitter flavour of the belladonna.

Mother was as capable as Father of adopting old-fashioned remedies, in fact, but would never admit it. Every couple of months, the Rawleigh's man called at our house with his double-sided suitcase. I waited expectantly until the full glory of the motley content of the suitcase was unfolded on the boards of the front veranda.

'How is Mrs Johanson today?' The polished salesman, in his suit and tie, removed his trilby hat with a flourish.

'Very well, thank you. Is there anything on special today?' Mother looked over the mass of colourful bottles and packets.

I tried hard to pretend that the theatrical display was just for my benefit alone.

'Our best vanilla essence is selling well. I think that you've tried it before.'

'Oh, yes. It is very good. I'll take two large bottles, please. And a tube of silver cachous for decorating my cupcakes. And do you have a large jar of barrier cream? It's so good for chapped hands. I'll try your vanilla tapioca dessert as well.'

I watched on in silent admiration, although tapioca was by no means my favourite. I have been told that barrier cream from Rawleigh's was purchased a lot by country women for soothing the skin on the udders of milked cows.

'We have a couple of new lines, Mrs Johanson…' but his voice trailed off as he noticed Mother losing interest.

Her regular purchases were predictable. A longstanding staple was Bates' Salve, a stick of brown goo (the size of a medium candle) advertised as a medicated plaster. Mother used it for many years on her children and grandchildren alike; the grandchildren still laugh about its supposed benefits. I have no idea how she found it originally; it was invented in 1833, and contained twenty-two per cent of lead oxide, smelt like rotting leather, and was supposed to be applied externally only. As the printed instructions explained, it was administered like sealing wax, heated by match or candle, and dripped onto gauze, or a Band-Aid, then pressed onto a sore spot on the skin (not an open wound).

Notwithstanding, an advertisement in one newspaper claimed that it was a cure-all – for cuts, bites, bruises, burns, whitlows, chilblains, sore lips, inflamed eyes, corns, rheumatism, warts, and many other ills. In practice as teenagers we treated it as quackery, yet another example of homeopathic delusions. Undoubtedly, it was warm and comforting emotionally to me on a Band-Aid as a child, but we now know that lead oxide may be fatal if swallowed or inhaled, and that it causes irritation to skin, eyes and the respiratory tract. Mother kept buying it regardless. When she died in 2009, I inherited three-quarters of a leftover stick of Bates' Salve from her, still wrapped in its original paper, including instructions. She let it go reluctantly.

Back in the night-time bedroom as a youngster, I pitifully called my night ghosts bad dreams but they were much more terrifying than that. Little wonder that I gnashed my teeth. I was petrified by all sorts of Brethren dogma – the threat of fire and brimstone in hell, the image of the bloodied holes in the hands of Jesus on the cross, the cruelty of the sip of vinegar when he was thirsty, and fear of missing out on the Rapture when the rest of my family might depart for nirvana without me. They were all downright alarming and I find it impossible to describe the levels of fear in me that they caused.

Another Brethren victim, Roy Daniells in Vancouver, has managed to describe exactly the same angst:

> I felt myself [at the age of 11] to be a sinner who might at any moment be irredeemably lost… Christ might come at any instant and take the saved, leaving me for judgment… I have come home from school, opened the kitchen door and found no one in the house, called 'Mother! Mother!' No answer. I would search the house and through the garden, full of fear. Nobody there. Then I've reeled against the door post with the conviction, Christ has come; they're all gone; I'm left for judgment.

Many times I panicked in the same way when I could not find Mother on my return from school.

Gloom

At one end of my bedroom was a deep, dark place where dry firewood was stacked for winter, to replenish the fireplaces in almost every room of our large house. David stirred me up about the dark with frightening facts. He called it the Black Hole of Calcutta, an historical dungeon where three-quarters of prisoners died of suffocation. Mother could not stop him from telling me about the ghastly torture.

But Brethren had begun with even worse; too many morbid genes plagued them. A heritage of suffering must have affected nineteenth-century fears. The horrors of novels of the time – let's say Thomas Hardy's Gothic – reflected mainstream attitudes. According to numerous accounts, since 1649 ghosts riddled the ancestral home, Leap Castle, of the aristocratic family of John Nelson Darby, the Brethren founder. Leap Castle in County Offaly, Ireland, had a reputation for horrible spirits of the dead – a dungeon tomb, murders and a prison fortress. A Darby ancestor was convicted of treason and sentenced to be hung, drawn and quartered. It was little wonder that spooks and nightmares were never far away from Brethren homes and communities. Current owners of Leap Castle attract tourists by advertising it as the most haunted castle in Ireland.

I was aware that unlike me, some others felt excitement and inspiration when they encountered the melodrama of biblical darkness and holy blockbusters. My brother David professed to be among them, but later I wondered if it was his literary affectation on show. Like David, the singer Bono got a kick out of apocalyptic dramas. He wrote in 1974 about a Brethren family who lived up the street from him as a child in a poor suburb of Dublin:

> That family were like an Old Testament tribe. I learned a lot from them. The depth and discourse of the scriptures. In their company I saw some great preachers who opened up these scary black bibles and made the word of God dance for them, and us… One minute you're reading it, next minute you're in it.

Similarly, the British novelist Rebecca Stott benefited, explaining that

> my imagination grew up on the Book of Revelation and the Horsemen of the Apocalypse and the great angels in Babylon and falling stars and floods.

Fantasies from the Book of Revelation and Old Testament violence had nothing but the opposite effect on me. I shrank in dread. For years (after reciting bedtime prayers mechanically), I talked in my sleep, walked in my sleep, gnashed my teeth, snored stentoriously, wet my bed and endured regular nightmares. My brothers slept in the same room as me and complained on a daily basis. Belladonna and a jellybean failed to stem the tide of trepidation. Fortunately, Mother cuddled me when needed.

When I was about sixteen, my prayers for a sign to show my future path failed. I can still feel physical tension in my chest at being let down after hopeful expectation of divine guidance. I could not have yearned harder, straining with effort. I was deflated that not only was God avoiding my sincere requests for assistance on life's path, but he clearly was not much bothered by my growing doubts either. At that time, I was preoccupied with the question of where I should go if I left Brethren. By any measure, it was a pressing problem which I dared not expose to Mother.

In parallel, new questions arose frequently with modern changes that challenged Brethren's antiquarian views. Earlier, I mentioned that my brother Peter was studying to become a surgeon. In our twenties when he and I were distancing ourselves from Brethren ways, when we were well beyond homoeopathy and childhood, heart transplants began in South Africa. Brethren were fusty. Although we had removed ourselves by then from their aegis, Father and Mother had not. We poohpoohed their bigotry that held that transplants were prohibited by the Bible on the basis that the heart was the centre of spiritual sensibility. The Brethren rump followed the instructions of King Solomon of Israel literally – of nearly three thousand years ago – when he advised 'Guard your heart, for everything you do flows from it' (Proverbs 4:23). A transplant was evil, supposed to destroy a person's unguarded motivations. Peter and I dismissed the narrowness as yet more confirmation of long-standing resistance to modern science. On similar pretexts, Brethren had rejected other medical advances in the past.

Recurrent tensions between submission to God's whims, homeopathy, and the latest medicine illustrate how my family muddled along. Willing to accept the unease of disequilibrium, no family member made any effort to reconcile the three competing practices, and none realised any illogicality in them not connecting. I was a child of more than one Cold War.

The contests showed how adults in my family adopted different preconceptions to interpret and apply their faith. They were not consistent. God's will depended on family submissiveness. Homeopathy was inherited. Modern medicine was a fifth column propagated by Aunt.

The wellness treatments followed stages of my own immersion in and then estrangement from Brethren. In my early days, the inconsistencies opened my young mind to alternative ways to solve problems. Then as a teenager the inconsistencies invited me to apply logic to try to reconcile the differences. Ultimately, the examples of inconsistencies multiplied to the point where I determined (importantly) that they represented incommensurable moral codes within Brethren themselves, as well as between Brethren and the World beyond. The life-changing revelation was that they were not capable of reconciliation.

Mother figure

In order to explore her other significant influences on my childhood, the rest of this chapter covers more of Mother and her role in our home and in the close-by Brethren community. Of lesser influence, Father and Aunt (Mother's sister, who lived with my family almost all of my home life) feature in the next chapters.

Moral dilemmas for us were as common as the home deliveries which arrived with regular precision, like the Rawleigh's man – and the milkman, baker, ice-man, woodman, postie, 'bottle-O', old metal collector, and others. Mother confronted religious conundrums daily. Painting a picture of her influence on me, my home life and my Brethren community requires representations of sturdy values, leadership, loving encounters, differences of opinion, compromises, fears, uncertainty, and the primacy of exceptionalism. Plymouth Brethren are more or less the canvas.

Mother never went so far as to give bottles of beer to the garbage collector at Christmas, he being a bit infra dig, although the uniformed postman always received a huge box of chocolates. Even though we did not do Christmas, the postie showed Mother coloured photos of his prize-winning cats, which he had affixed to large lids of metal containers of biscuits to sell. Mother bought several tins at the end of each year to give away to non-Brethren. But we still did not do Christmas – officially – while managing to keep a foot in both camps.

Mother made the postie busy. She was an inveterate letter-writer, penning in a bold, rounded, confident manner, and daily. Much concentration went into her compositions. God no doubt assisted because His grace and boundless love featured large in every letter. Letters ended always with the sign-off 'DV', which was an abbreviation for the Latin *Deo volente,* as mentioned. Indonesians say its equivalent to each other every day in Bahasa.

When I was born, one of Mother's holy correspondents (whom I never met) wrote some doggerel about me and posted it to her:

> So baby dear [that's me!] you've got our love,
> We thank thee and thank The One above.
> We love thee more as each day goes,
> Right from your head right to your toes.

That was only one of ten verses! Incidentally, my much-loved head was six centimetres bigger in circumference than average at birth, but Mother never complained about it.

Mother's writing compulsion indicated how happy she was to be surrounded by people and their letters which arrived regularly – morning and afternoon on weekdays, but only once on Saturday in the morning. Today she would be a social media junkie. When family members were away, she wrote instead of talking face to face. While David was at Oxford University, she sent him a letter every day for four years – that's about 1,500 blue aerogrammes. A complete list of her correspondents would almost outnumber the names in our old telephone books. Writing stimulated and entertained her. If she was up-to-date with letters to family and Brethren Sisters before the Separation of 1960, before Exclusive Brethren, she would send letters to people she had met elsewhere. Her distant non-Brethren relations were well informed of family events almost before they happened, and before the fatal iron curtain of Separation fell.

Her benevolent spirit always ensured that disadvantaged people were treated favourably. To her I attribute the beginnings of my own social conscience. She bought a new doormat from blind hawkers, even if we did not need a new one. Our piano was tuned annually by a blind man dressed in a black suit and tie – even if the piano was never really in tune. I stared at his white walking stick and his dexterity at the back end of the piano with awe. To perpetuate her concern for blind people, for ten years in later life Mother worked as secretary for the Christian Foundation for the Blind. She wrote letters and speeches for the director, Peter Sumner, and did the books. She helped with his travel plans to the Philippines, India and Tanzania. Her own much-loved grandmother was blind late in life.

Mother managed my household as well as the foundation. An unspoken domestic policy was to employ Brethren for work around the house if an opportunity arose. We supported deaf Brethren who often visited for meals. As children, we all learnt sign language, practising playfully with the patient deaf folk themselves. I loved the challenge. We children took advantage of the code by communicating across a distance using hand signs as a secret between ourselves when in the company of non-signers. Who needed new-fangled walkie-talkies?

One day when I was home from school, a Brother carpenter was fixing the warped wooden slats on our front veranda, when he chopped off his middle finger with an electric saw. As a Brother, he was not permitted to swear, but he could not anyway, because he was deaf and did not speak. Instead, he let out the most excruciating shriek, followed by a stricken wail such that I had never heard before. The veranda seemed to reverberate in sympathy. Mother drove him quickly to the Box Hill Hospital, where he was bandaged up. No microsurgery existed at that time.

As the crisis settled, when the howling faded, the problem arose as to what she should do with the leftover chopped digit? It looked dreadfully shrunken when the blood dried brown. Mother felt guilty about throwing it in the rubbish bin although the family counselled her to do so. She hovered around it as though it was a landmine about to explode. A mini-funeral in the garden seemed too weird, and other adults in the family were forced to point out that the Bible was deficient when it came to lost limbs. Surely the inner soul did not inhabit half a digit? She prayed for guidance and, after much family discussion that night, it went in the bin.

In addition to writing letters, Mother kept confidential diaries from the age of seventeen which I never read. She laughed, 'I've been bitten by the writing bug.'

Her cousin teased, 'Never give Marion your address, or she'll start writing to you.'

'She should have shares in the post office delivery service,' grumbled Father.

'I need her to write more because I collect all of the stamps off replies,' said David.

'Once I've started, I never want to stop,' confessed Mother.

Her diaries hid somewhere in her wardrobe, somewhat mythical, out of reach of prying eyes, occasionally mentioned in mysterious tones. Wardrobes were common hiding places in our home for all manner of secrets.

For more than eighty-five years, Mother was friends with Nancy Bastow. Nancy was a proud woman, sharp-tongued, opinionated, a veteran of many Brethren confrontations, and a frequent visitor to our home. Until she died in 2005, Mother had afternoon teas with Nancy, or kept in touch by phone or letter regularly.

The Bastow family was immersed in Brethren much longer than my own. Nancy's grandfather, Henry Robert Bastow, was a Brethren convert when he arrived from England in 1860. He is memorialised in a statue in North Melbourne, standing outside one of the 615 primary schools that he designed, as Victorian state architect between 1872 and 1892. Although an influential character, severe economic depression in Melbourne in 1892 forced Henry to abandon his job as public service architect and move on to other roles in the country. He established an orchard and meeting hall in Harcourt, central Victoria, with his savings. He converted neighbours to the cult.

Nancy and Mother were born in the same year (1912) and became close buddies by means of Brethren family connections. Nancy became the top preschool administrator for Victoria, having started work in the 1930s, along with Beth Stubbs, another founding preschool specialist, and close friend of Mother. Without informing Mother, we children decided that Beth and Nancy were gay partners.

In 1962, Beth and Nancy were thrown out of Exclusive Brethren, as our family was, but neither of the women showed any interest whatsoever in our tiny rump of leftovers. They were fed up. I remember a barbecue discussion in the rose garden of their damp home in the Basin on a Saturday afternoon, where the pros and cons of Brethren life were dissected heatedly, along with the blackened sausages.

Nancy's elderly mother was captured by Exclusive Brethren in Harcourt and forced to ignore Nancy altogether, because she was a turncoat and defector. They never met again. Nancy joined St Mark's Anglican Church, North Fitzroy, where the Rev. Martin O'Donovan officiated. I became friends with Martin – a wonderful conversationalist – when I lived in Ormond College in 1969, and shared a house with him while he trained as a priest in 1976. At the time that we lived together, he was trying to finish law and theology degrees together. As the loop of friendships came full circle, Martin became a priest and Nancy developed a deep respect for him spiritually. Mother told me, so it must be true.

Many of Mother's other friendships were disrupted in 1962. It is hardly surprising that her diaries were incinerated because of her loathing of the pain of separation caused by Exclusive Brethren. She felt no need to seek advice before burning all the diaries in anger. She continued to write enthusiastically elsewhere, though, in 1995 recording in her all-female Writing Group that writing was a noble pastime, that stimulated her and that heralded an inkling of better things. She was the optimist, Father the pessimist. If born outside Brethren, she would have been a professional writer or a counsellor of distressed people.

Just as she shared news in writing, Mother always welcomed a chat too. Her talk was cheerful. She professed to love airport lounges because there were so many interesting people to watch. Like a statue, she would sit quietly in a suburban park, happily just to observe passers-by, or to chat to anyone with the gift of the gab. In 1955, she found herself in a public gallery in a courtroom, to listen to David apply for non-combatant service in the army as a Plymouth Brother.

She was warned by the magistrate for gossiping noisily with a stranger, 'Will madam kindly desist from talking and keep silent in this court?'

Madam was struck dumb, crushed with contrition, afraid of being sent out.

The record showed that I enjoyed a chat just as much as she did. Mother wrote in my dirty book – that is, my childhood record – that as a three-year-old I had 'the most adorable sweet voice; he follows me around all day, talking as hard as he can, and is such good company'.

She did not want me to leave home for kindergarten. Communicating my views to others grew into an important part of my own destiny.

Home management

There was no need to leave home for social interaction because we entertained so many guests, temporary and long-term. I had no idea at the time how lucky I was to have a floating in-house community to hand, but then I had no experience of a social life outside either. I joined in at home exuberantly. Mother described home life sometimes as a human menagerie, but I reckon that she wanted it no other way. My aunt made the observation to David in late 1962 that 'it is the [Brethren] families who do not entertain who lose their children to the World'. And thus an adult ulterior motive was revealed shamelessly. In contrast to Aunt, Mother could not avoid exploring a relationship with any potential gossip whom she encountered, whether in the World or out of it.

An example of a short-term visitor was Mabel Spence, a Plymouth Sister from up the road (number 35), who dropped in whenever she ran short of cooking ingredients – butter, eggs, sugar or flour. Mabel wore a short apron. She arrived via our back lane to avoid having to remove her apron by walking down the street. One never displayed an apron publicly. An uninvited visitor was always a curiosity to me.

'Is Mother home?' she questioned on arrival, breathless, as she looked past me towards the kitchen.

'I think so,' I said, a little befuddled. 'Let me look.'

Before I had time to check, she dived into the kitchen in a flash. Did she have commando training?

'I just need a little, dear,' were her passing words (that was a little butter, eggs, sugar or flour). She always used the back entrance to push past me as though I was invisible.

'Oh, how lovely of you to drop in, Mabel,' were Mother's first words in her hardly detectable sarcastic tone.

Over the years, I learnt to deduce a lot about Mother's moods from her tones. She could never disguise them.

Mother opined that the real motive for Mabel's visits – some lasted longer than one cuppa – was that she was lonely and wanted to chat, mostly about her three marriageable Brethren daughters. Mother preferred to use the word eligible. They were Marjorie, Elizabeth and Mary.

Their father, John Spence ('He was such a dear'), died when I was three. His death notice in the newspaper informed that he died suddenly. Readers were reassured that he was with Jesus, which was far better. Better than what? I wondered.

My memory of Mabel's visits were after his death. I was horrified to learn that she opened and read her daughters' love letters while they were at work in the city, and resealed them for when they returned home. Mother learnt of all the intrigues, but never divulged the juicy details to me. Letters could be more intimate than any bodice-ripper.

In spite of the conspiratorial secrecy, the girls never married in the eleven years that I knew them. Mabel the Invader injected some colour into my domestic routines in any case. I did not understand the intricacies of human attraction as a five-year-old. I was not asked for an opinion, but I proffered one nevertheless – that the single Sisters *looked* quite appealing to me.

One long-term visitor was Aunt, Mother's younger sister, whose integration into family affairs will unfold gradually in this memoir. She was seriously discordant. In 1947, she was disgruntled in Hawthorn, where she shared as a boarder with cousins and aunts. She craved a closer family. Mother took pity on her, saying (when I was six months old) that she could stay with us in Canterbury for a year until she found another place. Aunt stayed for thirty-six years, long after I left that home. Father detested her, feeling his nest invaded, and he believed his wife was splitting her loyalties in half. Her residence set up yet another cause of tension in my home. When Aunt arrived at the age of thirty-three, she looked a diminutive version of Mother. But she was slimmer and more fearful and fragile. Mother and Aunt were close sisters, having lost a father as toddlers to Bright's disease (in 1914), and a mother to breast cancer (in 1940) when they were in their twenties.

Looks

There are few family photos because only Father owned a camera and, no matter how hard he tried, he did not work out how to use it effectively. Never could – and he refused helpful advice. A handful of poorly focused snapshots record the noticeable parts of Mother's face – her charming smile with loving blue eyes. She stood proud and dignified. My deep love for her was amply reciprocated. It never showed in insipid photos of her, but she sometimes dared to add the slightest glimmer of pale pink gloss to her lips, and a dab of skin-hued powder to her cheeks. All make-up was prohibited by Brethren, not to mention jewellery. I was not alone among toddlers in plastering her lipstick all over my chubby cheeks. Most do it, in front of a mirror. Mother was shocked by my self-decoration and rushed to hide me and remove the lipstick before it was seen. To discourage further abuse, she hid her lipstick by moving it from the right-hand drawer to the left-hand drawer of her dressing table. I never played with it again, though; sinning once was bad enough.

In addition to avoiding make-up, no shameful drop of moisture ever dared surface anywhere on Mother's neck. She insisted on calling it perspiration, which she regarded as more sophisticated language than sweat (of rougher Anglo-Saxon origins). If it surfaced, an embroidered hankie instantly soaked it up. Her nose was long, and sharp like her mind. Mother and I used to rub our noses together, in a welcome play which we thought was imitating the Maori. Anyway, that was what *Coles' Funny Picture Book* showed. A few brown curls capped her forehead, coaxed gently back over her slightly pointed ears. I inherited her long, piano-playing fingers but not her musical dexterity. In old age, cracking and craggy fingernails tormented her. Her great-grandchildren have her long fingers now.

Dressing well meant a lot to Mother, and Brethren Meetings were a suitable venue to show off. Entry into the local meeting hall became a unintended fashion parade. There was little else to notice – apart from the odd blowfly – so silently we asked ourselves questions, for discussion after the service:

What happened to that bright floral summer frock?

Why are the hairs on Gwen's chin curly, while the hair on her head is straight? (She was aged about forty-five).

How many hatpins does she use to keep that hat from falling off her head?

Does his walking stick really have an embossed silver handle?
Is Colin's coloured tie a bit too loud?
Did old Mr Hills spill some breakfast on his lapel?
Why are those eyebrows darker than his moustache?
What polish does Bert Rogers use on his high-heeled boot to make it shine so brightly?

Bert's left leg was shorter than the right, due to polio, which we were all vaccinated against at primary school. He was a serious thinker, bank manager in East Camberwell.

Insights about what we witnessed in the procession on a single day were shared with my brothers. Sisters had extremely limited scope for self-expression, because Brethren practised hard at being inconspicuous. Brothers were restricted to plain grey suits with plain grey hats.

One very old member – whose name I forget – attracted my special attention. Wherever he went, he carried a black box about the size of a Kodak Brownie camera. It was attached by thick wires to headphones slung over his bald head. If I wanted to speak to him, I had to shout into a small aperture in the side of the box. It was known as a vacuum tube hearing aid. I loved to play at chatting with him.

As a little child, I wanted to rub my face on the soft fox fur which Mother wound around her neck at special meetings. It was slightly perfumed and extremely sensual. To me, the glass fox eyes felt like tiny jewels. When neck furs went out of fashion, I was sad to see her fur dumped ignominiously into the dress-up collection. It deserved a more noble ending. When I actually saw a live fox years on, in the corner of my uncle's paddock, I was deeply disappointed to observe that it was so sneaky, stunted and scrawny in the wild. I expected a larger and more noble animal. Beatrix Potter had a lot to answer for by creating the fox character Mr Tod as such a sophisticate!

Seamstresses

Mother hated sewing and Aunt never did any handiwork. Together they paid willingly for outsourced dressing services instead. Changing seasons, pride in appearance and making the right impression motivated them. They kept a retinue of paid helpers for sewing (bespectacled Miss Oliver across our road), hat-making (the yappy Plymouth Sister, Winnie Way of Box Hill), and frock-and suit-making (grumpy Miss Alma Jemmeson in Maling Road, Canterbury). Their biggest challenge was not so much about deciding what was fashionable in the World, but how much flair Brethren would allow. It was never a lot. The competition was slight, most Sisters settling for looking dowdy. How to match tailored suits or frocks (made in Canterbury) with handmade hats (made in Box Hill) required extended negotiations between Mother and Aunt. I remember one hat that sprouted colourful peacock feathers. It was rejected out of hand by Mother, accompanied by snorts of disgust.

As a child, I was dragged along to their fittings. Work outfits as well as Brethren displays were at stake. Aunt never had enough time for the many fittings that were expected. Mother grumbled in desperation about broken appointments and tried dejectedly – on my Aunt's behalf – to imagine what might suit her sister, who was hard to please and suffered from crippling aesthetic indecision. Aunt cared little for appearance and lacked confidence in her choices.

At home, the rest of the clothes and linen of the entire family were cared for by Miss Oliver, who lived across the road. She was nearly a family member, having no children of her own, and was interested in all of our achievements, proudly conveyed by Mother and Aunt. She contrived, altered, reconstructed and shredded all materials. She was our very own seamstress. Her eyes were stressed behind her gold-rimmed spectacles with small circular lenses and tortoiseshell arms. I was amazed by the range of her skills. She wept openly when we moved away to another house in 1967.

Her regular income came from sewing soft toys – such as pandas – for a mysterious, swarthy middleman who came in a big black Humber car once a week to deliver raw materials and to remove completed products in big black bags. Mother and Aunt paid her handsomely for small jobs because in their view, Miss Oliver was swindled by the shadowy man in the big black Humber. They had no evidence that their suspicions were correct – as a family, we were not regular snoopers – but they watched cautiously from a discrete distance anyway. Miss Oliver was well worth protecting.

Mother and Aunt were allergic to sewing and knitting. When they were young, in the 1920s, their own mother (my grandmother) had no income when her husband died suddenly. A well-meaning Plymouth Sister in Kyneton suggested that she take in mending. Grandmother made an arrangement with the school principal over the other side of Epping Street that Grandmother receive a small remuneration for repairing any of the clothes of any of the children in their primary school. To my own Mother's embarrassment – as one of the pupils at the school – she was forced to bring home tattered clothes to her mother for repair and return them fixed to school next day, secreted under her jacket.

Mother and Aunt impressed on Miss Oliver – who always looked haggard – that she must never work on their behalf on Sundays (the Lord's Day). It is very likely that Miss Oliver laboured over her industrial sewing machine on her sunny back veranda every day. No one knew because the veranda faced east, away from the house entrance. In her virtual greenhouse, she was surrounded by lush maidenhair ferns and a forest of dangling and climbing plants. Hanging baskets were in vogue, often filled with droopy asparagus ferns. A visit to her on an errand was like peeping into a magical jungle. Where were the monkeys hiding? Apart from plants, her vast workspace smelt of desiccated textiles.

She could do any job from taking up trouser cuffs, to patching holes, or expanding waists, lengthening legs, or turning around collars or cuffs on white Sunday shirts, or hemming curtains. Or vice versa. She turned our old sheets into handkerchiefs. In those days, I was instructed to never leave home without an ironed hankie, the public icon of respectability and pre-emptive sanitation. Father often reminded me that 'Cleanliness is next to Godliness'. I still have a note with this aphorism – written in his Gothic script – which he placed carefully in the vacated centre of my untidy study desk in 1963.

More visitors

A distinct advantage to me of our copious hospitality was that a parade regularly visited home for meals and/or afternoon teas. I shall never know if Mother invited them strategically as substitutes for external entertainment, as decoys. We were forced to ignore ceremonial events in the World, such as cinema, sport, concerts, Easter, Christmas, Anzac Day and Moomba parades, and so on, so I developed an eye for the unusual in the passing parade of our patrons.

Little Mrs Roberts, a well-rounded Plymouth Sister, poisoned her husband by mistaking daffodil bulbs for onions and cooking them for his dinner. The old man spent weeks recovering in the Box Hill Hospital. He pecked at food gingerly at our place – Mother never served him onions.

Jan Vinje, the gaunt Norwegian sailor, was lonely when visiting the port of Melbourne. At the time of his visits, I had no notion that he was attracted to Turid (she and her family still lived in Norway). We did not know her family then. After meals at home, Jan tape-recorded our Brethren hymn-singing around the piano, so that he could replay the tunes for himself in his tiny cabin on return to the ship. I loved to show off by bellowing out hymns that I knew by heart, and he loved to eat dessert.

From near Highfield Park came a different Brother on a different mission, with the thinning slicked-back hair of a salesman. He drove a three-wheeled Goggomobil, with only one back wheel, for steering, a novelty car he was trying to sell in the 1950s. It was about the size of today's ride-on mower, looking and moving like a stingray. The imported German engines had bodies of fibre glass added to them in Australia, where the car cost $1,244. He told me that he managed to flog off three of them. As a boy of twelve, I knew all car types by name and had the thrill of sitting inside the domed cabin of the Goggomobil; I would have loved to own one.

From secondary school, David invited home a friend who was a Colombo Plan student from Malaya. He coped with our beef steak, boiled potatoes, peas and beans – smothered in a sticky dollop of white sauce – followed by a dessert of Spanish cream, a floppy white flummery, with strawberries and ice cream and cream. Boiling rather than steaming vegetables was common. The student reciprocated by inviting all my family to a meal of fried rice at his Burwood flat. It was our first Chinese meal ever. We agreed beforehand that we were not willing to try any Chinese dish other than fried rice. In spite of our shameful culinary ignorance, we all gave the student's cooking a unanimous stamp of approval.

Scrabble was a favourite board game at home that Brethren permitted. The accountant father of my special friend Gordon Stephens joined in. Nearing the end of a game, he became convinced that he could not win, and accidentally knocked the whole board on the floor so that pieces were scattered and no one could win. I was absolutely disgusted by his cowardice and could hardly contain my anger. He was loud and opinionated, willingly becoming a devout acolyte of the nasty Exclusive regime after 1962. We learnt to pick our losers.

Jim Wetherall made fine wooden furniture which reminded me of the Shakers' woodwork. Jim was stooped and leaning in his eighties. Standing under an equally old and bent peppercorn tree at the back of the hall after a meeting, he told me – in his gentle voice – that he remembered the police strike in Melbourne in 1923. There has never been another. He had stood in Swanston Street in the city and watched mobs of looters smash shop windows and make off with goods. They overturned cable trams. The conservative government of the day sacked 636 policemen to no avail. Jim remembered seeing the volunteer militias (brought in from country areas) trying to control the mayhem, which lasted for about a week. Finally the government increased pay and provided a pension.

Although I was aged nineteen, I welcomed his friendliness. He and his wife often came to Sunday lunch. Jean – a lot younger than Jim – worked at Stott's Business College and dedicated many hours to teaching me shorthand for free, which has proved extremely useful for notetaking and interviewing ever since.

With the traffic of Brethren (and other) visitors, our home functioned like a guest house. Housekeeping was familiar to Mother, whose home in Kyneton had taken in three or four boarders at any one time, in order to provide a living for the six women occupants – Mother and Aunt, their mother Frances and her sisters Aunt Amy and Auntie Olive, and the mother of Amy and Frances. Their weatherboard house was extended several times.

Once one of their boarders had no cash to pay for accommodation, so he gave Mother and Aunt an old Model T Ford instead, which they both drove with enthusiasm. In 1936, Aunt's face was cut by flying slivers of glass when a stone (thrown up by a passing car) hit her windscreen as she drove near Gisborne. She was returning to Kyneton from meetings in Melbourne. It is surprising that this unusual accident was regarded as sufficiently newsworthy to be reported in two Melbourne newspapers:

> She was treated at a nearby house, but, fortunately, the cuts were not deep, and she was later, able to proceed home.

Over years, the sisters drove the car until it broke down on a remote road, whence they walked home. The disabled car had been stolen when they returned to it with a mechanic next day. Easy come, easy go.

When Mother married Father for a new life in Melbourne, they closed down the house and all left Kyneton in 1937. Kinship bonds were strong.

Around the dinner table

Mother was never so light-hearted as when she was in her kitchen cooking. We often sang together as she cooked and I helped. Eating at home was a spectacle – primarily a maternal initiative. Meals were an opportunity for further fellowship, as Brethren called it, a carnival of cooking and presentation, as I call it now. A communion of chit-chat, a demonstration of genteel cuisine and devout testimony, a display of refined manners, and a celebration by lavish hospitality. As I grew up, I deduced that Mother used food as a form of communication. Good etiquette was intended to be as memorable as good witnessing to faith.

Everyday meals were less fancy than the bigger banquets and we enjoyed plenty of both. Domestic politics and personal anxieties inevitably roiled up to the surface at large formal meals because of the stress that accompanied formal guests. A Sunday lunch table of fifteen people – apart from being a feast – could be a forum for animosity. I felt severe discomfort about my family for bickering in public, as though I was responsible. They were my family after all.

Having grown up with boarders, Mother confidently strutted her catering stuff. When four-course meals were planned, we were often reminded by my lugubrious Father that we should all be grateful for whatever little might be served, because as a child he had to survive on bread and dripping throughout the Depression. The only snag with this claim (which my older brothers were quick to refute) was that he was aged twenty-two at the start of the Depression and had left home long before. Father dismissed the deduction with a brusque wave of his hand.

As well as being Queen of Cuisine, Mother was undisputed Supervisor of Seating Arrangements. Notable Brethren visitors had the doubtful privilege of placement next to Father at one end of the table. Great-aunt Amy, twenty years older, was placed at a generous distance – at the other end – from Father, with whom she disagreed on every imaginable subject of conversation.

Amy became extremely deaf, so conveniently was out of earshot of most banter. Essential messages were shouted into her hearing aid. Capable conversationalists were spread around among visitors. Peter and Aunt did not enjoy conversation, and liked to eat and depart the scene as fast as possible, so they were kept up at Mother's end of the table in the hope that their premature disappearances would go unnoticed. As was seen before, inconspicuous escape was an art which we all studied in searching for elsewhere.

No matter how ravenous I was, eating was always preceded by 'Giving thanks to the Lord for the meal'. Grace was only said by the oldest Brother present, who was occasionally me in the absence of older men. As usual after dinner, all diners except Amy lowered themselves to their knees beside their chairs on the pink, mauve and grey Axminster carpet, while Father prayed at length…mumble murmur mutter. Depending on what other commitments lay ahead for the evening, his monologic prayer could occupy up to half an hour after dinner. It was a strain on the knees. It was also the most sensational time for one of us three thrill-seeking brothers to fart. I only plucked up the courage once. Amy was not able to hear the explosion, and to her the prayer was just a murmur, as she fell asleep sometimes. She was exempted from kneeling in case she was not able to arise, and it would be indecorous to have to hoist her up. We all respected her honour, more or less, for the last twenty years of her long life. She was a monumental fixture at our meals.

The kitchen was a foreign territory to Father, whose self-appointed role was to sustain a stilted conversation at the head of the dining table, while dishes were cleared or the next course was prepared. Spaces between courses could last for ten minutes. This delay added to the tension in the air. Father held forth loftily, with exaggerations and elaborations added each time to the telling of his anecdotes.

One of his favourite yarns concerned Rupert Murdoch. Father worked through most of World War II at the Flinders Street headquarters of the *Herald* newspaper. There, he once happened to enter a descending lift at the same time as the famous stripling, Rupert – son of the newspaper owner, Keith Murdoch. Rupert worked temporarily at the *Herald* for his imperious father before leaving for Oxford to study.

As he jumped into the lift, Rupert was breathless. 'I am in a real hurry.'

'What for?' asked Father.

'I have to place a bet on a horse race which is about to happen.' Rupert rushed out of the opening lift doors.

There must have been a tote nearby. Father would not have been aware of it, because gambling was as far removed from our ken as prostitutes or opium, and just as wicked.

Father undoubtedly met Rupert, but the telling of his fleeting interaction became more and more elaborated each time as he told it. Father gave the impression that he knew Rupert intimately and worked with him closely, and that Rupert was ruthlessly ambitious even at a young age. The hope in this telling was that Brethren guests would be impressed by Father's breadth of Worldly experience. We were supposed to have no Worldly wisdom. Such whoppers were his self-crafted pushback.

At the dinner table, if the transition period to the next stage of the meal seemed too long, Father lost patience. He was electrified. Keeping time loomed large in our lives – as mentioned, thirty-two clocks were spread around far fewer rooms in our house. Father made sure that they were adjusted so that the noisy ones all pealed separately, in a sequence, never at the same moment. He inspected their mechanisms quizzically. The collection of thirty-two included a variety of chimers, each with a different tune. The cuckoo clock squawked first, followed by the Westminster chime, then the Saint Michael chime, and finally the Whittington chime. Just to make sure that the chimes were not enjoyed simply as entertainment by me, Mother stressed that special words were assumed to accompany the tunes. In a manic manner, in my home a patina of religion was spread all over any amenable activity. I still continued to hum the sounds, ignoring the text:

> All through this hour, Lord be my guide,
> and by Thy power, no foot shall slide.

Time could slide fast or slowly, depending on the context. If Father thought that a delay in the meal preparation was too prolonged, monitored on his Ernest Borel wristwatch, he bellowed impatiently in the direction of the kitchen, 'What's going on out there? What's happening?'

Visiting the kitchen to see for himself was beyond his territorial obligations, and in any case Aunt would have chased him out.

While guests recoiled into embarrassed silence at Father's shouting, I was paralysed with anxiety by his angry outbursts. What could I say? Mother oozed soothing words from a distance ('Won't be long, dear'), or scurried into the dining room apologetically with a precursor of the next course (maybe just a symbolic serving spoon). It made me wince.

Another cause of tension originated with Mother herself. At our dinners, she could not help monitoring the levels of etiquette on display. The monitoring occurred silently, so was impossible for any guest to notice. Expectations were high and the test was unapparent. As a child, I did my best to check on others and dutifully report them. Pity help the persons who did not use the ironed and starched white cloth serviettes, or who did not know which implement to use for which course, or who did not know how to hold a knife properly, or who did not eat every skerrick of food on the plate, or who did not know where to leave the knife and fork when the food was finished; they were subjected to intense scrutiny and whispering ridicule for long afterwards.

'Poor things, they don't know any better,' criticised my patronising Mother.

We were not allowed to forget. I was congratulated heartily when I learnt how to roll my white serviette and insert it precisely in my silver ring by the time that I was four. In fact, in my household admiration of anyone by anyone else was sparse: criticism prevailed over praise normally. I suspect that some of the obsession with conforming etiquette and contempt for the uninitiated, derived from the general Brethren intolerance of the enemy without, and from the insurmountable spiritual barriers that were thrown up around cynical, holy insiders.

Helen, the daughter of Joan, Mother's cousin, was about six years younger than me. On one memorable occasion, she stretched to use her spreading knife instead of the butter knife for cutting a slice of butter from a dish in the middle of the table at teatime. Her father explained that his eight-year-old, Helen, had never set eyes on a butter knife before. Or since? We were all astonished that a relation of Mother should have such lamentably lax standards. But then Ron, the father, listened to the test cricket on the car radio, and Joan the mother cut her hair in a bob and boasted bright red lipstick! – clear signs to us all that they were on the slippery slope to eternal damnation, of course. It did not matter that they were very conservative Presbyterians. In fact, contrary to the predictions of eternal torment, both Joan and Mary, daughters of my Great-auntie Olive, were never diminished in my eyes. They were always full of good cheer – gentleness, vivacity, love and genuine admiration. Great-auntie Olive gave a lovely hug. I basked in their sunny company.

My Brethren home

Mother led the team of the dominant three adults in my life at home – Mother, Father and Aunt – as my three siblings accepted the constraints of strict moral codes, implicit and explicit values, conforming practices, and dutiful relationships, for the most part. As I outlined, all were complicit in the moral conundrums thrown up by unconventional treatments for ill-health. No matter how hard we ignored them, they never went away. The consequences of avoidance and indecision were never thought through.

Mother had attributes that many – including me – admired: her ability to cook well, her openness to others, her expressive writing, her empathy, her dedicated friendships, and her generous hospitality. I loved her greatly. However, as time went on, beneath Mother's jolly polish I observed a degree of snobbery and hypocrisy, and a tendency to keep a foot in both camps in a confrontation. Do not strive for social superiority, I told myself, and do not prevaricate, but face up to hard decisions. I wanted badly to avoid any of her negative tendencies in myself.

I benefited from deep affection and companionable enjoyment with most family members. Home was a stimulating environment to share with like-minded visitors, to observe strengths and anomalies in human behaviour, and to accept foibles and pressing needs. But there were stresses – from trying to whitewash family tensions and putting a brave face on domestic discord. It paralleled religious discord.

I could not avoid the pain of excessive fear and guilt. There were few opportunities for relief and none for real escape in the early stages of my life. Belladonna was one of a few temporary sops. Lukewarm avoidance and internal questioning were my means of resistance, but they recircled endlessly inside my head. Mostly home life was happy and serene so long as demonstrative transgression was avoided, yet I was witness to too much that caused fright.

I became a marine bottom-feeder who chose to observe family alarms up at the surface, at a distance, and tried to avoid confrontation with any sharks up there. I felt protected from that low angle, out of reach of higher-level predator emotions, protected by remaining close to the solidity and simplicity of the ocean floor. It was more secure to follow black-and-white rules of behaviour because any thought of mine of breaking free at this stage was as remote as an octopus venturing to leave its den permanently. I was perturbed by the top-down disorder that resulted from set domestic conventions and religious practices as prescribed by Mother and Father.

Five

Father and his Nemesis

Together apart

Father and Auntie Bett were almost civil to each other once a year – on their birthdays. My conciliatory Mother tried hard to get them to lay down their hammers and tongs in between birthdays. Their biffo drained her emotionally, even when she managed to pacify them, but more often she failed. She felt deep relief when she and the duellers were separated when they were at work during the week, and on weekends Father spent hours in the garden or garage (his shed) while Aunt slept long hours and took refuge in her bedroom. Avoidance was their substitute for the biblical commandment to 'love your neighbour as yourself' (Mark 12:31). In this chapter, I track their influences because Father was a sincere disciple and enthusiastic manager of Brethren activities, and provided insights into that culture, whereas his handling of his relationship with Aunt was bumbling and savage. His contest with Aunt heaped bad feeling on daily doings. As children, did we dodge, obstruct, abstain or suffer?

Too often I had to second guess the impacts of my behaviour on both of them. Angry alienation spilt over into the relationships with all the children. If David or Peter confronted Father in any small spat, then Aunt could be relied on to back them to the hilt quick smart – regardless of the pros and cons of their issue – and to escalate disrespect.

My younger sister was one exception, indulged by all adults in the family, never bothered by any contretemps. Their aim was to protect her from negative contamination. The warring parties were aware that their aggression tarnished us all, but carried on regardless. Bettina grew manipulative, benefitting when her loyalties were wooed by both parties.

I was a semi-exception. I did not require Aunt as my second in any duel; I preferred to defend myself on my own, if I had to fight – which was rare. She deeply resented my independent stance. On the whole, I found that being a helpful character poured sufficient oil on troubled waters to enable me to function amicably with each member of the family independently. Another effective strategy for me was just to pretend that Aunt did not exist. Collective harmony was an ideal as remote as heavenly bliss anyway, while Father and Aunt were together apart.

The disagreements of Father and Aunt could all be sheeted back to the jealous ownership of Mother by both Father and Aunt. He loved Mother possessively and never stopped striving for her approval. They married in 1937 when he was already bald at the age of twenty-eight. When he was thirty-seven, I was born, and Aunt arrived to live with us the following year. She took advantage of having a prior emotional claim on her sister, my mother.

Father's tantrums were best avoided. He deeply resented the temporary residence of Aunt in the household for thirty-six years and resented her weighty dependence on Mother. David told me that he overheard Father threaten to murder Aunt, and we children felt terrible excitement and paid close attention, but I never saw action that evidenced such white-hot anger. Yet the kerfuffle was caused by more than just David's vivid imagination, because Father's jibes and constant sarcasm – usually directed towards Aunt – were sufficient to fuel our genuine apprehension. They turned him into a bitter man commonly around the home.

In view of their professed Christianity, it amazes me that the confrontations lasted for decades, that the protagonists never undertook any joint activity, nor attempted reconciliation, and even that they survived under the same roof. They were like two destructive prisoners in solitary confinement living in adjacent cells – hearing each other through walls, but never connecting face to face. They refused to acknowledge each other at every opportunity.

At times, I despised the behaviour of both Father and Aunt. I developed a clear impression that Father was lacking in courage – a coward? Aunt was a threat whose venom was aimed at limiting Father's influence at every turn. She was most satisfied when acting cunningly as his nemesis. In middle age, she grew more wealthy, more bossy and subversive, manipulated by using her gifts of money, and often tried to pressure me. Her behaviour alienated me as much as Father's. The story of her success and sudden decline occupy the next chapter.

A pleasure shared by Mother and Father, to the exclusion of Aunt, was their garden. Apart from their religious faith, gardening was the only activity that my parents shared lovingly and enthusiastically. Admittedly, they regarded the garden as God's handiwork anyway. Nature could not be separated from faith. From my hideaway in the old apricot tree, I looked down on Mother and Father planting and maintaining annuals. The difference between annuals and perennials was a concept that I found hard to comprehend as a child.

Mother's father (who died in 1914) was a nurseryman, so as well as feeling plants in her genes, Mother wanted to honour his memory. As for Father, he had lived in eleven houses before he left his Adelaide home at the age of fourteen, his own father (born in 1882) making a living partly by building and selling sandstone houses in Adelaide. At each new house, Father was assigned to help construct fresh gardens, yet he still loved them.

Native plants were not in vogue, so we had two only in the large garden. One gnarled bottlebrush required no care or attention, as my mother commented dismissively, indicating that it made it inferior. A glorious flowering gum tree had a staghorn attached (fed with banana peels), which draped over a large wooden and wire aviary of canaries which Father had crafted before I was born. Gum flowers never seemed to attract lorikeets or wattlebirds in those days.

Father bred yellow canaries successfully, with a genuine tenderness that belied his whippings of me in his angriest moods. I could never measure the mercury of his temperament. I watched the baby canaries hatch in the small nests made of half coconut shells, I watched when he fed them hard-boiled egg crumbled up in stale bread, I watched them grow their first feathers of yellow fluff, I watched them jump off a perch and fly tentatively for the first time, and urged them on, and I watched them chirp lustily in the sunshine as they grew. I was never allowed to touch them, but I caressed them with my gaze. I find all birdsongs – especially of canaries – comforting to this day.

The enemy of the canaries was the butcher-bird, which quickly switched Father back into a ranting monster. The butcher-bird would fly up and down outside the front of the aviary fast, frightening the canaries inside, some of which dropped dead with instant heart attacks. Father shot out of the house when he saw a butcher-bird out of a window, and threatened it violently with shouting and windmill arms. I never understood what the butcher-bird hoped to gain from creating an inside frenzy from outside the cage. It was a relief not to be responsible for raising Father's blood pressure on those occasions, when he found a villain far from me in the form of the harassing birds.

Army ambivalence

Breeding canaries was a popular hobby in Father's generation. Rudyard Kipling – whose beloved son was killed in World War I – wrote a short story about a breeder of deep orange canaries in London. The story focused on the 'Brotherhood of Man'. Being a man required toughness physically and emotionally in my Aunt's eyes.

I was amazed one day, when Aunt was in her seventies, that she asked me, 'What is that poem by Rudyard Kipling? The one that I like.'

'Do you remember the title of it?' I replied.

'It's something about being a man.'

'It's the one with "you'll be a Man, my son!"' I realised that Kipling's poetry and fiction were contemporaneous with Aunt's schooling.

'That's the one. And I think it's very true,' she said.

We checked the full poem together. It was published in 1910 to honour a British soldier who failed to suppress bothersome Boers in South Africa. George Orwell described the poem ('If –') as having biblical impact around the British Empire, not on Aunt alone. Kipling himself supported compulsory military service in World War I even though he lost his only son to trench warfare.

Aunt subscribed to militarism, espoused also by her Aunt Amy (my great-aunt). Amy sent Aunt postcards from her hospitals for wounded 'boys' in Palestine, Greece and England between 1916 and 1919, and Aunt replied from Kyneton with love in childish handwriting. Amy served as an army nurse. On most topics, Amy had emphatic views. But she was uncertain about what denomination she wanted to belong to during her War; she found it hard to choose between Anglicans, Methodists and Brethren, all listed by her in different official documents. However, she had no doubts about adherence to military service. In this belief, she and Aunt and Kipling were as one. Father was stuck on it too. Military service for men was the only topic that they mutually agreed on – absolutely unique in their relationships.

Their unshakeable attitude to war gave rise to disagreement with us boys of the next generation. Father's firm conviction was that the army is good for boys for reasons that he refused to articulate, maybe because he could not find the words to explain – he was no craftsman with words. He underwent a primitive form of compulsory military exercises himself as a schoolchild after World War I. He had made up his mind early in life, and his attitudes were unwavering in spite of life experiences that would tempt others to question or even to doubt war mongering.

Plymouth Brethren were officially non-combatants. They declared that wars were made on earth and belonged to the World, and not to us. We were far removed from war because 'we are citizens of heaven, where the Lord Jesus Christ lives' (Philippians 3:20). But Father and Aunt paid lip service only to pacifism, causing serious disagreement in the family. In character, they were both devoted to regimentation and control; their world views and ethics matched their religious narrowness. For many other Brothers, resistance to enlistment had serious real-life consequences.

Unlike Father, Brethren founders wavered in their firmness towards the morality of wars – the Crimean Wars (1853–1856) and Franco-Prussian Wars (1870–1871) – according to historians. Brothers refused to join armies. A petition signed by 590 Brethren (submitted to the Australian federal parliament) in 1916, pleaded for total exemption from military service for young Brothers on the grounds of conscience. I have read handwritten pleas for clemency to the government of Billy Hughes, prime minister, who had no truck with them, trying desperately to introduce call-ups and conscription. Great-aunt Amy lauded his stance.

When in 1970 I researched a master's degree based on government efforts to conscript Australian men, I avoided letting Amy know of my work in order not to become entangled in an argument. Many local Australian newspapers in 1916 reported that conscientious objectors were brought before magistrates to show cause. A few hundred Brothers were imprisoned.

During World War II, Father was exempted from military service altogether – his printing work on night shifts was treated as essential by the government. For most of the war his newspaper, *The Herald*, was regarded as serving a national need, except for the duration of 1943 when he was seconded to work as a machinist in an aircraft factory in Richmond. I never understood why he was so averse to tomato sauce – loved by me, as it was by most children – until he told me that the aircraft factory was next door to a Rosella tomato sauce factory, where he loathed the daily stench. Munitions and sauce were shipped to the war front in large quantities. No tomato juice, passata, or tomato relish ever passed Father's lips afterwards.

Being born just after World War II, I was too young to know wartime panic. But its remnants were close at hand. At the back of our garden, at 27 Wattle Valley Road, Canterbury, beneath the floor of the rickety garage, a mysterious large hole captured my curiosity. It had been dug by Father and Grandfather in 1942 – a deep bomb shelter in the earth, lined with wood, with numbered boards to be placed over the top of it, one by one, as potential refugees scrambled in via wooden steps. As I knew it, the shelter was dank and unused except by hordes of daddy-long-leg spiders.

As an early sign of my youthful curiosity, I noted that each unique board had a sequential Roman numeral chiselled into it. Roman numerals were fresh to me. Maybe they were aimed at confusing a Japanese-speaking enemy? I pondered whether the panicked family could arrange the sequence correctly in the rush for shelter? I imagined my parents and brothers standing on the edge of the hole in the garage, scratching their heads about how to align the boards correctly, and arguing about the sequence, while bombs rained down all around. Was Father obliged to dig the shelter by government decree, or was it a sign of his nervousness about a Japanese invasion? Did he fear that God would allow him to be obliterated by heathens? I was puzzled that Father avoided my questions.

As I grew older, I spared a thought for Brothers in totalitarian regimes such as in Germany, Italy, Spain or Russia during World War II. They were doomed to serve as soldiers or be treated far worse than our mob. Some ended up in Siberia, thanks to Stalin; some were imprisoned for twenty years in Communist China.

Just ten years after the end of that war, David was disgusted at having to spend months in compulsory training during his long university vacations in case another war developed. Korea was the place of the moment. Father expressed the firm belief that training would make a man of him. David was angry and despondent. He managed to wrangle non-combatant service out of a magistrate. Australia was the first of the few Western countries that allowed non-combatant service in law; in our minds we thanked the non-conformist churches and Irish Catholics in Australia for their lobbying for the exemption.

'We are going to visit David in Puckapunyal tomorrow,' informed Mother, oblivious to the legal origin of David's evasion.

'Can I sit in the front seat?' I begged. I never gave up trying. Even if I was relegated to the back seat of the two-tone powder-blue and grey FJ Holden, any relief from a Sunday of long meetings was a thrilling expectation.

'Go and ask your Father while I make lunch.'

'Your Mother has that spot,' was the predictable reply. Father held that pride of place, beside him as driver, belonged to his wife primarily. After all, he owned her as well as the car; she never drove when he was available.

Before long, I was animated, envisaging the flimsy eucalyptus forest of central Victoria flashing past the tiny triangular side back window of the car.

Aunt avoided these carefree excursions by needing to rest in bed. A mountain of food and drink was prepared and packed by Mother, to feed a handful of other Brethren boys in camp as well as her own boy. Fluffy cakes – always in Tupperware containers – were as essential as white bread sandwiches. Mother assiduously avoided all discussion of pacifism but her sympathies lay firmly with her boys in this family fuss. Father relentlessly taunted David for his stubborn resistance; Father and David were exceedingly pugnacious towards each other.

As a conscientious objector, David's duties were as boring as they could be contrived to be. He wore a khaki serge uniform always. With monotonous regularity, he had to march (rifleless) in dusty morning parades at sunrise, fight smoky bushfires with wet sugar bags, polish cumbersome boots, tidy dormitories, and sweep barracks floors over and again each day. He was closely monitored.

After collecting him with his Sunday pass, we slipped past the sentry at the gate of the army camp, with David hiding under my legs in the back seat of the car. On this hot summer afternoon, we could see a small grass fire near the perimeter fence that was spreading, and we realised that (if seen) David would be held back to fight it and could miss out on our picnic. I was as thrilled as Paul Brickhill in *The Great Escape* at our cunning conspiracy; I was reading that book at home. Lunch beside the Goulburn River was our reward. Among the ancient river red gums Father bowed his head in prayer and thanked God fervently for all our mercies. The delicious cream in the sponge with the passionfruit icing on top melted in my mouth. Pure sumptuousness.

One after another, Australian governments committed to overseas war after war, to keep our country safe in splendid isolation. The next war for conscripts was in Vietnam. My brother Peter missed out, but I was of eligible age. When I lodged an official conscientious objection in 1965 to my possible conscription by the government for the Vietnam War, I was still part of the little Brethren rump. Father was grumpy and unsupportive of my objection to service.

I was coached by David on how to present to a magistrate in the event that I might be unlucky enough to be conscripted after I turned eighteen. David held Lytton Strachey, a Bloomsbury Group author, and gay friend of Edmund Gosse, to be originator of the best put-down of an officious magistrate. It made no difference that Lytton was sickly all his life and perhaps would have been exempted on health grounds alone anyway (he died young). The following story is possibly apocryphal but appealed to David, who had a passion for lightning verbal retorts.

Lytton lodged a conscientious objection in London during World War I.

The wily magistrate asked him, 'What would you do if a German soldier tried to violate your sister?'

'I would endeavour to interpose myself between them,' Lytton answered.

David found this retort hilariously funny and quoted it with the poshest British accent.

If balloted for call-up, I intended to quote the Bible rather than Lytton Strachey, in an attempt to appear as fanatical as possible. Sniffing the establishment mood at the time, it was obviously not smart to be lumped in with the radical draft resisters who were using civil disobedience at my university to fight against government support for the Vietnam War. Lunchtime debates were organised and harangued by draft-resisters like Michael Hamel-Green, with his Che Guevara beard, and Harry van Moorst, beginning his lifelong commitment to supporting social causes. If the university refused to provide them with indoor space to vent their spleens, they delivered their messages by battling the wind and sun outdoors from a little balcony north of the Student Union. Both could project.

I was far more reticent than those political firebrands, and aimed to show that the origin of my resistance to service was entirely out of an ardent desire to imitate heavenly citizenship on earth. Whenever government impinged on perceived freedoms, Brethren were quick to quote John 17:16 from the Bible: 'They [Brethren] are not of this world, just as I [Jesus] am not of the world.' I hoped that my dreamlike rationale was sufficiently supernatural to impress any magistrate.

Deep down, I did not believe it fully, but camouflage was part and parcel of my survival. As it happened, I was rescued by my birthdate not being balloted into the government call-up at all that year. I danced and cheered about the house. It was rumoured that if a person lodged a conscience objection before the official draw, then that person's birth date was never balloted for call-up. I had no way to test the veracity of that rumour, but I was happy to try, and happy that the worry was ended and I saw off the last of the militaristic threats in my family. I have attended peace rallies since my auspicious avoidance – on one march, I was chased by a police horse down St Kilda Road, near the American Embassy, until I managed to scale a high fence and escape into a park.

The threats provided lessons. One was that a clash of politics and family values caused deep animosity, adding yet another layer onto pre-existing in-fighting. Perhaps the most significant lesson was that loopholes can be found in the most imprisoning of rules. And another was that Brethren dogma was not watertight, not adhered to universally by Father, Aunt and Great-aunt, nor all Brethren in the past, suggesting that if the pacifist rule could be ignored, then other uncertain tenets might also be overlooked. My forebears stashed their beliefs beneath the parapets. A further lesson was that being an oddball – at least at the time of the Vietnam War – was no longer shameful nor censorious amongst university peers. 'The times, they were a'changin'.'

Father did not expend a lot of energy at home on debating moral principles. He never felt comfortable engaging in abstract argument. He was an artful pragmatist, even when it came to another army – a Christian army. An exhilarating treat loitered outside my front gate on some Sunday afternoons in the 1950s, our corner favoured by the Salvation Army band as a resting place during their wanderings. Whenever we kids in the family heard the brass instruments and tambourines marching, we rushed out to sing along with them. Forget the words – the tune alone of 'Abide with me' still claims me and calms me when I hear the music on its own. I feel the same with other heritage hymns. For me, the arrival of the shiny brass instruments and dark blue uniforms meant just one thing – a fresh layer of excitement.

Father would never discuss Salvation Army beliefs with me, and would not join us on the footpath with the Salvos. Instead, he watched covertly through curtains at the front window of the house so that he would not be seen. I felt sad for him. I wondered what he was thinking. He allowed me to stand alongside the Salvos, tapping my feet and swaying to the music. Why was it so hard for him to be spontaneous himself? Was he holier than them? Heartily, we all sang 'Onward Christian Soldiers' in our lounge room, including Father, around the piano, but it was frowned on for me to do it publicly on the street corner. I puzzled over the acquiescence from behind the curtain. What were the boundaries of compliance?

Footy fever

When he was not gardening, Father was busy repairing fences, polishing shoes and washing cars. He kept a tiny transistor radio hidden in the remote depths of the garage, behind old paint tins under a bench, and I was pleased to corner him inadvertently one day listening to football commentators on the radio while he vacuumed the interior of the Holden. Their distinctive Aussie whine – common to race callers as well – could not be disguised. Brethren were highly unlikely to find out about his secluded wickedness. From that point on, I was emboldened to support the Geelong Football Club more openly than ever before. I was nevermore alone in getting fired up by footy. I found the excuse that I needed.

It felt warmly wicked to buy one pair of Geelong football socks at Adairs in Camberwell and I even managed to buy a woollen Geelong football jumper too. It prickled my hairless chest. I sensed relief on Mother's face when it shrank in the hot wash and I outgrew it after one season of clandestine use. I suspect that she washed it in boiling water deliberately but was never sure.

My footy fervour was unconstrained. Openness was one of my defences against manipulation, rumour-mongering and secret cabals. To keep up to date with football scores, I scoured the sports pages of newspapers; Brethren tolerated no radio or TV. I never attended a football match and was discouraged from even watching an amateur local game in the park. But Father was a proud newspaper man, so we received two morning papers via a paper boy (*The Sun*, *The Age*) and Father brought home *The Herald* after work. I made the most of them. On Saturday mornings, we also benefited from *The Argus*, where I eagerly consumed all the coloured cartoons. Reading all the papers one after another was exuberant escapism. No family member dared throw out newspapers without first checking that others had pored over them.

My football heroes (John Coleman of Essendon and Neil Trezise of Geelong) were no more than pixelated images frozen in black-and-white action on the back pages of the papers. Yet I strove to emulate them by playing against other boys in the mud of Highfield Park in Riversdale Road, soaring in my mind to the clouds. In winter, I rode my bike to meet friends to play there, often secretly. Riding home – caked with mud – I was twice as heavy as when I had left surreptitiously. Gritty mud was what I craved – proper Worldly immersion.

Pessimism

I always felt a tinge of sadness that Father was an incorrigible misanthrope. It seems strange to recount, but he was cheerful on very few occasions – as when he read an obituary out aloud. The day that he turned seventy, he was the happiest I have ever seen him. He was so proud to have reached 'three score years and ten' as prescribed by the Bible (Psalm 90:10). It was, in his own words, 'the allotted lifespan' and any more birthday celebrations were just the icing on his cakes.

Having cultivated a personal contact with a man called Bert at the main Melbourne funeral company of Le Pine & Sons, Father could arrange a Brethren funeral at great speed. At a funeral, it was regarded as essential that no outsiders, in this case undertaker staff, stayed in the hall while the Brethren funeral service was under way. Separation from Bert – representing the World – applied as much after death as it did before. Not that Brethren harboured any secrets about the realities of death and dying.

When Father was short of pallbearers, I was nabbed. From the age of thirteen, the job of helping to carry heavy coffins in and out of the hall was thrust on me. Gruesome. Father commanded me to miss school so that I was available for carrying. I remember trying to concentrate on a maths lesson in a morning class, with difficulty, when I knew full well that after a quick lunch I was required at the Chatham hall to heave a corpse of a Brother whom I never knew in life.

The wooden coffins were awkward, never designed with the task of the lifter in mind. Whatever decorative handles were attached to the polished caskets, they were designed to catch your fingers and squash your hands. These days, they are rolled on trolleys; then they were humped on our shoulders. Because I launched too many old fogies heavenwards, I developed a permanent aversion to funerals – which I still try to avoid.

Until I noticed an autobiography by a Canadian ex-Plymouth Brother, at 704 pages long, I thought Father was alone in his fascination with deaths and funerals, but then I realised that other groups of Brethren had much the same enthusiasms, in this case in Ontario:

> Brethren folk are pros at dealing with death. In fact death validates [their] entire world view and outlook on life… Whole lives are

building toward that final Brethren funeral for… Heaven-bound souls… Some of the warmest, most demonstrative, kindest, accepting, and outgoing behaviour…I have seen at funerals.

I do not believe that Father ever knew that there was a name for a love of funerals, cemeteries and death rituals – taphophilia – because he showed no interest whatsoever in language use.

On the rare occasions when Father smiled, crow's feet splayed across his upper close-shaven cheeks and his lips strained to curve. I tried hard to make him laugh, but he rarely did. Among Brethren, it was definitely unacceptable to joke around, to censure, to mimic, to satirise, or to challenge dour demeanour, so I tried to jolly Father along on my own. He was hard to amuse, as responsive as a limp, wet chamois. I remember reading a newspaper article a few years later which documented strike action by gravediggers at a Melbourne cemetery. The gravediggers demanded a joke allowance because their work required them to remain sombre at all times when in public, limiting their freedom to share banter on the job. I felt strong solidarity with that trade union, having been forced into keeping a straight face in Father's orbit for too many years.

Even Father's confined taste in art reflected the allure to him of tragedy. Before she married, his mother – my grandmother – had made a living as a colourist of black-and-white photographs, and that is why (Father said) he was always attracted to paintings. I failed to understand the connection myself, but did not question it. Past the stuffed racehorse, Phar Lap, in a glass cabinet in a foyer of the museum, lay the old National Gallery of Victoria where Father dragged me to see paintings by Frederick McCubbin, Tom Roberts and Hans Heysen. I was more interested in trying to work out how the taxidermist had managed to hide stitches in Phar Lap's carcass, and to hold it together, rather than the paintings of a brooding swaggie down on his luck, or mourning at a bush funeral, or felled gum trees – the scenes that appealed to Father.

Father harboured more fear than met the eye. On a Friday night in 1965, his first grandchild was born in Bethesda Hospital in Richmond. When David, the baby's father, arrived home after a drawn-out day at the birth, my diary recorded that Father showed characteristic pessimism.

'Is it normal, is it normal, is it normal?' Father kept asking David, exposing his fears that the baby might be born with a disability.

Father resented that Aunt had outwitted him by rushing to the Hospital (where she worked) at four a.m. that day, in order to monitor the labour from her office. He protested about the possessiveness of his nemesis. 'Aunt's in a panic. She's rushing around like a mad thing, sending telegrams and cables of the news around the world.'

Not to be outdone, Father spent the next day (Saturday) in the front garden, according to my diary entry, greeting well-wishers and telegram boys at the gate, and complaining about how much work was required among the new petunias. Telegrams were our SMS.

If Aunt was out of sight, and eventually out of mind, Father did manage to relax. For personal satisfaction, he needed projects planned well into the future. One of his favourite sayings was 'God helps those who help themselves.' It encapsulated his do-it-yourself religious practice as well as his work. He was admired much more for his contributions to the Plymouth Brethren community and in his work roles, than for any of his family bonds or domestic efforts.

Busyness

Brethren appreciated Father's organisational skills, and I helped him here and there, trying to extract from the group a glimmer of excitement for myself as the glow inside me faded inexorably. Father helped and helped, as though his life depended on it. He booked halls for hire, managed subscriptions to Brethren publications, arranged funerals, drove carless Brethren from one side of the city to the other, reserved suites for visitors at the Hotel Victoria in Little Collins Street (alcohol-free), booked tickets for plane and train trips, collected money to pay for fares for visiting Brethren, and ensured that a welcoming party of Brethren was formed, to meet or farewell a passenger liner at Port Melbourne or a country train at Spencer Street Station.

Many elderly Brethren from Melbourne travelled 'Home' to visit yet more elderly Brethren in England. In the 1950s, Mr and Mrs Le Souef from Burwood were entertained at our home after one such boat pilgrimage. Mr Le Souef's grandfather, Albert, established the Melbourne Zoo. I enjoyed many a ride on the back of an elephant at that zoo, once pulling a wiry hair from its rump to keep in a matchbox to admire. To focus on the morbid, Father often regaled us with the tale of the elephant keeper, a Plymouth Brother named Wilfred Lawson, who was crushed to death by Queenie the elephant in 1944. For forty years, Queenie had carried kids obediently around the zoo, but in the end she was just completely fed up with Brother Wilf and squashed him. Father was enabled to retell the tragic tale for the next forty years.

Appropriately – on return from the Mother Country – the Le Souefs gave me a small carved ebony elephant which smelt spicy. They bought it in Colombo, a favourite stopping-place for passenger liners. I revelled in their stories of the gully-gully man, the Ceylonese conjuror who collected donations by doing tricks with chickens, cobras and mango seeds for the travellers on a deck of the ship when in port. Eventually (aged about thirteen), I tired of elephant rides and of helping to make up the numbers at impersonal welcomes and farewells for Brethren, most of whom I never met again. Father pressed on alone.

It was common every couple of months for him to welcome overseas Brethren who visited Melbourne, mainly by liner from the UK. Welcoming parties of local Brethren swarmed onto the liners – like navy seals – to grab the visitors as high-level targets in order to take them home to prove our antipodean allegiance. They were farewelled by multicoloured paper streamers from Australian coastal ports, because Brethren had exempted streamers from the too-frivolous class of entertainment. I loved the colours of the streamers, and the way that the wind swung them in unison into semi-orbit, like a maypole. It was emotional when the rainbow colours stretched and finally snapped as the ship eased away from the dock, ripple by ripple.

In 1938, the grandfather of a friend in Wellington kept a diary (that she shared with me) of his migration to distant New Zealand, describing a typical progression of stopovers between Tilbury and Auckland. A group of thirty Brethren prayed with the family at Tilbury in London the night before departure. Fraternising with evil, the trip challenged faith. Reassuringly, Philip Cossham and his young family were hosted by Brethren along the way – at Gibraltar, Toulon and Naples for a start. In Gibraltar, they confronted a Spanish warship flaunting Franco's prowess; in Italy Mussolini's edicts 'prohibited them from meeting together' with local Brethren.

More than once, Philip had reason to resent the music and frivolity and the spirit of pleasure and amusement on board ship on a Sunday. In Aden, he 'spoke to a few natives as to God and they replied, I gathered, that God was the nephew of Mahomet whom they worship: they did not seem to know of the Lord Jesus, being probably in the darkness of heathendom'.

It was just as well for purity's sake that the loyal Cosshams were able to reaffirm belief in Colombo, where there were resident British Brethren as well as a 'colonised brother named Weenatne'. Things looked up. At least they were able discuss the Bible together, and Brethren 'came to see us on the boat before she sailed at midnight'.

Brethren groups met them and farewelled them with streamers at every Australian port. At Freemantle, they shared eleven o'clock tea and sandwiches with Brethren who made a good impression. After Adelaide, in Melbourne they met the Le Soeufs and Dr Vernon Seeley, mentioned in this memoir. At ports in Sydney, Brisbane and Auckland, the welcome pattern continued. At their final destination, they were greeted by the grandfather of a young Plymouth Brother who holidayed with me at our beach house thirty-five years later – Roger Clist. Thanks to Father and his efficient networks, we were glued together in a global connection of the faithful by pseudo-holy travel rituals. The web was vast.

Just as assiduously for car travel, Father applied his single-minded energies to the itineraries of our family holidays in country Victoria or interstate – arranged by slow mail and long-distance phone calls. If a trip of several days was planned, we obtained detailed strip maps from the RACV (Royal Automobile Club of Victoria) or COR (the Commonwealth Oil Refinery company). I got as much fun from following the maps as other kids did from serialised comics. They featured places of interest, side roads and distances. I always had a good sense of direction.

When motels replaced hotels (which had noisy night-time bars) and guesthouses (with none), Father was delighted to abandon the necessity of differentiating. Motels provided fresh convenience and simple service. We could be woken by a morning phone call from the office. I sampled the breakfast trays – pushed through a hatch in the bedroom wall – with great expectation, devouring the slight slice of cold white toast (resembling a piece of paperbark) and plastic sachets of butter, honey, strawberry jam and Vegemite. The boring porridge at home could not compete; I collected unused sachets from the rest of the family for future feasts.

Normally when we travelled to visit Brethren in the country, it was assumed that they would accommodate us with open arms, in the proper Brethren manner. Extended long-weekend meetings, called fellowship meetings, were a perfect excuse to escape the city in our much-polished Holden.

On the rare occasion we had to eat at a roadside café en route, Mother ran an incessant negative commentary, much to Father's chagrin. How limited the choice on the menu was, she remarked; the food was too expensive and, worse, it was badly cooked. It was bound to be second-rate! What else could we expect in the remote wilds of country meetings in Calulu, Lindenow, Nyah West, Bundanoon, Harcourt, Sutton Grange, Warragul, Thirroul, Waiai, Scottsdale, Gnowangerup, Warrnambool or Dalwallinu? Those small towns did not rub up against centres of fancy cuisine. I saw most of rural Victoria via meetings, and parts of other states in summer holidays. In country towns, Mother ordered an omelette because she believed that food should be freshly cooked, and she would never eat fish far from a coast. Regularly ordering an omelette, however, opened her eyes to the startling possibility that it could be concocted from powdered egg.

Before ending his working life as a lollypop man near Shoppingtown in Doncaster, Father had varied jobs in the printing and publicity industries. He was never content unless working hard. I suggested to him more than once that he should start his own business, but he never had the confidence.

As a fresh apprentice, he began his first job with *The Adelaide Advertiser*, profiting from a generous gift of £100 from the owner, Sir John Bonython. Bonython gifted money to all *Advertiser* employees on the death of his wife in 1925, regardless of their seniority. Father (then aged sixteen) had only worked there for one month. He used the gift – worth one-ninth of the cost – to help to pay for purchase of the large weatherboard home in Canterbury in 1940, where I lived for twenty-one years.

His winning continued in Adelaide. He was top printing apprentice in 1927:

> Mr. Johanson sat for four subjects, English, theory of trade, and practical work, and divided equal honours for first place in drawing. He also obtained the £3/3/- prize for the best all-round student of the grade.

I sometimes wondered if his skills were under-used. In the 1950s, Father printed small tracts – with effusive Brethren messages – for my distribution by hand, beseeching the masses of neighbourhood unbelievers to join the privileged ranks of the saved saints. The free tracts were not just any Christian propaganda – they were official pronouncements of vetted dogma. The Stow Hill Bible and Tract Depot in London controlled printing of true Plymouth Brethren propaganda, as hunky-dory as the Vatican Publishing House. I confess that I only ever read one tract from beginning to end, but that was quite sufficient to indicate the gist of all of them. They usually described a miraculous rescue from disasters by conversion to Christianity.

With Brethren mates aged about thirteen, I wore out leather soles whilst stuffing the picaresque texts into letter boxes large and small, ceramic and metal, wooden and concrete, decrepit and flashy, mounted on gates and walls, accessible and awkward. You can sense that even variations in letter box shapes and sizes provided some stimulation – there was very little else to entertain me on a Saturday afternoon. A short bike ride to Chatham amounted to a getaway.

'I'm going over to Geoffrey's to see if he wants to deliver tracts,' I called out to Mother.

'Make sure that your address is stamped on them,' reminded Father.

'Take an apple and be home by tea,' advised Mother.

Knick-knocking

I felt so self-righteous as I stuffed hundreds of the tracts into letter boxes of homes in surrounding suburbs that I could imagine a radiant halo hovering over my tanned forehead. What other kid was devoting Saturday arvo to tract dissemination? The halo only ever glowed briefly, however.

On these very streets, po-faced Geoffrey and I had strolled not long before, to victimise residents with our game of Knick-knocking. It should have been called 'Knock-knicking'. The game was simple: I quietly tied a thin black thread ('borrowed' from Mother) to the door knocker of a strange house, reeled it out the front gate and around a fence or corner, where I hid, pulled the thread hard to make the knocker work, then broke the thread and knicked off helter-skelter, to avoid the house owner finding me. I sweated in fear of discovery.

Ringing a doorbell and knicking off was even more risky than using cotton thread. Predictably the least satisfying part of the game was not being able to see the expressions on the face of the victims. As to effectiveness, I had to rely on a report by my partner, who positioned himself where the house-owner could be observed. My partner was not an informative interpreter of human annoyance. It was a risky game with too many variables – we soon tired of it altogether.

As a Saturday arvo activity, pushing the good news of salvation via paper tracts into narrow slots, seemed on a par with unravelling threads from front doors. I felt no obligation for moral comparisons. Both activities were virtual confrontations with strangers, reasons to hang out on the streets, waiting for something to happen. It rarely did.

Fine printing

Father travelled further afield with greater adventures. The Victorian Dairy Corporation commissioned a car tour around Victoria, to organise photography of prize cows on lush farms for its annual calendar. Father told me that it could take two days to get a cow to stand still to look at the camera for a portrait. From then on, I watched any cud-chewer in a paddock with greater respect.

But on the finished calendar, Father printed the groomed animals on shiny paper in a wash of pastel shades of sepia, blue and maroon. The rustic atmosphere was entirely lost in my view – not a green tree or gumbooted farmer was to be seen. The manicured cows may have beautified the wall of many a miking shed but I had no need for them on my own toilet wall. A glaring cow with impressive eyelashes was off-putting.

Years later, I worked with the wife of the manager of Exchange Press, efficient Patricia Owen, who told me that Father was so productive that sales increased by fifty per cent when he was taken into the company. Little wonder that he was trusted to tour the country for several weeks, in a chauffeured car, with a photographer, expenses paid, and was never unemployed, even during the Depression or wartime.

Father was modest about his work achievements, shyly avoiding contact between his family and workmates. I visited his printery, Exchange Press, only once in 1964 when I was editor of the annual school magazine with my co-editor, Miriam, as an excuse for a field trip. The press was printing our mag. Miriam was uncomfortable being jammed between Tony Pugsley, the teacher-driver, and me, on the front seat of his FJ Holden. At Exchange Press, it was fascinating to watch hot metal typesetting, which is now all but dead as a craft. The endless rattle of the machines took time to adjust to. I admired how the operators functioned as smoothly and flawlessly as piano virtuosos at a concert. My school blazer absorbed the unique mixture of pungent smells – of paper, metal, rubber belts, ink.

My older brothers were friends with Brethren boys of the McAlpin family – Bruce, David and John. They were the fourth generation of a dynamic dynasty managing huge sales of processed flour and daily bread around the country. In the 1950s, Father was persuaded to become advertising manager for the McAlpins, the family who owned the company, earning £33 per week. Aunt disapproved vociferously for reasons that I do not remember.

One of the McAlpin boys told me, with a sarcastic laugh, that when customers requested wholemeal bread, the McAlpin bakery would put molasses into the bland white bread mix, and sell it as brown, implying wholesomeness. We lived in an age of over-processed food, where white and brown were made to taste exactly the same. Modern culinary science was proclaimed from a spotless white test kitchen (inspired by US advertising) at the enormous red-brick McAlpin's factory in Richmond– I visited with Mother in 1960. In the kitchen, modern cooking was conducted by an officious woman in a white lab coat and pert hat who presumed to give lessons, and did not countenance questions from the sparse audience. Germs and queries were as unwelcome as baking imagination in her spotless steel cavern.

Father managed the printing of the McAlpin recipe books, complete with brightly coloured photos. I was fascinated to learn from him that photographing whipped cream under hot floodlights for advertisements required use of mashed potato instead of real cream (which would melt). I can vouch for the delicate, fluffy look of the mashed potato in coloured pictures of Jelly Sponge Baskets, the Sponge Sandwich, and the Chocolate Cream Tart, all printed to realistic perfection in *McAlpin's Test Kitchen Recipes; a Guide to Better Baking*. I forgot to ask him how the red jelly coped with the heat.

In special recognition of my responsible demeanour, I was permitted to serve at the tent of McAlpin's Flour at the Royal Melbourne Show two years in a row. It was no surprise that most of the customers for the *Guide to Better Baking* were middle-aged mums. They were fussy about correct change for their purchases – I got a kick out of calculating and dispensing it. The boring McAlpin's showbag gave away free a wooden ruler, a calendar, and a small sample packet of self-raising flour, which may have been sufficient for half a pancake. Apart from a token wage for this work, the main benefit to me of helping was to enable my wider exploration of some of the wicked sideshows nearby, when my supervisors were off-guard. Making evil sorties sent a thrill down my spine. Nowhere else could I see the Tattooed Lady, or Big Chief Little Wolf in a supposed north American Indian outfit, or a ventriloquist, or Indian rope climber, or, most amazing of all, a master of the stockwhip who could slice an apple in half when it was held forwards in someone else's teeth. If these performances were typical of Worldly shows, then I was all in favour of them.

Fashions in advertising more widely reflected Brethren preoccupations. Whereas McAlpins chose hygiene and cleanliness as themes for their products, in Fremantle another Brethren enterprise emphasised reliable construction and business transparency in its advertisement themes. The Plymouth Brother owner, W.J. Draffin, worked a mattress factory called Joyce (Bros) Ltd. Full US marketing hype was antithetical to his faith, as Draffin found out on a visit there in 1929. He was not allowed to boast of being the best or being proud of his products. To Brethren, those words were immodest, and pride was a sin. Instead, his beds and mattresses became hygienic, reliable, trustworthy, manufactured by machines (not human hands), giving 'guaranteed quality' without deceit, all words that were used in his catalogues from 1929 to 1959. His company dominated the Australian mattress market. In 1938, Draffin saw it as his duty to guide the visiting Cossham family around the Brethren cognoscenti in Fremantle. Hospitality was reliable, honest and guaranteed too.

Friends

Father had his own friends. On incomplete evidence, I always imagined that he had close male friends before he married. He talked a little of camping trips in Tasmania when he worked there with the *Hobart Mercury* in his late teens. He described country trips in Victoria with Vernon Seeley, a newly qualified dentist, who owned his own car. Vernon's involvement with my family was very friendly and long-lasting, but his cruel end at the hands of Exclusive Brethren was morbidly gruesome. It was the stuff of a Gothic novel.

Vernon was the son of a migrant named Adolph Seelenmeyer, as mentioned. He converted from Judaism to Plymouth Brethren because he wanted to marry a Plymouth Sister living in Parkville, Edith Le Souef, in 1914. My father – and many other Brethren – regarded this conversion as a divine miracle, clear evidence of the imminence of our heavenly ascent, known as the Rapture, the invention of the Brethren founder, John Nelson Darby. It became a central stressor to all Brethren children, who worried for years about being left behind.

A Scottish child of Plymouth Brethren parents (Professor John Richmond) born in 1926, while reflecting eighty years later, never let go of his childhood fears. He became a distinguished physician and wrote poetry late in life:

> … The Plymouth Brethren taught me as a boy
> to hope that we, the righteous,
> would escape death's agony…completely;
> we'd be 'taken' in the Rapture, captured,
> caught up, levitated, holy parachutists in reverse,
> to meet our Saviour in the atmosphere
> (joy unconfined, though altitude unspecified)
> and join the resurrected saints who had already died.
> And this might happen any time: next week, next year,
> tomorrow… What a way to go!…
> Well, that's all finished with. It's hard now to believe
> that I believed it then. I won't be up there in the ranks…

In contrast, Father believed until his end in the remote pleasures of the Rapture. He was enthralled that Adolph Seelenmeyer did not simply choose Christianity; he chose Brethren with its Rapture feature specifically. Such a conversion was unknown in Brethren annals and taken to be a clear sign that Jesus was on the verge of returning to our very doorstep. Darby taught Brethren to believe that when the Jews returned to Israel and Christian faith, as they surely would, then all Brethren would be elevated to heaven in the Rapture, the seventh and last dispensation of human existence. The excitement was palpable; I was as prepared for lift-off as the rest of my family when we discussed Adolph. No one mentioned that Darby had prophesied the year 1842 as the end of the world; that was conveniently forgotten.

Adolph practised as a dentist, only to be persecuted during World War I because of his German surname, Seelenmeyer. His brass nameplate in Collins Street was tarred and feathered in the feudal fashion. Changing his name in 1920 to Seeley seemed to be the means to bypass further discrimination.

Adolph's son, Dr Vernon Seeley (born 1910), was an unassuming and friendly man with a mass of black hair. He was a little absent-minded and other-worldly. Vernon graduated as a dentist in 1930 and became admired worldwide for his skills at reconstructing jaws and faces. In 1948, he was listed as Honorary Oral Surgeon and Senior Lecturer at the Australian College of Dentistry at the University of Melbourne. His minor religious status dwarfed in comparison to his stellar professional career. Once married, Vernon visited our home for meals with his wife and handsome kids, Graeme and Helen, who were older than me.

As a person, Vernon was quiet and compliant. Egged on by Brethren elders, in 1962 he tried to persuade Father not to leave the Exclusive cult. We left as a family anyway in spite of Vernon, who decided to hang in. At the same time, his daughter Helen bore an illegitimate grandson, George, whom Vernon rejected. As a single mother, she was thrown out of Exclusive Brethren hastily at the same time as us, and out of her family without support. I only had fleeting contact with her in our small rump, where she dropped in once or twice after she became a Mum. Most of all, I remember her fearful sadness, and then she stopped attending.

From the abandonment of Helen onwards, I rely on second-hand reports for Vernon's own catastrophe (mostly from Michael Bachelard, *Behind the Exclusive Brethren*, 2008) for the sake of completeness. After 1962, Father never spoke to Vernon again. In 1970, Vernon followed Exclusive Brethren instructions and was told to form a settlement of followers in Albury, where few had settled before. By 1989, he was cast out of Exclusives himself because he made a rude remark about an elect vessel – that is, a Brethren leader. His wife was not excommunicated.

He complied with a Brethren edict to sign over his estate to his wife, and then was forced to live alone and separately in a caravan at the back of his house. She left his meals outside the door. Aged eighty-two in 1992, he died in the caravan with a broken leg, just two years before Father died. As if the van humiliation was insufficient, his son rang the Brethren leader in Sydney, before the non-Brethren funeral, to seek a determination as to whether Vernon would go to heaven. Predestination was clearly not controlled alone by God in heaven, and arrogant cruelty despised that dedicated old generation.

Snooping

Brethren had such a terrified attitude towards external evil that it made them paranoid about their own. They were always looking out for sin, and had no qualms about snooping on one another, looking for faults and telling tales. I was caught playing a game of cricket that I should not have played. There was always one Brother or Sister more holy than the rest, who felt compelled to brandish their righteousness.

John Nelson Darby himself spent much of his life checking on his flock; in 1876, he visited Melbourne and Sydney for a few days and concluded that colonial Brethren were rough and ready and exercised far too much free will – an interesting comment that may have applied more broadly to early colonial culture generally. 'Home' was already becoming a distant memory for many.

Thirty years later, one zealous Brother spent his retirement – from school teaching – travelling the Victorian countryside checking on the quality of country meetings. J. Newell Barrett wrote a letter to Grandfather in a condescending tone in 1908:

> I have been moving around a good deal lately, and I shall continue to do so for some weeks… Stawell and Warrnambool have received some attention, and both needed it… In some places there is a certain decline which it seems difficult if not impossible to arrest… The Nhill meeting is not doing very well. Small as it is there is room for party strife, and instead of the uniting bond of peace there is the disintegrating force of criticism and dislike.

I can almost hear the hushed hearsay, loved by Grandfather, who absorbed the inclination himself to pry on Brethren, snooping for problems. Father shared his enthusiasm. He benefitted from the strategies gained from checking on Aunt, his arch-enemy at home. Prying only led to more prying.

The experience of living through global wars and spending thirty-six years avoiding one another would affect most people deeply, just as it left an imprint of the meaning of lonely separation on the whole family. Father and Aunt were never reconciled before they died; bitterness and jealousy dominated until their ends. Their consensus about the errors of conscientious objection was coincidental, and never led them into any meaningful alliance. They both worked very hard at their careers and were well rewarded, and Brethren praised Father for his lifelong support of their devout activities. In an earlier era, he would have been the wily abbot of a monastery. Mother suffered a lot from their envious competing claims on her.

The only men whom Aunt really admired were her medical doctors, especially those who employed her, although other doctors were treated as gods as well. As a result, she doted on Peter, my brother, who became a doctor. To her, Father was a mere irritant. She was overly dependent and clung to Mother like a limpet to a lonely rock. In contrast, Father remained genuinely committed to his faith, reviling double-dealing, building community and continually asserting his primacy over Aunt.

The mythology of Nemesis, the vengeful Greek goddess, was taken over by the Romans, who made her the patron of gladiators. We had two resident gladiators at home. Nemesis dealt out justice, supposedly ensuring that no one benefitted from more than their fair share of happiness, aiming to keep people humble. Father hardly needed Aunt. Brethren alone (like Nemesis) kept him on the straight and narrow. In a way, he had double burdens – from Aunt and Brethren both. In statues and frescoes, Nemesis is depicted as carrying a tally stick and scales for weighing, and she wields a whip, dagger and sword. Father went up against a relentless monitor, sufficient to make anyone groan. The classical Nemesis was as bothersome and frighteningly omnipotent as the Christian God to come.

Above: Graeme, aged nine months, 1947.
Below: Graeme at left in a studio with his family, 1956.

Above left: Graeme's mother, 1964.
Above right: Graeme's father, 1935.
Below: Graeme's Aunt Bett, 1943.

Graeme with football, third row from front, second from left, Grade Four, Canterbury State School, 1956. Teacher: Mr Baddeley.

Above: Graeme's passport photo, 1962.
Right: Graeme hiking in Tasmania, 1967.
Below Left: Graeme, 1969.
Below right: Graeme with loaded bicycle, Sri Lanka, April Fool's Day, 1970.

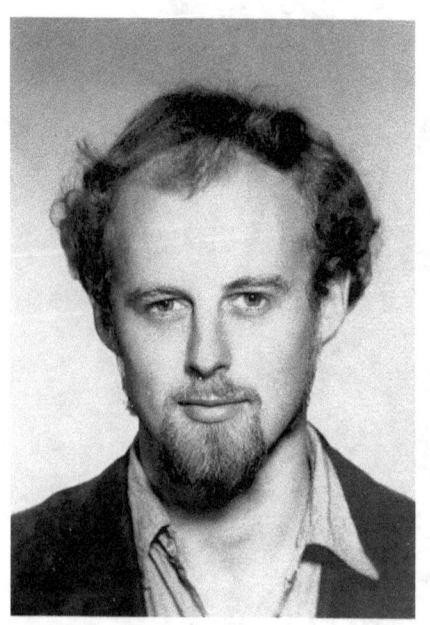

Top: Impounded bus, Iran, 1970. Franko in the long white shirt.

Centre: Typical Brethren meeting hall, Calulu, country Victoria, 1959.

Right: Hats and long hair. Plymouth Brethren in Moss, Norway, 1955.

Above: Wylie family, Devonport Brethren, 1966.

Left: Turid, friend and partner, 1969.

Six

Can't buy love

The power base

For my aunt, work at the diagnostic group at Bethesda Salvation Army Hospital in Richmond was her chosen retreat, her fortress and her control centre. There, she expressed herself in her own style. Although they overlapped in small ways, our home did not serve the same purposes as work for her. Known as Miss-saireee (that is, Miss Airey) at work by servile secretaries, she tried to resist a radical loss of influence when obliged to leave the hospital campus. At home, the playing field was more challenging.

At work, she had enormous influence. She rushed always. She was well-regarded by her peers not only at Bethesda, but at six other networked hospitals as well, where she managed about a hundred pathology and secretarial staff in the manner of an army.

In the wafting formalin atmosphere of all the pathology units, her role was unequalled. Her word was unchallengeable fact, and her terse requests were instant orders. Because her doctors trusted her implicitly and she ostensibly performed to their expectations, over decades she was able to deprive them of millions of their profits via their unguarded back pockets. Her blunt barrister informed His Honour 'that she was responsible for the administration and accounting of the group, including the payment and receipt of all money'. What a temptation!

I witnessed Aunt's power at first hand. At her invitation, during two university vacations I took over the work of Mac the courier, for a few weeks for the partnership of pathologists, while Mac went on a camping holiday with his family to Dromana. In taut tones, Aunt explained that the job required me to deliver pathology samples and messages to group branches continuously and fast by car, all within the inner city. With this temporary job, I had income (always welcome to a student) and access to Aunt's office – guarded watchfully by Patty and three other hard-boiled typists – in the pool outside the secretary's office door.

'Yes, Miss-saireee.' 'No, Miss-sairee.' 'Certainly, Miss-saireee.' 'Of course, Miss-saireee.' 'Straight away, Miss-saireee.'

These sibilant replies were mouthed always with a final rising intonation, as though pleading for mercy. The acknowledgements from the four devoted secretaries – dressed unnecessarily in white uniforms – hissed around the spotless white walls of the outer office.

Sometimes I forgot formality, forgot to knock on the heavy wooden door to her office, forgot the guardians, and barged straight in to ask for advice or give her news from another branch. I could hear the four typists gasp with horror in unison, then realised my error and froze in the opened doorway, suspended in space. I was neither in nor out. Normally when a typist entered the Holy of Holies, she invariably knocked first and awaited a signal of a green light – the size of a traffic light – installed over the door lintel. Aunt's office was designed as a watchtower with an easterly window that allowed her to check anyone coming along the outside path to visit. Why was she so wary?

To my mind, Aunt's morals seemed superficial – including her faith. I learnt to be on guard when she spoke in a lowered voice. 'You mustn't tell anyone about this,' was one of her favourite sayings.

Her subterfuge activated my impulse to broadcast her secrets instantly. She imagined that she cleverly juggled her many secrets as control devices. She was easily provoked and I enjoyed giving her cheek – more than any of my other siblings. I felt no special obligation towards her, no matter how long she lived with us. I never thought that she belonged properly in the family; I treated her rather like a pet that we offered to mind temporarily for an absent friend.

There is no doubt that she invested years of energy into her job; she was no freeloader. She functioned with meticulous precision. She was not medically trained, and she had no non-Brethren role models other than her bosses, who were all doctors with varying degrees of wartime experience. Strangely, doctors were the only males in her life whom she looked up to; she became close to them all and they depended heavily on her hard work. She was very well-respected, knowing all the staff, having interviewed most of them for jobs at their start, and she was in demand for handing out prizes to nurses at annual graduation ceremonies. But she was never comfortable with people.

Forgetting to wait for the green light once more, on another visit to her office, I was allowed to see more of her inner sanctum than I bargained for. As I pushed her door shut, she opened her top desk drawer silently to show me a black revolver that she kept loaded there. She was proud to display the squat, sinister weapon. One of her favourite doctors, Dr Kurt Schwartz, told her to buy it, but I doubt that she knew how the revolver worked. Whenever I ran across him, Schwartz thought of himself as a spontaneous wit, but I failed to ever get any of his jokes. The revolver in the drawer was no joke.

I asked why Aunt had the weapon, and she told me that thousands of dollars passed over her desk on fortnightly paydays, and it was for protection. At that time, pay was distributed to staff as cash in small paper envelopes. She had never fired the gun. Although it indicated her nod of acknowledgement in the direction of the military lineage of her doctors, and it gave Aunt a sense of power, the revolver caused me to reflect on the supposed pacifism of Brethren philosophy which she clearly flouted. I needed no more emphatic evidence that at work she ruled the roost. In retrospect, protecting her group's funds from outside robbers with a weapon was tantamount to defending her own income as a white-collar robber.

Aunt took plenty of years to embed herself in the senior ranks of the medical partnership. She first joined the hospital in 1936, when Dr Douglas Thomas, a pathologist, realised that his specialisation was rapidly expanding. Three further pathologists were employed in the young business in the 1940s – Doctors Geoffrey Harkness, Kurt Schwartz and Howell Hosking. The last two possibly conspired with Aunt later on, but it is not certain. The longer Aunt worked as a secretary for them, the wealthier she became. Sometimes, I wondered that she did not sleep at the office. She often started work at five a.m. and finished at nine p.m.

It is notable that her closest associates and mentors had all been soldiers overseas. Was it a coincidence? One could easily assume that an essential qualification of her bosses was army service. It is likely that the military heroes at her work permeated her consciousness early on. Implicitly, she revered the patrimony and endorsed military service for men. She grew into the role of commander-in-chief herself.

As a young woman in Kyneton, her first job was with Dr Downing, a major in the AIF, who had served in England from 1915 to 1917 in the Australian Army Medical Corps. She developed competency by accompanying him on his home visits as well as managing his appointments, and became a close friend of his family.

Her next boss in Melbourne, Dr Thomas – at the age of nineteen – had spent five months at Gallipoli in an ambulance corps. He was elevated to sergeant, and then again to colonel in World War II. In 1923, he was appointed medical superintendent at Bethesda Hospital, where Aunt soon worked. He was a strict Methodist.

I met Dr Thomas only once, on a winter trip with Aunt to Olinda. One snowy day, she took me to his home, where he was ill but had to review some papers. We drove there in her little Austin A40 tourer, and I remember having to use the crank handle from under my seat to start the engine twice. I made a snowman on the bonnet of the car while she talked to the doctor. I felt very excited – it was my first contact with snow, but without gloves I was freezing. Although hard to believe, the mascot-sized snowman atop the radiator cap melted only slightly, and lasted all the way back to Canterbury that afternoon. On arrival home, Mother was suitably admiring.

Aunt's next supervisor was another ex-soldier, Dr Geoffrey Harkness. He took over the diagnostic group in 1954 from Dr Thomas when he retired. In World War II, he served with the AIF in a medical corps in New Guinea, and from 1947 he continued military service as Deputy Director of Australian Medical Services, for which he received an OBE. From brief acquaintance, I remember him as urbane, handsome and affable, with a blue-blooded wife and five boys. Although the official obituary of Dr Harkness in his professional journal praised his absolute integrity, he seems to have led Aunt into a series of illegal embezzlements, and his estate was pursued successfully by the remainder of the Bethesda pathology partnership for recompense soon after he died suddenly of a heart attack at the age of fifty-three.

Medical assistance

With her medical knowledge gained on the job, it is not surprising that Aunt felt competent to make medical decisions on my behalf. I began life in her hospital in 1946 at the cost to my parents of £8, according to the receipt for my birth, an amount that was equal to the average weekly wage of the time.

When I was just one-and-a-half-years old, Aunt arranged for an X-ray to be taken of my buttock at her hospital, because a sewing needle had lodged in it, collected as I manoeuvred clumsily around the dark-stained wooden floor at home. I did not crawl on all fours, Mother said, but instead shuffled along on my buttom, remaining upright. Mother noticed the needle because the eye of the embedded needle pricked her hand once when she changed my nappy. She estimated that it had been in my bottom for about three months. Crawling must have caused me pain, although by all reports I was a jolly baby. Aunt organised for my X-rays, which I still have, on Eastman Ultraspeed film. The needle – about 3.5 centimetres long – was removed with pliers by the family GP at home, but it became rusty and I threw it away long ago. The unwanted breach of my epidermis did not put me off injections generally. But I am glad that the needle was no longer – in both senses of the word. It gave me pleasure to relegate it to the rubbish.

That Aunt loved to cuddle young boys I discovered fully when I had my own children. Up to the age of four or so, she regarded boys as saintly cherubs, as much as did the Renaissance painter Raphael. They gurgled and she pinched their chubby knees playfully. As they grew, they became less saintly and far too independent for her to cope with. Mother described me (in her record in the dirty book bequeathed to me) as a gorgeous fat boy at the age of one who called Aunt Bee-Bee. I sat on her lap to listen to the tick of Bee-Bee's cuckoo – as I named her wristwatch. Her full name was Olive Elizabeth Airey, named after her aunt, grandmother and father. She chose to be called Betty. But always Miss-sairee in the office.

My reliance on Aunt's absolute devotion to the science of modern medicine took a deep slide in my teens. She disliked illness intensely. She brought home several bottles of Waterbury's Compound as a tonic for me, on the advice of Dr Schwarz. It was stinking muck that I left to sit inert for so long on the pantry shelf that its use-by date expired eventually. Far from tasting like a tonic, it smelt like putrid prune juice. I expected it to grow fur in the bottle. Aunt threw up her arms in anger, stressed how ungrateful I was, and complained about how much money she had wasted on the imported cure-all. I reminded her simply, 'I didn't ask for it.'

At the age of fourteen, I could not see the blackboard in the classroom, and was prescribed glasses. For unknown reasons, perhaps because of spite about the waste of the tonic, Aunt derided my myopia, claiming that I invented it to gain attention. Actually, I was embarrassed about having to wear new black-rimmed spectacles at all. In a passport photo from the time, my face looks overwhelmed by black plastic. Around the same time, she also denied my pain from massive carbuncles that developed on my side and posterior. You can imagine my discomfort from sitting on top of carbuncles while spread on wooden chairs for hours in meetings. On Mother's advice, the family GP lanced them to relieve the horrible pressure. I still carry the small scars.

In contrast, a welcome contribution by Aunt to my well-being was almost coincidental, having nothing to do with tonics or doctors. My pleasure came from access to her gramophone when I was occasionally sick and home from school. Thanks to her, home was endowed with the treasure of the heavy box. Because it was old, she wanted to throw it away, but I loved to use it like a toy.

When Aunt was nine, she was confined to bed for months, because, according to her family GP, Dr Downing, she had tuberculosis. Late in life, she adamantly denied the diagnosis; her relationship with medicine was very conflicted. It is tantalising to think what a psychologist would make of it. Brethren did not believe in psychology.

Uncle Bill gave the gramophone to Aunt in 1924 so that she could listen in her sickbed. Bill was not an uncle, in fact, but an orphan, named William Croft, having been adopted by my maternal great-grandmother before World War I in order to attract a government allowance of five shillings per month. He rejected strong overtures to join Brethren, or any church, and I blessed him for facilitating my access to the ancient gramophone.

I benefitted from his generosity in other ways; he brought bags of the juiciest snowballs in the universe when he dropped into our home – all the way from Bunbury in Western Australia, which seemed an inordinate distance to me. His bouncy wife was an extraverted joker, covered in perfume and make-up, noisily filling our home in her flouncing frocks and busty blouses on the rare occasions when she stayed. Aunt found Bill and Ede too frenetic, but I delighted in their posturing. They may have sensed that we lacked stimulation at home. Bill was a chain-smoker, reeking of nicotine, and found our tobacco-free household an inconvenient strain; inevitably, he died of lung cancer.

His memorable music box was covered in thin black leather. It smelt musty. Permission to play with it depended on the severity of my sickness, so naturally I felt very, very ill when I wanted to use it. It stimulated every sense that a child could desire. A soft rubber turntable revolved when a large chrome handle was used to crank it up tightly, and old steel needles were inserted in an arm to wobble on the surface of the Bakelite records, making a harsh scratchy crackle, like a distant bushfire burning. To Brethren, record-players were sinful, but illness led to weakened rules for Aunt, and to Worldly songs and stories for me, which I welcomed. I played the records hundreds of times. All of the equipment was kept out of sight in the recesses of Aunt's cupboard, revealed only for entertainment when I was far beyond the purview of Brethren. Again in our home, a wardrobe served as a secret store for forbidden impedimenta.

The few records which Aunt owned had not been added to since the 1920s. I recall a few of them – sombre jazz (Paul Robeson), 'The Volga Boatman' (why was he vulgar?) and the reading of 'Little Red Riding Hood'. My sad reaction to the wept tears in 'Old Kentucky Home' was strong, even though I had no real understanding of the background to its nostalgic banjo.

All the much-loved records were pitted, and smooth narration of 'Little Red Riding Hood' got stuck in a worn groove regularly, the narrator repeating the ominous words 'into the woods' over and over. The ill-fated innocent never stopped walking into the woods, never reaching her grandmother's house, as long as the needle was not moved manually over that unwanted groove. At least I had the option of moving the needle right over the section with the Big Bad Wolf on it, if I wanted.

The metaphor of my life journey was laid out before me repeatedly by this old record. The mythical woods were undoubtedly the World beyond the security of Brethren. I repeated the niche message over and over in my head up into the 1970s. The Red Riding Hood woods sounded just as frightening as the woods in *The Hobbit* or the Wild Woods in *The Wind in the Willows*. Would I get lost in future in those woods like Mole, see too many evils among the nasty denizens, and experience sheer panic? It was a daunting prospect.

Beach holidays

Temporary retreat into fantasy was allowed via the treasured gramophone, but by far the most valued contribution of Aunt to my health was a beach refuge. I was lifted to the top of a wave physically, emotionally and spiritually by respite at the vast ocean sanctuary.

The hassle of renting holiday houses to accommodate all of the growing family, such as that in Rosebud mentioned already, led my mother to buy two adjacent blocks of land on an old dune covered in tea tree at Ocean Grove for £50. They faced the rolling Southern Ocean. Conveniently, a Liberal government introduced a child endowment payment in 1941 which Mother saved assiduously. She received 5/- per week from the government for her third child (me), and 10/- per week for the two older boys. My arrival boosted her weekly allowance to £1/5/-, which today would pay for one kilogram of porterhouse steak. I was well worth it.

For ever, I have cherished beaches, where I regularly scavenged, always looking forwards to a fresh discovery on rocks or vast stretches of sand – sombre abalone, crinkly sea horses, pink anemones, scurrying crabs, plastic-like ray eggs, pristine scallops, royal sea urchins, and even a coy crayfish every now and again. Aunt enabled long beach holidays of perpetual pleasure, during regular breaks at school and university, turning me into an avid beachcomber. Just walking along the sand with the perpetual swish and thump of waves was hypnotic. At night, the roar of waves under a star-filled sky lulled me to sleep.

Aunt was beginning to share her money furtively, thus underwriting the investment in the land at Ocean Grove. She funded the construction of a fibro-cement holiday house on the highest of the two beach blocks, starting in 1950, that was two storeys high, with views of the ocean, where twice I spotted whales. She paid a house-builder whom she employed otherwise for jobs at her work at the diagnostic group. My oldest brother David was assigned the task of naming our new house – he chose 'Karnkendi', an easy-going word from Kaurna for place of laughter. Father tried to stay there on holiday when Aunt was not, so that they did not overlap, thereby avoiding emotional fireworks. The sparks that they generated were far from a laughing matter. My only memory of relaxing with Father was of playing with strands of giant kelp in the waves with him during a swim together.

Dozens of Brethren children joined us at holiday time, often from other states. The long dining room could accommodate about twenty holidaymakers. At least four other families of Plymouth Brethren holidayed in other houses in the town, and with a Brethren meeting in nearby Geelong, the holiday retreat was ostensibly within reach of essential worship. My strongest memory of the Lord's Days in Geelong is having to wear stiff white collars and tight ties around my tanned neck during summer heatwaves. I wore as little as possible all week, then was bound up like an Egyptian mummy at the end. The burden of respectability added to the bombast. Tracking blowflies in and out of the windows in the hot hall brought some small relief to the Spirit's shenanigans. I envied Aunt, who regularly gave herself permission to stay comfortably in bed at the beach house all day.

At the beach, I bodysurfed at every opportunity all year round, sometimes in the nude in summer. But never on the Lord's Day, of course.

One sickly bout of sunstroke was enough to ensure that I thoroughly covered myself in zinc cream or sunscreen, to prevent sunburn ever after. Wetsuits and rashies were as foreign to us as fibreglass surfboards or bikinis. Our bathers (togs, trunks, cossies) were made of wool.

The isolated walk from Ocean Grove to Point Lonsdale along the beach, and back, took a day, depending on the height of the tide and the firmness of the sand. It was not unusual to meet fairy penguins onshore, or stingrays and dolphins in the shallows. At a remote spot on the beach, I always rested by the rusting funnel of a steamship embedded in the sand – perhaps from the nearby remnants of a 1940 shipwreck of the small passenger ship the *Orungal*, stuck fast on a rocky promontory at Barwon Heads. My parents told stories of walking along that beach collecting flotsam and jetsam from that wreck, including blocks of chocolate. It made me wish for another shipwreck.

For the twenty-one years until I left home, the beach house was a happy refuge at holiday time and at weekends. Driving along the monotonous, flat Geelong highway was a necessary gateway to freedom.

The misty blue You Yangs mountains marked halfway. Through the car window, we watched passengerless-planes practising their landing and take-off at Avalon. My siblings and I spent ten schoolless weeks a year relaxing at Ocean Grove, exploring the endless dunes, and fishing, swimming, catching rabbits, yabbying, riding bikes, hitchhiking, playing games and walking on the boundless beach. There, we did things together.

At each holiday, every family member except Father took a load of books for leisure reading, in an encircling armchair during the day or in a bunk bed at night. Aunt's favourite books were mysteries written by Raymond Chandler and Agatha Christie. Who knows whether she discovered in them any dirty tricks to use in her real-life frauds? At least via them she could maintain a modicum of mental tension when far from fiddling the figures at work. She subscribed to all Readers' Digest Condensed Books to avoid reading full tomes; we teased her about lack of diligence. Any leisure time of hers was occupied by fiction – she never read any Brethren 'Ministry', compulsory exegesis for all faithful adherents. When tired of reading, we played board games or charades or darts or table tennis. Radio and TV were unheard of. During university swot vacs, I spread papers out over the table tennis table overlooking the ocean, ruffling my hair, picking scabs, doing revision, practising exam answers.

Slowly but inevitably in the 1970s housing development impinged on the dunes and surrounding farmlands, converting our wilderness playground into symmetrical, bitumen-bound suburbs of Geelong. I grieved. After Aunt went to gaol, the family could not afford to maintain the beach house, which deteriorated rapidly, and it was sold for demolition.

Other states

Even when we had the option to hide out at our ocean eyrie, Aunt's spending on interstate holidays became a fresh avenue for amusement, in addition to the beach. In 1956, the whole family toured Tasmania for two weeks in two hired cars. Why did we need two cars? Because Aunt could never co-exist with Father on any journey. We stayed in hotels and motels, visited ruins of convict prisons and witnessed all of the energy that could be generated by new hydroelectric dams in the highlands, and by means of the Spirit moving Brethren at meetings along the east coast. At Scottsdale, Peter Unwin showed me the fun to be had from hand-milking mottled cows and mowing hay with a Massey Ferguson tractor, a Brethren invention. Peter's unkempt mop of tousled hair stood on edge, scrubby above his rosy cheeks.

At the end of 1958, my family headed west by overland train to Perth, Western Australia, for four weeks. The train passed through tiny settlements (of one or two iron buildings) on the Nullarbor Plain on Christmas morning. At one brief stop, I watched a small child on his brand-new bike who raced in the dust to try to speed faster than the train. In Kalgoorlie, we hired two cars for touring among country Brethren again. It was always a mystery to me as to why the sparsely populated south-west wheat belt harboured Brethren congregations in parched wooden halls in insignificant towns with only a handful of residents. Their origins remain a mystery. Typically in towns, Brethren ran small businesses: a grocer, a clothes shop, a service station and a manufacturer of farm equipment and water tanks.

At the age of twelve, I sported a crew cut that my parents abhorred. They told me it was wicked. At school, it was the height of cool. In Dalwallinu and Gnowangerup, on massive wheat farms, no one else seemed to care about my hairstyle, and I spent a lot of time under water sprinklers on lawns in home paddocks, playing happily with other Brethren children.

Teenage jaunt

The year 1962 was a turning point for my family, and for Aunt. Exclusive Brethren excommunicated my family in a dramatic blow – although Aunt seemed unruffled. Another big change was a long overseas trip after excommunication. For months, Aunt strongly resisted going overseas but her doctors insisted that she take long service leave at their expense. She had not been on extended leave for twenty-six years, nor travelled outside Australia ever.

As an eager fifteen-year-old, I was ecstatic to be chosen as her chaperone because Aunt's favourite – my brother Peter – was in the throes of matriculation and could not go away. I jumped for joy. David was in Oxford and wanted us to spend weeks with him. Bettina was aged only twelve. The round-the-world trip was a stunning gift for me to experience at that young age, and it was the closest that I ever came to knowing Aunt as a person. I already knew that she was generous, and when she committed to a project, she supported it whatever may militate against it. I benefitted from her adherence to the adage that blood was thicker than water. I could add a few insights from my trip: she was hesitant, evasive, quick-tempered and cunning.

I dissuaded her from taking a hatbox on the trip. I willingly carried suitcases upstairs or loaded them onto car pack racks. I helped her find our way around Beirut and Balleyboffey and Banff. I bought stamps to post her letters and numerous presents home. I swore never to include her in photos without her permission, nor to challenge her expenditure. Many rewards came my way. For instance, I happily celebrated my sixteenth birthday in the Piazza Santa Croce in Florence, within sight of a basilica as symmetrical as a white wedding cake, and for the tastebuds, juicy scampi and a carafe of red house wine. It was the first time that I enjoyed wine. In consultation, David and I agreed to avoid exposing Aunt to Michelangelo's *David* in the Gallery of the Academy of Florence. We contrived a visit without her.

Aunt was a lesser conversationalist than my mother. She lacked many social graces. Whereas Mother had a genuine, welcoming face and courted interaction, Aunt looked like a poteroo. She fossicked about like one too! She wore a worried brow permanently and forced a smile when she had to, approaching newcomers with a slight forwards tilt. To me, she was always a figure in motion, frozen in action, as in Eadweard Muybridge photographs. Muybridge took the first series of still photos to demonstrate clearly how people (and animals) moved forwards. He invented special cameras that froze their movement.

New York stresses

Cameras became crucial to our adventures. We began our global wander together in Japan, Hong Kong and Bangkok, toured the Middle East, drove from Rome to London with David in his tiny Mini Minor, saw a lot of the UK, stayed briefly in Oslo, then crossed to the USA and Canada en route for Hawaii and Australia. The thrilling excursion took nearly four months.

Halfway around the globe on our trip, Aunt's rude rebuff of a well-meaning New Yorker on the subway still sticks in my mind. In spite of the racket of the subway tunnels, the enquiring local expressed a genuine curiosity about Australia. He was friendly, but Aunt sensed New Yorkers as nosy and brash, and impatiently dismissed people as an annoyance after very brief acquaintance. She shook her head and growled in recognition; New Yorkers were a threat. She had heard a lot of bad rumours about New York. I was often left to pick up the pieces.

To begin her self-fulfilling prophecy, on arrival at Idlewild Airport she argued with a Customs officer, possibly the worst person to pick a fight with.

He asked, 'Madam, please open your suitcase.'

She complied.

He poked around among clothes, until he struck a stone. 'What is this?'

'It's a stone that I collected in Israel,' said Aunt.

'When did you travel there?'

'About three months ago,' said Aunt.

'Do you have any other stones?' asked the Customs official.

'I think so,' said Aunt, rummaging around, pretending to find others, actually trying to waste time.

Impatiently, the Customs official picked up the suitcase and tipped it upside down. I had never before seen such a cascade of female undies, bras and stockings. They were mixed up with several labelled stones and eighteen matchboxes with dirt in them. We carried empty matchboxes from home, to fill with bits from places in the Middle East, including (for instance) sand from the Dead Sea, a beach in Tel Aviv, the banks of River Jordan, and earth from the Via Dolorosa in Jerusalem. I can still feel the dust in my nose. My brother David suggested that we collected these earthy souvenirs, because they seemed more real as keepsakes than our fragile geisha doll from Japan, made of bamboo, or toy Thai dancer from Bangkok. A lot cheaper too.

Aunt was an expert at procrastination when it suited her. The official was curious about her motivation for carrying stones from the Sea of Galilee and from the Garden of Gethsemane.

'Why are you carrying these?' he pressed to know. It did not require a genius to discover a Christian rationale for the bits and pieces.

'I just wanted to collect them,' said Aunt lamely.

'Get them out of my sight,' he concluded curtly, abandoning the content and the suitcase for repacking.

I stood by bemused, having been waved to the exit long before. It was a bad introduction to the USA.

Aunt was shaken as we caught a cab to the shabby Abbey Hotel on 51st Street East. Next day, my movie and still cameras were stolen from the locked hotel bedroom. We were spooked. I was despondent. Aunt's instant reaction was shock, but then revealing: tomorrow we would go and buy two more cameras for me, a new Polaroid camera, and a movie camera for David as well. She made the decision on the spot, stiffening her jaw in resolve. Expense was of no concern.

I had to try hard to encourage her to report the theft to hotel management, pleading, but she was reluctant. The manager told us to go to the nearby police station to make a report. The police politely filed a detailed report; she looked uneasy. At no point did Aunt think it was worth the bother. In her view, only a murder in New York might stir police into action. 'And maybe not even then.' She was convinced that the theft was an inside job, and that the stolen cameras would never be traced. Her pessimism surprised me, but it took a thief to know a thief.

Effects of Separation

Brethren never travelled far without a cache of names and addresses of saints abroad. Such a list was a Brethren visa against the evil World at large. One such network was mentioned in the previous chapter. If we had the urge to look over the city from the top of the Empire State Building, or to take a ferry on the Hudson River, we were surely expected to ferret out the mousey family of Bob Smith, Brethren in the New York suburbs, who celebrated the Lord's Supper with one other couple, acting out the Biblical prescription: 'For where two or three are gathered together in my name, there am I [Jesus] in the midst of them' (Matthew 18:20). The Smiths spoke with a whining drawl that was harsh to our ears. Grey Bob Smith worked in insurance.

Doctrinally, we had been assured that the Smiths were the equivalent of our small Melbourne rump. There had never been large numbers of Plymouth Brethren in the USA, and it turned out that the two white families that we joined up with chose to remain isolated in New York, regardless of alliance options. Racial discrimination separated them from a far larger meeting of black Brethren in Harlem; there was no continuing contact between black and white. Our Smith Brethren drove us in a massive Lincoln Continental car to watch the Afro-Americans pour out onto the street after a meeting in their squat brick hall. It was like visiting a human zoo from behind glass. We peered and inspected from a distance, but we met none of them. Racism proved far stronger than Christian fellowship and it made me feel weak, embarrassed and disaffected.

Wherever we travelled, the same absence of fraternal support and lack of shared vision unfolded. In places where Plymouth Brethren numbers had been meagre before the rupture of 1960, Exclusive dogma reduced many a 'congregation' to an even sparser quorum after it. We were unwilling witnesses to many community wreckages.

Aunt had a passion for all things Irish. Her own father (who died before I was born) had left Ireland for a better life in New Zealand and Australia. In Dublin, we encountered a pitiful group of ex-Plymouth Brethren who were on the verge of joining Open Brethren. They were heirs to my grandfather's communion. The two families which comprised the tiny group reported to David on the Lord's Day that the Spirit was not moving them any longer. Two families hardly viability made. The leading spokesman, Tighe Taylor – proud to be married into the extended Melbourne families of Seeley and Le Souef, mentioned in the last chapter – confessed that he was bereft of inspiration from either the new or old ways of Brethren. He wore a green tweed waistcoat and suit. In my mind, I silently congratulated him for at least being honest and realistic.

On Monday morning, we ignored the problem of the Spirit's lack of revelatory energy and went sightseeing. After all, we were on holiday, not a crusade. While David found a garage to repair a petrol leak in the little red car, Aunt and I ventured around the corner into the crypt of Saint Michan's, a Norman church built beside the Liffey River in 1095, on top of an older Danish-Viking chapel. The Vikings founded Dublin in the fifth century, in order to enslave and export Irish men and women around their empire for use as thralls.

In the vault of Saint Michan's Church was a stunning collection of parched corpses. A cheery local guide with a lilting voice showed us around. Aunt felt disgust, but tolerated my fascination; I was enervated by the pace of the commentary.

'Here are two headless bodies that belonged to a couple of rebels, the Sheares brothers, executed in 1798,' she began in her musical voice.

Rebellion in Ireland has a long history. The Sheares had studied law forty years earlier than John Nelson Darby in the same college. Undoubtedly, the spirit of liberation moved them. They witnessed the French Revolution in Paris and tried to transport it to Dublin. At that time, clergy in England and Ireland feared for the end of Christianity in the UK altogether.

The guide was unstoppable. 'Have a peek inside this crusader's body. His hand was hacked off by medical students three hundred years ago. If you look here you can see how his chest has opened and clearly visible are his heart and intestines'.

Along with others I took a quick glance at what might – in that degraded condition – be any part of any anatomy of any mammal. The melodic voice encouraged me to shake hands with another corpse, 'because his hand is just like new, and, look, it still bends so well at the elbow.'

It creaked. I recorded in my diary that the skin felt like shiny leather to my hesitant handshake.

A few weeks earlier on our long trip, Aunt and I had encountered another impractical juxtaposition – as a result of Separation – among Brethren in northern Scotland. We visited Gardenstown, a tiny fishing village clinging to the sheer cliffs of Banffshire. Gulls wheeled over the ocean spray continually. The whole congregation in Gardenstown – about three hundred of them in a cramped hall nestled among the dark stone cottages – had separated from the entire congregation in the next fishing village that was just a few kilometres along the misty cliffs in the next cove.

Crews on fishing trawlers had to be changed to accommodate new eating rules introduced in 1960 by Exclusive leaders. Exclusive fishermen could no longer share meals with other types of Brethren fishermen nor any other crews on boats. The fleet – settled in the stone harbour below – was split as well as the congregations. The Exclusive Brethren along the cliffs were in a minority. I wondered which group of those rugged fishermen would make it to heaven later on. Would they carry badges saying Plymouth and Exclusive just to make it easier for God to check them in?

Aunt loved the gusto with which the men sang hymns but I could not understand their burr. All I wanted to do was record their unique nook on camera, but I was not permitted to take photos of the remote village or the cliff-dwellers themselves, because it was the Lord's Day.

On any day at home, happy-snapping was common. I loved composing photographs and felt as hampered as if I was tangled in one of their fish nets.

It was hard to settle back into normal school and home life on return. In those times, international plane travel was less common than today, and my coloured slides and my eight-millimetre movies were in heavy demand among Aunt's staff in her hall, supper shows for Brethren, and schoolmates after class teaching had tapered off. My throat went hoarse from commentating on my pictures. For weeks, my main attraction to others was to tell of my trip away, how I had managed to explore elsewhere. Marco Polo must have felt the same on his return from the Silk Road. Settling down was hard and made me dizzy. Fortunately, coming back was near the end of the school year, as I was forced to ease back into reality. On my global search, I had separated emotionally from my old haunts completely. There was much, much more to human endeavour than Brethren ever dreamed of.

Philanthropy

Aunt was well resourced to assist Brethren other than me. She was born into a tradition where Brethren supported their own as compliantly as police in a force. It was fashionable, among well-off early Brethren, to prune their accumulated possessions, to anticipate eternal bliss as much more important than riches on earth and to share earthly wealth about. But Aunt's motivations to give and give and give had additional drivers. She had lived with genteel poverty as a child, relying on five other women in her household for support and income. When of working age, she was determined to use her chance at wealth to live as comfortable a lifestyle as she could without impinging on the expected image of Brethren abstinence. She pruned her assets for effect and deliberate influence.

From the year after I was born (1947), our family home became her hospice. She needed to help others generously with boundless gifts of money in order to feel free about enjoying her own prosperity. She paid for renovations to our old weatherboard house. Deep guilt about her theft drove her to share so that she could not be accused of selfishness? That's how it appeared.

Generous support of poorer Brethren by the richer had a very long history. Back in 1838, a few years after the first Brethren got together, the Great Masonic Hall in Plymouth, UK, hosted an auction of the valuables of wealthy Brethren for the benefit of the poor, including

> silver plate, silver-mounted plated articles; about seven hundred volumes of books, handsomely bound; paintings and prints, valuable jewellery; table linen, glass, china, wearing apparel; household furniture, etc., etc.

The local newspaper informed that

> It was quite simply and freely [given to the poor], as desiring to express [Plymouth Brethren's] then indifference to the world, their separatedness to the Lord, and their waiting for His coming from heaven.

Well-off nineteenth-century English families – both nouveau riche and old money – toyed with the Brethren way, which became fashionable, so to show off their conversion to saintliness, they gave a lot of money and chattels away. In spite of trying hard to appear abstemious, John Nelson Darby was supported permanently by family inheritance. The pretence of holy poverty coexisted side by side with discreet affluence.

Aunt's largesse was spread generously outside the family. Winnie Way talked loud and shrill. For her, life was lived as an endless fiesta of gossip, like the prattle of hairdressers. As well as chatter, Winnie was committed to running a hat shop in Box Hill, where for a long time Aunt bought her original designs. Winnie's father owned the shop. When the father remained with the Exclusive Brethren in 1962 and Winnie opted out, the father shut off his finance to spite her.

Aunt stepped into the breach quickly by purchasing the shop, and its stock, to give her, to ensure that Winnie joined our little rump of

Brethren rejects – and stayed in business. Such displays of Aunt's wealth were unexpected and swift, but became more and more spectacular. She paid for a son of Brethren, of about my age, to attend a private college in order to get through year twelve, after one failed attempt, and then more funds for his four-year university course. He was embarrassed to talk about it.

Final flings

By 1960, Aunt was buying blocks of flats as investments, one lot in Elsternwick given to Mother (sight unseen) and another to Peter, as well as a Carlton mansion. Overseas trips for all of us children were funded by Aunt. She manipulated remotely, as though we were shadow puppets. Most of the family assumed that Aunt was being paid handsomely because of her workload and responsibilities. Little did we suspect.

In 1965, she decided that it was time to move the family out of our comfortable home in Canterbury to North Balwyn, without any consultation with me. She paid for building a massive solid brick house on three empty blocks of land in Hill Road. The interior spaces were as vast and vacuous as the empty Hall of Mirrors in the Palace of Versailles. The air-conditioned house had five bedrooms, four bathrooms, five toilets, a heated swimming pool – used more by a neighbouring teenager than any family members – and a burglar alarm that did not work. The house was robbed four times in the first couple of years of residence, causing me to snigger snidely.

Around the same time, Dr Howell Hosking purchased a large house in Winmalee Road, Balwyn, with a prized garden by Edna Walling, a much-awarded landscape gardener hired by rich house owners. Dr Hosking was a senior partner in the diagnostic group. He added a new wing to his house, two garages, a swimming pool and a tennis court at the time that our move to Hill Road was planned. I wondered if Hosking inspired competition in Aunt.

What else could Aunt do to gain our seal of approval? It seemed impossible to switch off the charity cascade. Father succumbed to the temptation to enjoy her wealth, and skited to visitors about his new home in North Balwyn, but it did not improve their relationship in any way. Mother squirmed with discomfort at the ostentation of the mansion. Peter left for Europe for study and work. I had moved out of home altogether. One morning in 1974, Aunt was arrested for embezzling from her partnership of pathologists. The police claimed that the crime had begun in 1967, although we quickly realised it started much earlier. Father complained bitterly that – after Aunt served her gaol sentence – he would have to share his house with a convicted robber. It looked likely.

Trial

Our resources became more complex. The precise time when Aunt started to embezzle was never known to anyone else at all – in the family or out – even after she left gaol in 1977. Her escapades with money were her own disguised rebellion. She never talked about her time in prison or her crimes – which probably dated back to about 1950, we calculated. Her story has to be pieced together entirely from external evidence. It is painful to recount.

The essential facts of Aunt's capture and conviction were conveyed by my brother David, who worked hard with her lawyers to develop her defence, and from records in newspapers of the day. David was keen to take on the job of gathering data to assist with Aunt's defence both as the sort of drama that aroused him, and because she had funded many of his activities, including his three years in Oxford. I helped collect and file documents for her trial.

I was in shock for months and unsure whether to tell anyone outside the family, bothered more by my imminent divorce from my first wife and separation from my two precious children than by Aunt's arrest. She had given me little directly by way of cash. My brother Peter – working in Paris for a multinational drug company on a massive salary by that time – refused to answer questions about Aunt's financial dealings, and never contributed an iota of his intimate knowledge of her many property dealings. By proxy, he quickly sold off his properties.

Bettina – frozen with fear – did not speak about her gifts at all; Aunt had given her (in quick succession) a house in Doncaster, a honeymoon in Asia, a speedboat and a red Monaro car.

The immediate cause of Aunt's arrest was that the managing partner of the diagnostic group, Dr Harkness, died suddenly in 1971 of a heart attack. He was Aunt's senior boss. Dr Kurt Schwartz, the next most senior pathologist in the group, closely scrutinised the accounts and found discrepancies, but records that were available to him stretched back to 1967 only.

Early in 1974 – before her arrest – Aunt complained to me that the rearranged partnership of doctors had appointed a new business manager, without consulting her. The official reason she was given was that he would take over once she retired. After three months in the role, he began to make indirect insinuations about her honesty. I am uncertain about why she confided in me that she felt suspicious of him. Soon after, two fraud detectives interviewed her at home, then took her to the police station to make a statement. The so-called business manager turned out to be a police plant, inserted to collect evidence against her.

She had to wait until the end of 1975 for a Supreme Court appearance. Her barrister, John Winneke, a criminal law heavyweight, was her special gift from Legal Aid. He managed to reverse the guilty verdict in the trial of Lindy and Michael Chamberlain, of dingo fame. In Aunt's case, he advised that the paper trail clearly showed that she had forged Dr Harkness's signature on cheques in payment to her (after he died), and forged a letter from him, and that she had taken money from petty cash to the tune of $410,175. She told police that Dr Harkness was her accomplice.

With David's assistance, she sold off blocks of apartments, expensive Carlton houses, blocks of land, and the new mansion in Hill Road, her cash sinkhole, which had been built as our home in North Balwyn, ousting Father and Mother to a ramshackle rented house belonging to a hoarder. The proceeds of the fire sale amounted to $316,500, which she refunded to the diagnostic group, to impress the court with her contrition. In her defence also, her sharp barrister alleged that Dr Harkness had embezzled together with her, and thus it was hard for police to determine who was the bigger thief. The prosecution agreed.

Inside gaol

Early in 1976, Aunt was sentenced to goal for four years in Fairleigh Women's Prison, but with good behaviour she was released on parole after a little more than a year. A few months into her gaoling, prison authorities gave her the job of inducting new prisoners (many of whom were drug addicts) into prison customs. She enjoyed organising newcomers, and made good friends with a couple of women who continued to socialise after she was released.

Visits to prison on Sunday afternoons for one hour were restricted in numbers, so my family arranged a roster to go to see Aunt. When it was my turn, I took my two small children with me, as entertainment for Aunt; they were blissfully unaware that they were in a gaol, and they had fun playing with the security equipment at the entrance. If the family took presents of food along, they had to be shared among all prisoners. So we would buy a wooden case of oranges or apples from the market, for example, and leave them near the entrance for all inmates to enjoy.

The strained atmosphere was eerie and surreal, a whirlpool of whispers. We spoke in hushed voices, hoping to overhear the conversations of other inmates maybe, but never quite managing to do so. It was impossible to ask Aunt how she was being treated or how she had coped since my last visit, without threatening to upset the chunky warders. We all knew stories of prison abuse. As well, I did not feel like expatiating too much on the family news from the outside in case it made Aunt feel more cut off than she was. Conversation had to be very confected for the occasion. It was stilted.

'How are you getting on?' seemed a sufficiently neutral opening question in the charged atmosphere.

'Oh, well, thank you,' Aunt always replied, properly and politely.

'Are your cellmates OK?' I ventured.

'Fine, thank you.' She fixed me with a piercing glare.

'We're leaving you a box of apples from the market.'

'That's very kind of you, I'm sure.' She looked as grim as Queen Victoria.

'Is there anything else that you need?'

'Your Mother is bringing me some new stockings.' It was Mother's turn to visit next week.

Prisoners and visitors were directed to sit around the perimeter of a very large hall in small huddles, talking, while women warders circulated around the empty centre of the room like blue-clad fish in a bowl. The room was vast and the feeling was oppressive. No kissing or hugging was allowed in case outsiders used the greetings as a chance to swap concealed drugs.

Later that year, the estate of Dr Harkness was sued in the Supreme Court by the seventeen partners of the diagnostic group for $1,201,118 of funds that were embezzled by Harkness and/or Aunt. The group also alleged that their bank was negligent in not detecting fraudulent cheques to the value of $914,832. Both the Harkness family and bank settled hastily out of court, to avoid adverse publicity, and Aunt was not charged with further offences. The average cost of a house in Melbourne in 1975 was about $34,500, indicating that hypothetically Harkness and Aunt could have bought thirty-five houses with their stolen funds – even more if the swindle began two and a half decades before when residences were even cheaper. The scale of the crime was breathtaking.

My foil

Aunt's aberrant behaviour was the last blow by Brethren to my ultimate liberation; that is, during my life when I lived at home, she used her empty devotion to God as a device to cover up her crimes, and to deceive those in the family who altruistically tried (and failed) to live up to Brethren aspirations, like me. Of course I benefitted from the fact that she splashed money around – on holidays, overseas trips, book-buying, renovations at home – while we assumed that it was all the result of her hard work. All the family dipped gladly into her largesse, but I was angry afterwards. Her insatiable hunger for endorsement from grateful and innocent recipients of her stolen funds led her to deviate from norms, to transgress all moral boundaries.

Her conviction in 1976 was a fitting end to decades of hypocrisy. She was my foil. Her behaviour was a childlike response to wildly-improbable religious demands, a deliberate subversion of the atrophied theology of Exclusive Brethren, a blatant sabotage of the trust shown by her adopted family, my family, and a degradation (if a parallel degradation) of my drawn-out struggle for an independent identity, for freedom in open and sincere ways. If she was aware of her offences during the period of crime, none of it showed. Until well after the arrest, there was no hint that Aunt and I were both aligned to escape, although the inadvertent end of her search for elsewhere – prison – did not resemble my own relatively innocent trajectory out of Brethren. She attended the Church of Christ in Hurstbridge after her release from goal, in a different congregation from my parents' church of the same brand.

She used her money to seduce Father into accepting her calculated insertion into the family's prosperity. He used her beneficence to bolster his ego. The palace in Hill Road, North Balwyn – funded by Aunt – was sterile and phoney to me. The beach house at Ocean Grove was registered cautiously in Mother's name at the very beginning, suggesting a collusion that was never spoken of.

What astonished me more than anything is that Aunt managed to maintain a semblance of Brethren holiness for at least twenty-five years without being found out. The holiness was a cover which fooled everybody. Her shallow piety hoodwinked most. I never trusted her because of her incorrigible scheming at home, but during the years of crime, I had no grasp on her ability to plumb the depths of deception of everyone around her. Instinctively, I was trusting, an open and honest person, perhaps to a fault, which made Aunt's eccentric cover, immorality and lack of remorse all the more startling once revealed.

Moral consequences

To add to my panic, the lawyer prosecuting Aunt, Bruce Sundberg, I had befriended at law school, where we sat next to each other in most lectures, comparing notes and sharing ideas. He and I learnt a lot together. We both scored very high marks in Criminal Law. Fortunately, there was a considerable gap between me abandoning law studies in 1969 and Aunt's arrest in 1974, and in the meantime I had no further contact with Bruce, a decent and clever man. He became a managing partner of a large Melbourne law firm. I assumed that he never realised Aunt was related to me but I still feared that he might make the connection.

Ironically, back in 1969, I had rejected Aunt's overtures to pay for my extended stay in Ormond College, to finish my law degree. I had left Brethren and home by then. Did Aunt think about how I would have managed my loyalties (or my career) at the time of her arrest, if I had become a fully qualified lawyer? Probably not: robbers often lose a grip on reality and are completely carried away by their inevitable successes. Aunt was close to retirement but – like a gambler – she had no exit plan for escape from her devious entanglements.

Aunt's debacle had a weird final twist. She moved to the country, and needed a car, which she bought from a city dealer. David and his generous wife, Turid, took the ex-prisoner under their wing, extracting her from the intolerable bitterness of living with my angry Father (and my bewildered Mother) after prison, and helping her build a cottage of her own on their remote rural property at Strathewen. It was idyllic. She was relieved to spend the last ten years —the happiest of her life, she said – in a peaceful environment and in a fresh, accepting, rural community which knew nothing of her past. Along with a new Toyota car.

Because Toyota was about to sell its millionth vehicle in Australia, Aunt was automatically entered without her knowledge into a lottery to celebrate. Entirely by chance, she won first prize, and received the yellow car free. She drove the automatic car over the gravel roads like a maniac, always pursued by a cloud of dust. Her habit of using her right foot on the accelerator pedal and left foot on the brake pedal simultaneously did not lend itself to a smooth drive.

A self-righteous observer, anonymous to the world at large, noted her win in Toyota advertisements, and, also knowing of her crimes, rang the radio shock jock Derryn Hinch, to inform on Aunt. Hinch was known as the 'Human Headline' for his notoriety, going to prison himself three times for contempt of court. In personality, he was a free radical, a law unto himself. Derryn Hinch rang Aunt unannounced in her country retreat to alarm and harass her live on radio about her lottery win, which he thought she did not deserve because of her old embezzlement convictions.

'Is that Elizabeth Airey?' Hinch asked on the phone, trying to surprise her.

'Yes it is.'

'Did you once work for the Melbourne Diagnostic Group?'

'Yes.'

'Have you recently won a Toyota car?'

'Yes.'

'Do you think it is just and fair that you are given a car when you have just been in prison for embezzlement?'

A long silence followed. The imprisonment and winning were logically unconnected, but Hinch wanted to stir up anger and indignation among his radio audience. Aunt was befuddled and muttered before hanging up on Hinch on the phone. She was lucky no social media existed at that time. We advised her never to speak to Hinch again, although he tried to ring her more. Dirt makes for cheap journalism.

Two years after Hinch's bold attempt to vilify Aunt, the two senior partners in the diagnostic group were named in the Victorian parliament as swindlers. Our family always suspected that Aunt had more accomplices than she ever mentioned, but we never had evidence. As the shadow Labor spokesman for health, Tom Roper accused Doctors Schwarz and Hosking – senior partners – of charging patients fees for medical services that they never received and for overcharging them for the services that they did. The group was more than doubling patients' bills.

Tom Roper was my local member, with boyish ruddy cheeks. I knew him briefly from university and municipal politics, which never attracted me for long. In the Victorian Legislative Assembly, Roper declared,

> It is tantamount to a fraud… Groups like pathologists…are robbing the community and giving good doctors an extremely bad name… Any person who robs a bank will receive a substantial sentence… These people are getting far more in the way of rewards but they are never threatened with imprisonment.

The skeleton in my cupboard

At least Aunt did her time. All her working life, she was driven to devote herself to keeping her nose to the administrative grindstone, doting on her doctors at all times and dedicating her considerable energies to running two businesses – a parallel business parasitically on their thriving legitimate business. She showed no remorse about purloining huge quantities of the doctors' money even when her secret enterprise ended in imprisonment.

Aunt's main influences on my life were to teach me how to confront her self-seeking power and to refuse to be corrupted by her access to immense wealth. At times, I was crude in my reactions. She adopted Brethren as a convenient sheen and focused on buying their favour and respect when she needed recognition. She craved love more than anything, and felt cross that I treated her as outsider from the family unit, but I did support her post-prison welfare when she was lost and became a vulnerable husk of her former cunning self.

It always surprised me that Aunt never seemed to have any suitor, nor vice versa, but instead she harnessed her hunger for wealth into a personal mission, using it as a means to overcome loneliness. Understanding her influences on me, mainly in the form of gifts, connected directly with the effects of Brethren on my continuing march away from them – especially during 1962. Travelling overseas with her opened my eyes to fresh cultures and many alternative ways of life.

Her contribution in my family life revolved around medical treatment, based on her informal access to doctors and Bethesda Hospital. She funded the family holiday house, which served as a wonderful refuge for years. Generously, as we children entered the education system, she expected us to open accounts with booksellers and paid the bills. The broad benefit of this investment will become more obvious.

Brethren supported needy Brethren always, and Aunt splashed her money around on worthy causes, as did other well-off Brethren, but by growing too ostentatious, finally drawing unwanted attention to the massive scale of her supposed income, she was imprisoned for embezzling amounts that would equal many millions of dollars today. Her moral failure caused immense stress to others, not least to those who had accepted her largesse in good faith. She died in 2001 after a drawn-out convalescence caused by stroke.

Brethren cannot be blamed for causing her crimes. At least she was not in the class of the Acid Bath Murderer in the UK, who did blame a Brethren upbringing for his recurring religious nightmares in childhood, including ghosts. As a child, he was forced to live behind a two-metre fence and was not permitted to play with other boys. He pleaded,

> I had none of the joys, or the companionship which small children usually have. From my earliest days my recollection is of my father saying: 'Do not', or 'Thou shalt not'. Any form of sport or light entertainment was frowned upon, and regarded as not edifying. There was only, and always, condemnation and prohibition.

As an adult, he left a trail of convictions – not just for embezzlement, but also for theft, impersonating a lawyer, gambling, fraud and the murder of six people. He destroyed the bodies of victims by dissolving them in barrels of sulphuric acid. His plea for incapacity because of insanity was rejected at his murder trial, the court believing that his crimes were premeditated, and he was executed in 1949 at the age of forty. In comparison, Aunt's ending was benign.

Seven

Eccentricity

Reputations

In spring of 1990 in a London park, 'two young dudes in baseball caps, Hawaiian shirts and Bermuda shorts...and with deadpan senses of humour' sang along with two acoustic guitars and a trumpet. The buskers called themselves the Plymouth Brethren. An enthusiastic crowd of people gathered around to listen.

The stall selling deep-fried cashews and peanuts coated in spices smelt tempting.

'Are they really Plymouth Brethren?' a middle-aged man on the fringe of the crowd asked loudly.

'I think so,' replied his girlfriend hesitantly. 'They've changed a bit, haven't they?'

'It's hard to recognise them.'

'Their clothes don't look right and how about the songs?' she queried as they moved on.

The encounter was reported by a journalist in *Cross Rhythms*. The two students had no connection at all to real Plymouth Brethren, but cleverly co-opted the brand in order to attract attention to their original lyrics and blues/acoustic music. The stunt succeeded in commandeering a widely known image of eccentricity to help to launch their careers in public performance.

The role of eccentricity in bolstering identity and how that eccentricity can highlight and legitimise abnormal behaviours, are themes of this chapter. I also outline how eccentricity affected my release from the grip of Brethren. In some ways, eccentricity was a fulcrum for me. This chapter reviews five ways that eccentricity influenced my first twenty-one years: it encouraged me to adopt a holier-than-thou attitude in the face of external threats to my faith; it amused me to notice it as entertainment in others; it reassured me inside the Brethren tent that I was not alone in my cultic religiosity; it embarrassed me when I mixed with non-Brethren, exposing my oddity; and it frightened me when taken to extremes, to the edge of sanity.

Selected features of the Brethren show how collective eccentricity served their objectives – primarily to reinforce boundaries while at the same time pushing them. The novelty of their non-conformity attracted much attention and helped increase congregations initially in the mid-nineteenth century. They were entirely unapologetic about their assumed status as predestined saints, and lacked interest in the views of other Christians, except to reject them wholeheartedly. They showed interest in others only in order to persuade them to the Brethren – the correct – opinions. In the 1960s, Brethren harboured secrets about their unique community, limiting public exposure, in order to impress on each other their select status.

I sometimes wondered if the Brethren preoccupation with eccentricity was due to the complete absence of opportunities to observe other normative forms of performance – no sport, no theatre, no circus, no comedy, no music, no shows, no radio, no TV. Intense scrutiny of a proximate Brother or Sister substituted for observing conventional performativity. I scanned my memory for clues and decide that as a teenager I was more alert to and more observant of eccentric behaviour in daily life than Brethren of other ages.

This type of obscure discourse was served up commonly to entertain all Brethren:

'The saints are sanctified and holy of the Spirit unto obedience and the sprinkling of the blood of Jesus Christ,' contributed one Brother with a deep frown.

'We are set aside and consecrated to God's service,' a self-congratulatory elder added.

'The inner soul has new and everlasting life imparted which it never possessed before,' suggested an innovator.

'Practical holiness becomes an immediate and heartfelt responsibility of every day.' The final contributor added a burden.

They all nodded sagely at each other in silence, overtaxed by their carefully crafted efforts. No effort whatsoever was made to appeal to kids.

Little is known of the Brethren founder, John Nelson Darby, as a child. He was born into a family of eccentrics, one of nine children, to a distant mother who may have died in a mental asylum, to whom he professed perpetual devotion, and to a strict father focused on his London business. Home life was cold and uncomfortable. His family expected him to leave home when young and shine at law.

Darby loved to write in order to share his inimitable thoughts. He was described by one of his biographers as an eccentric friend, an ascetic mystic who, after a leg injury at twenty-seven caused by a shying horse, was physically weak. He looked bedraggled, with bloodshot eyes and a fallen cheek, badly shaven, shabby clothes, showing a careless exterior, and he might eat one boiled egg only as his main meal of the day. It was reported that his dogmatism and impetuosity were an embarrassment to his few friends, while his brother called him potted arrogance. His writing style was pedantic, flowery and deliberately obtuse, and his sentences ran to hundreds of words each. He was a supreme polemicist, always on the lookout for a ding-dong argument.

Darby did not need to work when he left the Church of England in Ireland. His family made a business out of victualling the British navy, and although his father was disgusted by John's faith and disinherited him, his unmarried uncle, Admiral Sir Henry Darby, came to his rescue with an inheritance. The eccentric aristocracy of Britain looked after their own first and foremost.

Darby involved himself in a very tentative liaison with Lady Theodosia Anne Powerscourt, a cultured, well-educated aristocrat. He told her that he might marry her after she hosted Brethren faith conferences in 1831, 1832 and 1833 at her stately mansion in County Wicklow. She left the Church of Ireland, imitating Darby, and gave away her belongings in order to join Brethren, only to be jilted by her lover soon afterwards. Later, he wrote poignantly, 'I turned down a marriage and broke a heart in doing so.'

It was a scandalous tragedy, presaging his lifelong celibacy. Both the former husband of Lady Powerscourt and her only child had died recently. When she died three years later at the age of thirty-six, some said that the abandonment by Darby killed her.

In my time, to outsiders Plymouth Brethren were an esoteric minority, speaking gobbledegook, hardly worth noticing in passing amongst millions of Christians, but on the other hand, to Brethren the World outside was wild and weird, and the forty thousand of us worldwide were taught to remain on high alert. By living with Brethren for my formative years, I observed and absorbed some of their strange ways and came to appreciate some amusing tendencies of eccentric thinking and behaviours and (importantly) to deprecate some others that were nothing short of antisocial or downright dangerous.

Witnessing eccentricity set up a boundary in my own mind, an invisible demarcation that was impossible not to find bothersome. I worked hard to avoid sticking out like a sore thumb, feeling very self-conscious about being part of a zany religious cult because membership bestowed unavoidable stigma. Within the cult, the pressure for conformity was enormous, on setting a good example both to insiders and outsiders. In a strangely contradictory way, conformity worked in unison with eccentricity; I was expected to flaunt my righteousness come what may. Outside, I only ever did it in the company of other Brothers, never alone. The upshot was that, in whichever direction I turned, I could not avoid the pressure of the boundary between conforming and being unconventional.

School idiosyncrasies

A contemporary from school who had no idea of my Brethren alliance spoke to me as an adult recently, because he observed me at school as very shy in the playground, trying to avoid repartee, being ignorant of popular sport and culture. Was I eccentric? I felt intense isolation at primary school at times. My only exposure to pop singers like Elvis Presley occurred at the recess times when I overheard other children singing the latest hits and I picked up some words by heart. We had no radio at home. I must have looked odd as I walked home from school bellowing out whatever segments I could remember of 'Rock Around the Clock' or 'That'll Be the Day' or 'Purple People Eater' at the top of my lungs, before reaching my high side gate. Rebellious and rough the singing was, but still invigorating.

I was not alone in my enforced remoteness from boyish passions. In 1974, the Rowen family with twelve children, who lived in a poor suburb of Dublin, belonged to Plymouth Brethren. One of the Rowen boys, Peter, was friends with the musician, Bono, leader of the rock band U2, and recalled struggling on the margins of teenage norms:

> Myself and Bono, we weren't like the other kids in the street and we knew we weren't. I was seen as an oddball, a freak. We didn't know what to say when they would want us to name our favourite football players because we didn't know any names.

Although Peter belonged to Brethren, he was photographed and persuaded to appear on three U2 album covers as a boy, and paid in Mars bars to do it. Chocolate and caramel outranked holy devotion.

At a reunion of my high school peers in 2014, I met a bunch of what we used to call 'ockers', that is, macho boys devoted to sporting muscles, six-packs and chicks. They assured me that at high school at the age of eighteen I was regarded as moralistic and staid, a real brain with strict self-discipline. Another friend remembers me 'as very studious and scholarly, highly organised, quietish, serious, non-demonstrative and exuding a sense of all-knowingness'.

Because it was not cultivated deliberately, I was surprised by the reports of my imperious image. I had little self-awareness. Appearing all-knowing was due to not knowing much about the fun of interacting. I only knew what not to do.

Images of Brethren respectability and self-righteousness stretched back a long way. The media included a fascinating account back in 1836, an early mention of Brethren in Australia. Captain Morgan of the migrant ship *Duke of York* sailed to South Australia, and because he was a Plymouth Brother, according to the *Adelaide Chronicle,* the twenty migrant passengers

> never heard a single bad word used on the whole voyage, and there were prayers each night. There was no drunkenness aboard, although the sailors, as customary in these days, had their regular allowance of grog every evening.

Did the generous supply of rum keep the peace, or was God in control?

Respectability troubled me at school; it troubled my teachers too. Being good, breaking rules and suffering guilt were part and parcel of my unusual daily behaviour. Paradoxically, for me punishment in class was more rewarding than the tedium and loneliness that I experienced a lot. I had perverse power over punishment; it gave me a degree of emotional control by asserting myself. I could make it lie at the heart of any activity of my choice, whether as part of a mundane act of stupidity or planned hubbub resulting from showing off to a group. As a result, I continually got the cuts at primary school.

And yet my grade five teacher seemed to put his finger on the nub of my dilemmas. At 11.05 on Tuesday 9 December 1957, Mr R.G. Matthews caught me playing ball outdoors after the school bell had finished ringing. The bell called for a return to class, so I should have been settled back at my desk five minutes earlier. The offence was minor and Matthews chose writing an essay as my experimental punishment, with the title prescribed as 'Doing Things at the Right Time'. As well as using this heading, I added the date and time. I kept my nose down near my nibbed pen, making a serious effort in Italic script; I was a little afraid of him and wanted to impress.

I had topped my grade four the year before; he knew I could write. By some means, Matthews must have become aware that strappings were ineffective for modifying my erratic behaviour in the previous year. He had respect for my honesty and integrity, and (in retrospect) his mission must have been a clever ruse to force me to reflect solemnly on my misbehaviour. My spelling was perfect in the essay that I still have. The thin paper is brittle and smells stale. Inevitably, my words were bound up in religion, as I began in a Biblical tone,

> There is a time to play ball…and a time not to play ball. It is a natural instinct that children should play, because if they didn't their muscles would gradually fade away… All children and even adults have done wrong because it says in the bible, 'all have sinned and come short of the glory of God'… Children should do as they are told, but when you are not told I suppose that you can do anything you like. You should not be inquisitive, you should try and be a help (not a hindrance), you should not laugh at old people, you should be cheerful and happy…

I cannot be sure that writing the essay changed my attitudes but at least it forced me to seriously explore them. It is clear that moral self-talk was never far from my mind and I could easily quote slabs of the Bible. The Bible functioned as a permanent carapace of burdensome conscience.

Matthews was pleased with my thoughts and thanked me for setting them out. I expected some argy-bargy from him but there were only polite thanks. His mild manners deeply impressed me, promoting in my mind the value of calm and reasoned understanding of authority. Spending excessive time in the pressure cooker of a Brethren home and community, then being released into the open school community daily, was bound to unsettle my emotional equilibrium. The contrast showed up in my behaviour when I let off steam and showed uncertainty about what was acceptable in my Worldly roles.

As for displaying a strong moral standard – a Brethren feature – in another incident to my shame I betrayed Miss Pettit's trust in me at high school in 1959. It was my very worst example of bad behaviour at school. Maverick Mavis Pettit was fatter and bigger than three of us at the age of thirteen, stacked together. Her lipsticked smile betrayed her over-didactic manner.

She tried her hardest to teach us French but left herself open to ridicule. She wore a tattered old black academic gown, covered in chalk dust, over a bright red flannel dress. Her bulky waddle cut a swath through any crowded corridor. She could shriek louder than a wounded cockatoo, and for longer, as she raised her eyes to the ceiling in despair, gathered in a very long breath, then spat chips at my entire junior class.

On a hot summer afternoon in a stifling portable classroom, side-on to the hot north winds, we watched her saliva launch into her aura. Lucid sermons on decorum and polite behaviour could occupy the entire forty minutes of class time as she blinded herself with the topic of etiquette, while we egged her on (very easily) with the desirable prospect of avoiding French altogether. In some lessons, the topic of manners became the entire content.

With hindsight, I wonder if she anticipated that moral degeneration was in the offing in the 1960s as a range of social movements got under way? Perhaps she wanted to pre-empt their effects. She volunteered to teach religious instruction when outside volunteers were in short supply.

In Australia, a large proportion of the rapidly growing population was young – the term teenager emerged for the first time – and generational differences became a common topic of casual conversation. Political opposition to the Vietnam War was beginning, rebellious music and fashions spread, the mass media unearthed rampant permissiveness and anti-authoritarianism in every nook. Women's liberation and environmental concerns were peeping out from every cranny. Greater participation in tertiary study got under way.

Miss Pettit's antennae sensed moral decline in every direction.

'I cannot accept rudeness in any form. It's just wrong and destructive.'

'In my day, there was respect – respect for elders, respect for parents, respect for others. What has happened to it?'

'I dread to think to what depths you lot might sink to before you wake up to your futures.'

'I came here this afternoon hoping to talk to you a little about French food, to tell you about the rum baba. I am sad to think about how unproductive we've been.'

On and on and on it went.

Once when her back was turned to the blackboard, sitting at the rear of the room, in protest I made a deafening bang on the floor just to create a disturbance. Miss Pettit swung around, demanding to know the cause. I refused to own up. We waited. And waited. I still did not own up. The bell rang for the lesson to end. We waited. Then a pimp in the front row suggested that I might be the culprit.

'Oh, no,' said Mavis, 'it could not be Graeme. He would not cause a disturbance like that. He comes from a good family of faith. I have taught his brother.' She fixed her stare on me, as if to say, 'Not you, surely?'

I shrank onto the sticky desk lid in scathing self-reproach. I never did bring myself to disillusion her about my faultless reputation, but I behaved thereafter with better discipline always. It was one thing to act the eccentric class clown, but I did not want the responsibility for undermining the essence of the family reputation and Brethren mores in one simple act.

Media stereotypes

The high status of Brethren's moral standards was repeated over and over in media treatments. The contrast between do-gooder and tyrant has already been noted. In fact, two conflicting attitudes to Brethren eccentricity can be found in print media.

In media generally (on the one hand), Brethren are depicted as consistently helpful, trustworthy, honest and completely reliable. My friend Don describes theirs as a reputation of always doing a good job. On the other hand, in printed news items Brethren concealed a dark underbelly that drove them to extremes, associated with tricksters, madmen and even murderers.

Thus as an example of the first trend, in 1924 a Sydney newspaper reported on the death of an altruistic Brother sympathetically:

> The philanthropic Edwin Cocks, of Sydney…was a unique character and was known as the good Samaritan. He belonged to the sect of Plymouth Brethren, and for nearly half a century preached his gospel every Sunday afternoon under the trees of the outer Domain… He was fearless in his denunciation of evil and at times was assaulted by the crowd for his outspokenness.

In a different guise in a court in Brisbane in 1950, Edwin Elliott, aged thirty-five, took advantage of the upstanding image of Brethren. He was convicted of swindling people of £106. He posed as a Plymouth Brother and as a clergyman of other religions. He was described as a cunning, plausible criminal who found the religion of his intended victim, and then posed as a minister of that religion to borrow money which he never repaid. As well as Brethren, he pretended to belong to Presbyterians and the Salvation Army. How he succeeded with using Brethren as a ploy is hard to comprehend because they had no ministers. His victims knew a little about the honesty of Brethren, perhaps, but not enough to help them to avoid him. Elliott was fined heavily and gaoled.

Borderline entertainment

Fashions in ideas wax and wane – some insidious, some forceful, some eccentric, some barely noticeable. In the 1840s, some Brethren in Plymouth decided that if they were to follow the Bible closely they should wash each other's feet; Jesus showed by example how to wash disciples' feet (John 13:1–16) and explained why it should be done. The early Brethren tried it, but soon decided that it was a bit unhygienic and ceased the smelly practice altogether. Later on, John Nelson Darby came to the rescue by casuistically relegating foot-washing to symbolic cleansing, pronouncing that 'Jesus certainly intended it as a proof and example of humility and condescension', but it was just figurative. It was obvious that eccentric beliefs of a low order were entirely disposable, easily shrugged off, even if explicit in the Bible. In the 1930s in Melbourne, Eustace Kelsey posited such an opinion about the sky. His black fedora hat and matching sooty moustache added gravitas. He refused to fly in aeroplanes because the heavens were God's domain alone, he told my Mother, but thirty years later he willingly flitted around the globe by air. God's airy domain must have been symbolic only; it shrank back towards the stratosphere as plane travel became more and more common.

Activities as well as attitudes were shared by eccentric entertainers with my family. Mother and David were skilled at cultivating friendships with eccentrics. The friends fascinated me and helped me to become cautiously aware of the limits of out-of-the-ordinary behaviour. It was not enough for Mother that as a cult we were already odd ourselves in the eyes of outsiders in every way. Eccentric behaviour was tolerated – if not encouraged – by my family. Welcoming eccentrics into the fold kept us right on the edge of normality.

In 1951, I enjoyed Mr Blount stumping noisily down our wooden passage on his wooden leg. Short and stout, he arrived by train from Kyneton, where Mother knew his Brethren family. I was awestruck by the wooden leg and two brown suitcases – a large one for his collection of tricks and a small one for his pyjamas. He gave a comprehensive performance of basic magic at our dining room table with flashing silk scarves, disappearing cards, collapsible sticks and hollow balls. Fortunately, no one raised any questions about the morality of his magic. Officially, magic fell within the realms of miracles and luck, all of them irrelevant to us because of Providence – God's well thought-out road map for us, as the predestined few. Chance and probability played no part in our single-minded pilgrimage to heaven.

Mother told me that Mr Blount learnt magic – and lost his leg below the knee – when young before he joined Brethren. The magic performance was followed by the removal of the wooden leg before he got into bed that night. Both were brilliant. I was permitted to watch him in wonder in the guest bedroom as he unstrapped the prosthesis from his thigh and swung his stump under the blankets. I got a close-up peek at his pale scar below the knee. He suffered from an injury from World War I service, after which he saw the light and converted to Plymouth Brethren (supposedly pacifists). Brethren numbers were enlarged by several veteran converts like him.

My Aunt made a few Brethren friends, usually single women of her age. One year younger – at thirty-eight – was Annie Vernon, who lived on a vineyard in Nyah West. To a degree, her eccentricity related to her times and environment. During the parched summer of 1952, I travelled in Aunt's tiny convertible car to visit Annie, the gaps in the rough canvas roof and window flaps allowing for plenty of rushing air.

Tall and gangly, suntanned and skinny like a giraffe, Annie greeted us in dusty working boots and a thin cotton dress. "Ow yer goin'?" she wanted to know. Her nasal language was as dry as the dust.

'We're glad that we've arrived,' said Aunt diplomatically.

'Well, yer certainly brought a spot of hot with yer,' Annie replied, waving away flies. 'Wanna see some grapes? Yer can see it's nearly time. We'll be pickin' all of 'em 'fore long.' She gestured in the general direction of the vineyard across the hill that she worked with her shuffling widowed father, specialising in table grapes.

The ground was red sand, heavily irrigated from the nearby Murray River. I had never seen such well-formed willy-willies of dust before.

I met no other Brethren in Nyah West. Soon after my arrival, measles showed up. Annie put me to bed in a darkened bedroom in the stifling weatherboard farmhouse. She made me drink red wine, poured and re-poured from a green bottle on the dresser which was supposed to help with reducing my high temperature and fever. It was the first time that I tasted alcohol and I felt so merry that I could have danced to the ice cream shop in the main street and back. I convalesced for five days in a euphoric mood, fantasising. Never had Brethren felt so welcoming.

Homeward bound, we transported a precious cargo of green grapes picked and placed in two large metal crates (covered with holes), that rattled all the way home. Gradually it dawned on me that Annie did not just pick them for tables.

Odd choices

Mother cultivated eccentricity. Did it open a window onto another world for her – beyond Brethren? Maybe she harboured eccentric feelings in herself and had intuitive empathy. Of what benefit to her were her eccentric connections? Where did she draw the line between acceptable and way-out behaviour? I cannot fully answer these questions.

Some clues assist. As the eldest son, David engaged in precocious behaviour when he was still a child. At the age of seven, he wrote a letter to the manager of Bethesda Hospital in Richmond, Major W.B. Parkinson, whom he had met at Aunt's workplace there. The hospital was owned by the Salvation Army. As well as family news, David informed the major that he hoped that his two-year-old brother (Peter) would soon become a Christian, as we thought of that text 'Ask and it shall be given to you.'

Dutifully the major replied 'I like your text very much and, like yourself, believe that God answers prayer when we ask sincerely.'

My admiring Mother often regaled us children and captive guests with David's early spiritual prowess, as she proudly shared the letters around as evidence. It made me cringe.

Ten years later, David felt the urge to protest at Saint Patrick's Cathedral in East Melbourne. It was hard to determine why. Was the target of his idealism political or religious? I never understood David's need to confide in me (aged about ten) that he had committed sacrilege; I was uncertain how to react. He and an Anglican school friend called Peter plotted to annoy Catholics, no doubt feeling conspiratorial, but it was a naïve act that seems insipid now. Mother was always eager to defend David's strange behaviours as just unusual, even when they hurt others.

At that time, all secondary school students wrote with fountain pens, filled with deep blue Quink ink. Use of ballpoint pens at school was prohibited on the grounds that they enabled writing that was too quick and undisciplined. Neatness was an educational obsession. Making a long detour on their way home from Melbourne High School, David and friend Peter took it in turns to empty their fountain pens of ink into the holy water font in the Cathedral lobby, while the other kept a lookout. They turned the font azure.

Brethren regarded Roman Catholics as very remote on the spectrum of redeemability. I worked out that David's motivation was political ultimately and indicative of the sectarianism of the day. The Australian Labor Party was dividing, between left-wing secularists and non-Catholics who were pro-trade union, and right-wing Catholics (the Democratic Labour Party) who strongly opposed perceived Communist influence on Australian trade unions. A secret Catholic society called the Movement set up to try to control the Labor vote nationally.

The conservative federal government aligned with the Democratic Labour Party, sometimes relying on its preferences in votes at elections, and wanted to ban the Communist Party altogether. The Labor Party split into two over the ideological differences and became electorally weak. The spilt ink relieved some of David's anger about Labor and his annoyance with the Catholic Movement. He assured me that he was proud of his daring stance, but my opinion (at the time) was that his impact on the real target was as wishy-washy as the resulting pastel colour of the font water. I never revealed the secret of his font behaviour to others in the family; his impulsiveness and obscure motives confused me.

Seb and Addie

The most absorbing yet frightening eccentrics whom I met, befriended my mother. They were a couple called Seb and Addie Bean (that is, Sebastian and Adeline). The comedian Mr Bean was more amusing but much less absorbing. Mother found the Beans at the Church of Christ, so strictly speaking they were not connected to Brethren. But they make my point strongly about the oddity of some Christian boundaries.

Mother wrote about them in 1993, hardly able to decide whether to express acceptance or ridicule. Her pen portrait of them seems super-critical:

> [Addie] is always making sniffly, snuffly, snorting noises... Her mouth is toothless except for six teeth... Her cheeks are sunken and tanned... She works tirelessly for the Epileptic Society... [Seb] wears very thick black spectacles. His nose is out of shape owing to frequent falls when he has an epileptic fit... A black crash helmet sits on his head to save his skull, and he carries a small black suitcase for his tablets. He mooches along in a long shabby black overcoat behind Addie... They are my friends. She is an accomplished pianist and he is a talented violinist.

The last sentence gives a clue to the enduring affection of the friendship. The musical skills added an air of solid sophistication. I never heard the couple play music but was assured more than once that Seb's brother was a leading surgeon. Superior, that is.

Over decades, Seb and Addie supported causes. When the one-cent and two-cent coins were abandoned from Australia's decimal currency (in 1992), Seb and Addie went on a hunt to collect all the copper coins that they could find. A photograph in the Doncaster newspaper showed them standing admiringly next to their bath full of copper coins which they had sorted over several weeks for the Salvation Army. How did they bathe, I wondered. The coins' value totalled $5,800. If all them were of the two-cent variety, then they collected 290,000 of them, and twice that if they were all one cents.

Mother told me that the Beans tried to hand out Christian tracts as they pounded the pavements, but kids ran away from Seb and Addie in fear and home-dwellers refused to open front doors to them. Seb and Addie could not drive, nor afford public transport fares. Whenever I met them briefly at Mother's home, they were getting stuck into a lavish afternoon tea of cakes and biscuits, which probably made them even more appealing to Mother. Enjoy her biscuits and you were a friend for life. She gave them money for bus fares. To me, they seemed to grow more and more reticent and evasive each time that I saw them.

Self-abnegation and an ascetic lifestyle were features of many Brethren devotees in my time. In the nineteenth century, excess wealth was even more sinful. Thus the son of a merchant family, Robert Chapman, abandoned his wealth and chose to live simply in Barnstaple in Devon in the 1830s, at the height of the early ostentatious wave of Brethren self-sacrifice. He chose to rise at three in the morning for a cold bath. Then he walked for nineteen kilometres over the hills for breakfast. Returning home, he spent the next seven hours in prayer, Bible study, and writing some of his 165 hymns. All day on Saturday, he fasted and meditated. His credo was

> You see, God has given us a valuable body, and He expects us, as good workmen, to keep it in good order. I open the pores of my body at night with a hot bath, and close them with a cold bath in the morning.

Chapman and his busy pores died at the age of ninety-nine. He prayed daily for Queen Victoria who was born after him and who predeceased him by one year in 1901.

When Addie Bean died in 1996, Seb showed how differently the Bible could be interpreted. He went right off the rails and abused his body. He pulled one of his eyes out of its socket on the basis of this section of Bible: 'If thine eye offend thee, pluck it out: it is better for thee to enter into the kingdom of God [heaven] with one eye, than having two eyes to be cast into hell fire' (Mark 9:47). Seb told Mother that the reason for his self-mutilation was that he looked at an immoral image he believed he should not have looked at, so he punished himself according to the biblical command. In its early phase, Seb's behaviour was charming because of its originality, but his later self-abuse went far beyond the limits of my idea of acceptable eccentricity.

Pushing boundaries

When I was called on to confront the World head on, it was affirming to have the Brethren community behind me. Sticking my neck out in an eccentric way did not feel so hard if others backed me up.

Our preaching method seems crude now, but in the past, Brothers bore testimony to their faith by shouting at sinners. With prearranged police permission, on one bleak Sunday at dusk, a rabble-rousing Plymouth Brother proclaimed in Canterbury Road, via our loudhailer, that sin was sterile and God was full of love. It was never clear to me about why we had to shout about it to passers-by. Surely there must be more effective means.

The police licensed us to occupy part of a footpath each week next to the Canterbury Gardens, probably because few pedestrians passed by that point at night. The pong of car exhausts was strong.

'Do not be afraid. God loves everyone who puts their trust in Him. Why not come in from the cold?' blared the loudhailer.

As usual, complete with my pork-pie felt hat, I dutifully joined three loyal supporters on the sidelines, shifting self-consciously from one leg to the other.

'I feel a bit shivery tonight,' I said.

'You need a thicker overcoat,' said another.

'A scarf would do the trick.'

'How about a hug from your mama?' joked a third.

The hailer's noise was drowned out by a cacophony of honking car horns. We started a war of noise.

A few dog-walkers prudently crossed the road to avoid us – just the opposite effect of what we hoped for. Our unfulfilled aim was to engage in conversation about the warm embrace of our loving God. The chasm between fantasy and reality could not have been greater.

Standing in the same place weekly was an invitation to troublemakers. A modern Guy Fawkes – in the form of a young pedestrian – was on the prowl. Unexpectedly from a distance, he threw a lighted firework – a sparkling tuppenny bunger. I watched it sail starlike through the sky to land right beside the loud hailer, threatening to explode in a ball of fire and a stink of burning sulphur.

Next to me, amidst the threesome of recoiling Brothers, was an ex-soccer player, our athletic saviour called Johnny Johnson. (He had abandoned his sport to conform to Brethren tenets). He earned full redemption in my eyes by quickly kicking the sizzling bunger deftly right back to where it originated, and the offender, waiting on the other side of the road, had to flee as it exploded. Our rewards were meagre, but they were assured. God protected us on that frosty night in the person of Johnny, to be sure, and we felt obliged to point the finger at the non-believing disruptors of divine promise, who undoubtedly would suffer from eternal fireworks in hell.

An ex-Brethren member (from Devon again) described the perverse attitude towards interactions with non-Brethren in the 1940s – just as I remember them in my time:

> No sinner ever did come in [to join Brethren]…and I wonder how the Saints would have reacted if one had. Plymouth Brethren were essentially born not made. They proselytised all their lives, distributing tracts and buttonholing strangers, but unsuccessfully. Perhaps they really preferred it so.

For me window-dressing was sufficient demonstrative piety. Arm's length felt comfortable. I did not have the necessary commitment to stretch my ardour further.

Eccentrics at school were not uncommon among students and teachers; I do not aim to leave the impression that Brethren were alone with their quirks. Mathew Perceval fascinated me in 1960. He was in my French class, regularly scorned by Mavis Pettit. Tall, thin and bedraggled, he defied all authority continually and behaved exactly as he chose, asserting his independence with flair. The son of the accomplished artist, John Perceval, Mathew was soon to establish his own reputation as a painter and ceramicist. To gain attention to make a living, artists need self-promotion to live boldly.

At school, his determination to defy or destroy educational structures of every sort – classes, curriculum, yard games, detentions – astonished me. He stole from shops, he despised school uniform, he provoked, he destroyed playful outdoor games, he attended classes only when he liked, and he answered to no one. I never met anyone so footloose, so devoid of basic politeness, principles or constraints. His recklessness took my breath away.

'Why bother?' he asked me after playing truant for half a day.

'I suppose I'm expected to turn up,' I stammered.

'What good will that do you? I don't care if I get thrown out of this school.'

'Where will you go?'

'Dunno. Probably to Preshil, if I have to. At least it's friendly.'

Preshil was an alternative school not far away in Kew where rules of behaviour were limited and children controlled their own curriculum and learning, assisted by teachers; Mathew's father had attended there when young.

Up to a point, I envied him secretly. In the world of theology, Brethren were as iconoclastic as Mathew (without ever admitting it). I wondered if Brethren could cope with his sort of personality. The only artist that I knew was an old-fashioned Plymouth Brother, a bank manager who painted for relaxation in pastel watercolours on the Mornington Peninsula. His simple seascapes – decorating two walls in our home – were formulaic and prudent.

Mathew left the impression that he needed no conventions or friends. His world was completely foreign to me – he made me feel that I was boringly over-dependent on my spiritual community and social orthodoxies. He was expelled from school at the end of the year and he moved with his artistic parents to the south of France. Maybe he reflected then that Mavis Pettit was of some value for him. The director of the National Portrait Gallery in Canberra described his 1960s art as 'wild and abandoned, so loosely painted that it is as though the artist doubts his own identity'. The director could have been describing Mathew's school shenanigans rather than his electrifying portraits.

In 1961 R.A. ('Eddie') Hart professed to teach maths in a very odd style. He had special mathematical ability, others said, but only one arm – but an arm that could throw a blackboard duster at me more accurately than anyone. He was a source of amusement to all students and of my frequent detentions. He would set a problem on the blackboard with his one arm for the whole class to work on. Then – while we were supposed to find the solution individually – he wrote the answer on his desktop in chalk. Often, he fell asleep at the front of the class, and mayhem erupted for the duration of his snooze. Terry Martin and other students would go for a walk outside and return in time for the denouement (the solution explained). Others would fight a noisy pitched battle with paper darts; I remember that one errant dart hit Eddie on the nose and woke him suddenly. Eddie's enduring hangdog expression resembled a bloodhound, probably because he still felt pain in his missing arm, as he said, and another teacher told me that he suffered from being henpecked at home. I enjoyed the odd circus of Eddie's raucous classes but was guilty of adding to his misery.

In 1961, my good school friend Terry Martin died. I had been comfortable in his company because his mother cleaned the house of a neighbour who was a Plymouth Sister. Terry knew my parameters without me having to explain them over and over again. Although he was a little bandy, he loved to play hockey and keepings-off, to swim and ride his bike. I joined with him enthusiastically, unbeknown to my parents. I was jealous of his membership of Scouts. How lucky was he? In a school essay in 1960, I described him as having black hair, brown eyes and a dark, healthy-looking face. Sad to say, it was not healthy enough. Within a year, he contracted leukaemia and could not be rescued by intensive chemotherapy. His handsome thick hair disappeared, making his head look like a mammoth smooth mushroom.

When he died, I was in a quandary about attending his funeral. For a start, he had not behaved like a Christian (swearing lewdly was his appealing forte) and also Brethren were not permitted to attend non-Brethren funerals. Did he go to heaven? Brethren ruled that if he was older than twelve, and if he had the opportunity to commit to God, and ignored it, then he was a dammed sinner. He probably did have the opportunity because his mother cleaned for Gilbert Brown and his Brethren family, over the road from his house.

I did not attend his funeral, but felt that I should. I was torn: how could I pay tribute to our friendship without paying tribute? I internalised my feelings, awash with confusion and swamped with inadequacy. I felt uncomfortable, not knowing whether to grieve or not.

An unexpected event in my final year at school illustrated my sober effort to assert individuality while at the same time conforming to Brethren expectations. Without any campaigning at all, I was elected as a prefect at school in February 1964. Eleven other students were elected to leadership roles as prefects for the year. That night, my parents were unimpressed by my new status and shocked at the possibility of my contamination by evil. They required me to visit the principal, Roy Andrews, next day to point out that I could not hold the office of prefect, especially because it would require me to attend a social dance late in the year. Dancing was an extreme form of wicked fraternisation. I felt humbled by the unsolicited trust conferred by fellow students and deeply embarrassed about the insistence to confess to my incapacity to fulfil it. I was trapped, fearing that my secret eccentricity might leak into the public domain.

The stress of resignation was lessened because it was short and accepted quickly without the need for elaborate justification. Old Roy Andrews, the principal, mumbled equivocally. He had taught my mother maths many moons before at Kyneton High School, he had boarded in her house next door, so he was familiar with odd Brethren ways.

I gazed fixedly into the distance out of his office window as I tried to make my stance on the issue clear. An empty teacup wobbled on his desk, making a tinkle, and drew my focus back.

'Sir, I need to point out that I cannot be a prefect because it would require me to attend social functions that are outside my faith,' I blurted out. It felt like a very long explanation, but it was what I had been told to impart.

'Yes, you would need to attend the end-of-year social.' Andrews squeezed the ridge of his nose, where his spectacles normally sat.

'I am not allowed to do that.'

Andrews mumbled something barely comprehensible – indicating that he understood my predicament. So my election was rescinded without further ado.

I felt the back-up of Brethren righteousness behind me, even though I had discussed the problem only with parents and no others. It was a prop to know that I was not alone in my other-worldly stance and I swore to myself not to endure any further embarrassments ever again by exposing such odd beliefs to outsiders.

Tragedies

My final experience of eccentricity was much worse than school exposure, touching on criminality and trauma when a few Brethren went over the edge into insanity. Although Brethren courted privacy and obscurity as much as they could, every now and again they burst into the public eye by means of evidence provided by bizarre events or court cases, or both. Disasters exposed freakishness.

Stern, severe, sullen Brothers were not uncommon, sad to say. My own father was inclined that way. A euphemistic snippet of 1926 news from Wellington, New Zealand, indicates another characteristically glum frame of another mind:

> Archibald Gray of Eltham, a former Inspector of the Public Health Department, who murdered his son, aged sixteen, was acquitted today on the ground of insanity, and committed to a mental hospital. The evidence showed that he was a member of the Plymouth Brethren faith, and was rather religious and inclined to look on the gloomy side of things.

Closer to my own experience, further Brethren deaths startled me. Petite Rose Waddell from Austinmer, on the New South Wales coast, spent summer holidays with my family at the beach at Ocean Grove, with her cheery optician husband, David, and daughters. In 1968 in her shrill voice, she expressed strong dislike of my fashionable tangerine beach towel and luminous green socks, but was relaxed otherwise. She did not seem washed out or depressed, but she went home and hanged herself, aged only fifty, overwhelmed by despair because she had recently lost two daughters (and grandchildren) to Exclusive Brethren, who would never allow Rose to see them. The remnants of that sad family retreated to Open Brethren, and never crossed my path again.

As noted in the previous chapter, when Brethren holidayed, they were enjoined to visit other Brethren to consolidate social networks. In the late 1960s, Anthony Panes came from England, from a family of well-endowed landed gentry, to investigate our colonial outpost. His pink cheeks looked as polished as any apple, but it was his patronising accent that invited our parody. He stayed in our guest room while he toured the city and took in the countryside. In spite of his sheen of English manners, he took advantage of the hospitality of members of our little Brethren rump wherever he travelled. When he exhausted ours, he charmed others.

His parents followed Anthony on holiday here soon after he returned Home. Like us, they belonged to the expelled Brethren. In a tweed waistcoat and polished brogues, the paterfamilias looked every bit the aristocratic squire. Mrs Panes complemented him with her golden hair in a braid wound around the back of her small head. She was dainty in size and mannerisms but a pompous know-all in conversation. I had met the old couple first in Oxford in England in 1962 when visiting my brother David there. She irritated me but impressed Mother with her plum-in-mouth accent.

Predictably, they were invited to dinner with all the members of our family who could be gathered together in 1971. David, Peter and I had left home. David and his wife were separated in fact, which we all pretended had not happened.

'Lovely weather we are having,' observed Mother. Weather was a much-used antidote to awkward topics of conversation.

'Back home, the wild weather has reduced our success with young calves,' said Mr Panes.

'What type of cattle do you breed?' asked Father.

Before he could answer, David's two-year-old daughter – who sat in a high chair with a bowl of green peas – accidentally knocked them all onto the floor. 'Oh fuck!' she protested loudly.

Total silence descended like an impenetrable fog. David dived beneath the table to retrieve lost peas. Rachel's mother tried hard to suppress her giggles.

After a long pause, conversation resumed awkwardly and gradually; Brethren in extreme shock talked staccato out of the sides of their mouths, non-Brethren family (including me) desperately tried to think of any topic (other than peas) to chat about. Peas and cattle breeding had departed the agenda rapidly.

Little did the Panes know that a worse disaster was about to befall them. When they returned home to Hampshire, the Exclusive Brethren lost patience with another of their sons, Roger, a cattle dealer, whom they excommunicated for a slight sin of some sort. The terms of his ostracisation – complete isolation from his wife and three children – sent him around the twist, and he retaliated by killing them all with an axe, then hanging himself from banisters, leaving a nonsensical suicide note. A jury decision that Roger Panes had killed his family while the balance of his mind was disturbed was an extreme understatement:

> The Exclusive Brethren is notorious for the severity of its discipline and was ruled with an iron hand by its world leader...

I was deeply hurt by this disaster; it seemed so far away, and yet so shocking to us all as a family emotionally.

Means of rejection

Maintaining eccentric behaviour, attitudes, ways of thinking, self-perception, motivation and relationships inside the Brethren could themselves be forms of escape. But they were severely inwardly focused and inclined to tip a minority over the edge into madness. They also formed an elite refuge for others. If adherents wanted to leave Brethren, they were believed eccentric by those who remained. They came to be treated as complete unknowns who were never mentioned again. An exit required a leap from one realm of eccentricity to another. New arrivals on the outside had few guidelines as to how to behave in the World that had been despised as so threatening in their recent past. Their new reality – yet to be discovered – had ample scope for eccentricity, but was as yet a mystery. I have alluded to several of my struggles for fresh identity outside.

Bizarre notoriety was recognised in 1967 by the Beatles, when they chose a portrait of Aleister Crowley for the top left-hand corner (second from left) of their album cover of *Sgt. Peppers Lonely Hearts Club Band*. Aleister had a reputation. He squatted tightly alongside Mae West, Carl Jung, Dylan Thomas, Marilyn Monroe and Mahatma Ghandi. Aleister's notorious lifetime (1875–1947) began with Plymouth Brethren and ended in loneliness, quite the opposite of the implied connectivity of the Beatles' music cover. Aleister's extraordinary exploration has been chronicled almost as widely as the Beatles' own saga of fame.

Aleister's father Edward made a large fortune from beer manufacture, a business which he sold when he converted to Plymouth Brethren. At the same time, he withdrew all investments in railways because they were not mentioned in the Bible. John Nelson Darby applauded his stance, declaring railways and the telegraph unnecessary and immoral. Edward swore that while young, Aleister could have access only to the Bible and to no guidance from literature, government, articles of religion, catechisms or rules. For him, all Worldly outlets were slammed shut. As a child, Aleister was allowed no non-Brethren friends. His mother called Aleister the Beast (which he encouraged) and acquaintances in the 1920s labelled him the Wickedest Man in the World. Aleister wallowed in his weirdness. His scary bulging eyes protrude in photographic and painted portraits.

An Australian publisher undertook the printing of his extensive autobiography. In it, he professed that he was predisposed to suffering as a child:

The Bible was [my] only book… [I] was fascinated by the mysteriously prophetic passages, especially those in Revelation. The Christianity in [my] home was entirely pleasant, ...and yet [my] sympathies were with the opponents of heaven...[I] preferred the Dragon, the False Prophet, the Beast and the Scarlet Woman, as being more exciting. [I] revelled in the descriptions of torment. One may suspect, moreover, a strain of congenital masochism. [I] liked to imagine [myself] in agony.

I have mentioned that others in contact with Brethren – Bono and Stott – shared his obsession with Biblical prophecies, but not in such literal thoroughness perhaps.

By Aleister's own accounts, his closest friend was his benevolent father, who spoilt him, but when Aleister was twelve, Edward died. A sadistic uncle took over Aleister's custody, sending him to a Brethren boarding school and to private Brethren tutors, where he endured bullying, neglect, sexual abuse and extreme harassment for his idiosyncrasies. Teenage angst and trauma turned him into an inveterate loner and led to his absolute hatred of Plymouth Brethren.

At twenty, Aleister received control of his inheritance and spent lavishly while a Cambridge University student, excelling at chess, poetry-writing, experimental sex and mountaineering, but never completing a degree. He began using heroin and claimed to work as a spy.

It was a vivid vision that led him to believe in the truth of magic alone. By 1904, he created a new religion of his own called Thelema – where he was the head – which he was convinced would replace all other religions globally. According to theological analysts, the new religion plagiarised liberally from Gnosticism, tantric Buddhism, chemistry and Freud. And perhaps from Brethren in terms of its extreme intensity and comprehensive ideology?

During World War I, Aleister published pro-German propaganda. Authorities were less than impressed, and upset as well by his erotic books, way-out rituals and much-publicised erotic lifestyle. He was expelled from many countries, making a living from publishing and suing in courts for libel. He died lonely in a residential hotel in Hastings, United Kingdom.

Aleister Crowley's experience shows how extreme reactions to Brethren developed, how contrary the views of escapees grew, and how – although he escaped from their grip – he inadvertently replicated some of their values and habits, dressed afresh in his own outlandish guises. In his case, from the seeds of dissent from Brethren, grew a life of rebellious adventure, pain, havoc and self-inflicted alienation.

I am glad to say that removing myself from the Brethren orbit did not lead to such dire consequences, yet echoes of some of Aleister's experiences reverberated for me. The experience of being outside the fold was familiar. I accepted early in life that belonging to Plymouth Brethren marked me as odd and on the margins of normative behaviours, living separately from the World, and paradoxically it may have made it easier for me to be courageous about being different when I escaped the cult altogether. But I was frequently puzzled about the limits of eccentricity, about how to conform but still continue to assert sufficient individual identity at the same time, because in their extremes, they both felt uncomfortable to me. Eccentricity could augur tragedy, but at the same time in my experience it more often proved productive, amusing, entertaining, and a means to rehearse my own liberation.

Work challenges

Well after my escape from the cult, later on at the State Library of Victoria in the 1970s, I worked in the Picture Collection of the La Trobe Library. Eccentricity continued to present itself there in several forms. I did not seem able to escape it. Was it universal?

For me, the main interest was the one million pictures in the collection, mainly historical photographs of Australia, but they had been neglected for years, desperately in need of careful arrangement, indexing and conservation. The subjects ranged from the lavish photos of Aborigines by the French gold-digger, Antoine Fauchery, in the 1850s, to the stylised fashion photos from the 1950s by Athol Shmith in Melbourne.

Arguably the most valued and famous collection of artworks were by Samuel Thomas Gill (1818–1880) of life on the Victorian goldfields in pastel watercolours. Gill had been brought up among Plymouth Brethren in England, whom he escaped on arrival at Adelaide in 1839, at the same age (twenty-one) that I escaped them. His search for subjects included lurid depictions of street life and the libertine activities of all sorts of posh and destitute characters, attesting to his quick immersion in non-religious lifestyles in Australia. Gill captured the colour and crudity of the social melting pot of the goldfields.

My boss in the Picture Collection wrote a book about that artist. In my experience, she was often very anxious and eccentric, erratic and fractious herself, and had recently left her husband in Sydney, who conducted voluble and drawn-out arguments with her over the phone at work. Shouting that emanated from her tiny office grew shrill and strident. Overhearing it was unavoidable.

As a result of her regular cigarette-smoking, the collection and staff were subjected to unhealthy clouds of smoke. Once, I had to extinguish a billowing fire in her metal rubbish bin, because she dropped her burning butt into the paper rubbish impetuously and rushed downstairs for an impromptu meeting.

Her most eccentric act was managing to step through a famous oil painting by William Strutt called *The Burial of Burke* (1911), of the Burke and Wills expedition. Her clumsy foot made a hole right through the canvas where a black Bible lay on the ground near the open grave; it had been used for the reading at the Burke funeral. Would the Bible ever stop popping into my life uninvited?

Another strange experience in the same part of the library involved three young librarians who were feminists regularly calling out loudly to each other across the workspace as they moved from task to task. They were assiduous at appearing worldly-wise. Sometimes it was just 'What did you do last night?'

I could not avoid hearing parts of a more intimate discussion as I looked for an 1880s painting of a corroboree by William Barak to show an art historian. The women chose to ignore my presence.

'Last night was no better than the previous night,' Anne called out, hoping that the others might suggest a solution.

'I sometimes have the same sort of pain,' shouted Kirstie, 'and I reckon it's the size of his penis pressing too hard on my cervix.'

'I've had similar pain which was certainly caused by inflammation,' said Tina. 'What I do is use more vaginal cream.'

'Be careful not to get fibroids. Ooooh, they are soooo painful,' contributed Kirstie.

It was a salutary offbeat lesson to us all. The stridency of secular eccentricity could be as shrill as religious eccentricity.

Eight

Learning

Unorthodox waste

At my primary school, the toilet paper in the draughty outdoor toilets was of two colours. In the boys' toilets, there were green sheets, and in the girls' toilets (I was told), there were pink sheets. Why this colour segregation?

A clue lay in the collection in our school library – jammed onto the shelves of a tiny converted classroom, supervised by a round, snappy teacher called Mrs Macdonald. As a fixture every week, I had ample time to share her company and to absorb the stuffy library surroundings, because I was not permitted to attend religious instruction classes at school – they taught the wrong sort of Christianity – and during RI I was consigned to the library, not an exciting initiation for a kid.

All available wall space was covered with pinewood shelves, many of which were packed tight with weekly Hansards, that is, transcripts of parliamentary debates, printed on green paper (for the House of Representatives) and pink paper (for the Senate), stapled together for each house. The federal government sent them to every state school library in the country regularly, although how many Australians up to the age of twelve would read them, let alone understand them, are open questions. Room in the library for books of interest to me was limited because of the permanent proliferation of Hansards. When I told my brother David about the encroaching Hansards, he explained to me how parliamentary debates worked, and why they were printed in the interests of open democracy.

My school put the Hansards to an alternative use; lack of shelf-space probably led to their deconstruction. Broken into single sheets, they were halved by guillotine, bundled together, hole-punched in one corner, and held together with a piece of twine, so that they could hang on a nail next to the toilet bowls. Who decided to recycle the Hansard in this way and who was responsible for choosing the gendered colours, will remain a mystery forever.

Imagine a discussion in a staff meeting of teachers.

'Our librarian is relieved to be rid of a whole year of Hansards,' reports the headmaster, Mr Bright brightly.

'But is green the right colour for boys?' questions Mr Baddeley, bursting with leadership potential.

'Well, certainly pink would not look right,' chimes in Miss McKevett, the deputy.

Mr Baddeley is incapable of looking chastised.

'The caretaker is concerned that the paper is too durable and will block our pipes,' says the secretary. She has oversight of maintenance services.

'Can we ration use of it?' a new teacher asks naively.

In fact, the shiny paper surface of Hansard was not very functional but it was the only thing that our bottoms were provided with. Toilets in other places in the 1950s – such as public parks – used old newspaper (instead of Hansard) or pages from telephone books, which performed slightly better.

Learnings dawned on me. Parliament's serious purpose – to broadcast debate as part of democratic obligation – was corrupted at my school where surplus Hansards were commandeered for a putrid purpose. It also taught me that library disposals were known as weeding, although sludging might have described it better in this instance. Typically, my school's unusual sanitary treatment was explained properly for me at home, which was often the place where conundrums from formal learning were expanded on, or reviewed for my better understanding.

The fate of Hansard at school provided a lesson for my search for elsewhere: tradition and convention could be adapted (even violated) for local needs. The special use of Hansard was powerfully symbolic of an effort to demonstrate democracy in operation, of economy (avoiding purchase of commercial products), and of careful reuse of a valued resource, paper.

The meanings of learning

Education fed into my crossroads with Plymouth Brethren and swept me along in its path. For instance, I could hardly avoid learning textual exegesis very thoroughly from Brethren, with whom I sat through 10,000 hours of Bible discussions. Eventually I was able to apply a few of the early acquired skills during my tertiary education in the World. A few spin-offs were a small reward for the tiresome sacrifice of childhood sufferance. Many laborious hours of interpretation of legal statutes and case law in my studies at university were made easier by my understanding of the need for stoical, close scrutiny of texts, their syntax and meanings, and the same applied to original sources (often handwritten) in my history courses. I quizzed always with predetermined questions. Who wrote the texts? Where did they come from? Why were they written? Were they authentic first-hand accounts? Who was the intended audience for them? By what process did they arrive in my hands? Were they comprehensive? These types of questions inevitably required an element of scepticism which added to my quiver of critiques of Plymouth Brethren thinking; I stored them up as a squirrel keeps nut supplies for winter.

But first of all the facts of my educational progression. I loved to learn. From the age of three and a half, I attended kindergarten at Saint Paul's Anglican Church, then at five (in 1951) I went to Canterbury State School for seven years. In 1959, I started at Camberwell High School, finishing as dux of school in 1964. All three places were within walking distance of home. Between 1965 and 1968, I rode my motorscooter to, and completed a Bachelor of Arts Honours degree at, the University of Melbourne, but fell one semester short of a Bachelor of Laws degree, abandoning it because I felt less and less ambition to be employed as a lawyer. I never mastered the technique of thinking confidently and fast on my feet at university. I reached conclusions best by ruminating and reflecting.

The federal government paid a small allowance to study undergraduate degrees; I did not take up the offer of a more generous studentship because it contracted a student to the Education Department to teach in schools on graduation. By 1975, I had researched a Master of Arts degree in Australian history from the University of Melbourne, per favour of a scholarship. A thesis for the Doctor of Philosophy degree in 1995 (from Monash University), a cultural history study, was also funded by scholarship, and published as a book. The investigative and enquiring parts of learning always inspire me; unearthing knowledge is infinitely rewarding in its origin and usefulness, and leads to fascinating discoveries and more challenging questions.

In this chapter, I use the word education to include informal learning and powerful experiences that shaped my knowledge and understanding of my family, home, and community. They led ultimately to irresistible urges within me for liberation from Plymouth Brethren. Education was the most important general influence on my search for elsewhere, and all the more important because of the vast openings which it enabled, in distinct contrast to the extremely narrow benefits of immersion in Brethren dogma. It rescued me. Learning to remain astute and analytical ensured more than mere survival: it revealed fresh ways of rethinking and exploring new worlds forever. Horizons expanded.

Mother's influence

My enthusiasm for reshaping by learning began with Mother's robust beliefs in the enduring importance of education, driven initially by her regret that she was deprived herself, having to leave school and start work in a solicitor's office in Kyneton at the age of fifteen. She married at twenty-four. She told that her vigorous promotion of learning all her life benefitted from participating in the growth of her kids. They sustained her. In 1982 – after her four children had completed university degrees – she was emboldened to apply as an adult to study at La Trobe

University herself, and as part of her entry test she was required to write about why she would like to study. She wrote,

> In the 1920s I had no hope of studying…formally at all. By convention no one – especially a female – remained at school beyond what was then called Intermediate Standard. Of my own generation only one girl, the bank manager's daughter, did so and was immediately alienated from us all, through awe on our part and arrogance on hers.

Father had even more limited opportunities for study, but he acquiesced in Mother's commitment without directly promoting scholarship himself; he felt inadequate about formal learning, and limited his involvement to boasting widely about his children's successes.

Mother wrote in her application for university that she learnt a lot by spending many hours with each of her four children hearing notes, by which she meant that we volunteered to be tested by her orally on our knowledge of written summaries of texts, before our formal examinations. Very effectively, she devoted hours to such pre-testing well before the main events, especially in sciences and maths where the answers were inclined to be factual. My mind was sharpened on many fronts (for example, place names in geography, vocabulary in languages, recitation of quotations from literature) by her dedication. I have never encountered another parent who cared to pre-test to such an extent. She soaked it all up.

In earlier chapters, I have described significant learnings that contributed to the development of my independence. One was my cautious separation of the school world from my home and Brethren worlds, caused by the many cultural differences between them. Another was the lack of interest in me by my brother Peter and my loneliness at times at school. My alienation from the insincerity involved in family plotting and scheming, which presented as sanctimonious on the surface, taught me much about honesty and openness in dealing with people. The realisation that self-knowledge was liberating as well as challenging, along with discovering the usefulness of some Brethren ways of thinking, to analyse the internal inconsistencies of its own doctrines, taught me about connecting ideas. Cumulatively, all of these discoveries pointed me towards taking personal responsibility for independent choices.

Independence seemed to come easily to me at a moment that is thoroughly documented in Mother's writings from 1998. Conveniently, Mother wrote that on the morning of 13 February 1950 she sent me off to kindergarten as usual, telling me that when I came home at lunchtime, if she was not home, I should walk on to the home of Mrs Wilson – a trusted Plymouth Sister – up the hill in Bryson Street. I had no idea why I should go to her place, but I always did what Mother asked. No one had even whispered to me about a new sibling; in our family, pregnancy was an utterly taboo topic. A recent writer describes Brethren in Ireland refusing to use the word pregnant, even in the 1960s; they disguised it by requiring use of *enceinte* instead. I was about ten when I first heard the word pregnant in the school playground.

Unbeknown to me, Mother's fourth pregnancy came to a finale when her waters broke in the shower at seven a.m. that day. She wrote that during the morning she remained duty-bound, ironing, cleaning and cooking, refusing to acknowledge her labour pains. She relates that by late morning she was forced to drive alone to Bethesda Hospital in Richmond, where my aunt worked. Mother took a risk: our green Austin A40 tourer sometimes needed cranking to start, as mentioned already, sputtering like a blocked drain.

Typically, the engine stalled – in Bridge Road, Richmond, en route to the hospital – but fortunately a helpful tram conductor and tram driver offered to push the car off the tram tracks, and to restart it. With her teeth clenched in pain, her knuckles white on the steering wheel, and moaning, the helping hands must have wondered what was going on inside the car. Ten minutes after arrival at the hospital, my sister Bettina was born in a rush, just in time for lunch, Mother recorded.

When I came home for my own lunch, the door was unlocked with no one home; Mother had disappeared. Had the Rapture arrived? Giving it a passing thought, I walked up Bryson Street to Mrs Wilson as instructed and felt proud to manage myself and have the opportunity to show personal responsibility. I was very keen to grow up.

Mrs Wilson's garden boasted a laden nectarine tree and a vine of warm grapes, which I raided, supplementing my lunch. She had no children of her own. She was a gentle, considerate woman, and I was happy to continue to visit her welcoming house for the week while Mother languished in hospital – the normal lying-in period at that time.

Mrs Wilson's old mother, Mrs Bryant, fascinated me to the extent that I felt inspired to sketch her portrait in pencil. I remember feeling very pleased that Father praised my drawing. The smiling octogenarian arced her back, reclining in a large rocking chair, stroked her hair behind an ear, with a wispy bun perched on her head, and a long black hairpin threaded through it. She smelt pleasantly of 4711 eau de cologne. Her peaceful retreat contrasted with the hubbub of my own home.

Cross-examining the evidence

Later, other opportunities arose to exercise my independence – I select just one. I concocted a challenge to test the strictness of Brethren's reliance on the Bible as a complete source of all truth and wisdom. By the time that I reached seventeen, my concerns about Brethren methods of interpretation had flickered earlier sporadically, like a strobe light in the gloom, but I had never set myself the onerous task of testing their methods systematically, as with the beam of a spotlight. Being bored with studying French one day, I struck on the idea of checking the reported genealogies in the Bible. I found a large sheet of butcher's paper. The repetition in the text was a monotonous task to submit to, as I laid the details out on the huge sheets, there being no computer family trees then. I registered each name from the first book of the Bible, which said, for instance,

> These are the generations of Shem: Shem was an hundred years old, and begat Arphaxad… And Arphaxad…begat Salah… And Salah…begat Eber… And Eber…begat Peleg… And Peleg…begat Reu… And Reu…begat sons and daughters… And Nahor lived after he begat Terah… And Terah lived seventy years and begat Abram, Nahor, and Haran (Genesis 11: 10–26).

And so on. I noted every name and place in the sequence, but I do not recommend this exercise unless you happen to need a drawn-out diversion from more boring tasks!

All the strange names merged into a mashed-up muddle as I annotated them – hardly surprising with all that busy begatting going on beneath my very eyes! Aware that language is never meant to be precise for all circumstances, after spending hours tracing the supposed family tree of all humanity, by plotting every name and event in the Old Testament part of the Bible, it became clear that the text was not a comprehensive historical document, and that it contained as many errors and omissions as holes in a sieve.

The Bible proved to be full of ambiguities, anachronisms, metaphors, symbols and internal allusions, not to be taken literally. Yet our Brethren Bible translator, the inimitable John Nelson Darby, insisted that God had spoken definitively and with universal truths 'with the very fullest conviction [that] the divine inspiration of the holy scriptures [w]as the revelation of the infinite wisdom of God'. Darby glossed over anomalies. How to share this disturbing discovery was a major headache which I kept secret, but huge gaps in the Brethren net were widening in my mind, independent thinking developing alongside my applied knowledge.

It was obvious from my internal assessment that literal interpretation of the Word of God failed miserably. For example, executions were carried out frequently in the Old Testament, but was it still a valid authority for punishment today? Far from a hypothetical question, it concerned all the thousands in 1967 who opposed the punishment of Ronald Ryan by execution in Pentridge. His was the last execution of a prisoner in Australia.

Another problem was that the Bible begged the question as to authorial intent. Half the Bible was written after Jesus died: how reliable was an author who wrote up the verbatim sayings of Jesus but who never knew Jesus? What was the effect of multiple translations? What about blanks – what was God's Word on war technologies or land rights or plastic pollution? The Bible presented no guidance whatsoever.

Close cross-examination of texts, having a little chat with them, as I suggest to my own students these days, inevitably helped me to elucidate their intended meanings. That skill I absorbed in the beginning from learning to read, taught largely at home, then Brethren added to my knowledge of textual analysis by insisting on my daily exposure to unrelenting dissection of every word in the Bible. I learnt a lot about subtexts and hidden meanings. Formal exercises in comprehension and clear thinking at school enlarged my self-control, focus, discoveries, memory, and analytical and communication skills, by taking analysis beyond religion, and ultimately beyond printed texts into images and the spoken word as well. I did not acquire long-term problem-solving and good decision-making skills until later in life, after real experiences in the World, but up-close and immediate assessments became second nature to me when still young. You could say that for insights I was equipped with a microscope rather than a telescope at that stage.

Arguments

Presenting an argument, advocating a point of view and taking a moral stance were important skills that I acquired at home and school. They had little direct connection to Plymouth Brethren. However, I suppose that they could be seen as a reaction against the Brethren inability to manoeuvre, because of their tendency to fixate on one narrow perspective on every issue. Brethren inherited a formula for life that served to achieve their historical ends, and soaking up black-and-white diktats were all that was required from emergent, unthinking victims; there was no scope for contestation or wavering doubt. For Plymouth Brethren, the evidence was all in the Bible, only in the Bible, and nothing more nor less. Rote learning of doctrine was the sole basic requirement. Accepting their dogmatic interpretation of the Bible by heart was unchallengeable. Contemplating any contrary point of view was just bound to be a distraction, to cause worry and heresy. Unhelpfully, my parents advised, 'Don't let your brain overrule your heart.' This mixed metaphor helped me very little, because I could not work out how to separate the religious functions of the brain and heart, nor how to interpret the word rule.

Preaching to the unconverted, to persuade them of the values of a Plymouth Brethren way of life, had less and less meaning among the Brethren that I experienced. This was because they grew narrower and narrower in outlook by the mid-1960s, when in practice they courted no converts, in the manner of some orthodox Jews today, relying instead on inbreeding for population growth.

Haranguing passers-by through a megaphone on a main street – as we did up to the early 1960s – could no longer be respected as carefully reasoned persuasion. Although I did preach a sermon in a hall to three hundred people in 1966, all of them were card-carrying members of Brethren already, and I was left with the empty feeling that my performance was a hollow charade, an exercise in warm and fuzzy self-affirmation with no originality and no kernel of genuine appeal to any outsider. It lacked fervour or purpose. A long-term value of preaching lay in my understanding of the need for projecting a message to a large group – useful for later university lecturing to six hundred students in a large theatre, for instance.

I veered off the straight and narrow path at school in form four (1962), when I volunteered to lead a team in a debate supporting apartheid in South Africa. My sincerity was not required at all. It was a different game altogether, intended as a mental exercise, just playful argumentation. I welcomed the freedom to avoid any pretence of sincerity; Brethren were so nervously earnest that their every utterance was subject to censure by others.

My inspiring history teacher, Dr Joe Rich, child of refugee migrants, needed three students who would present the case for apartheid, even if we did not agree with that side of a confrontation. Although I was fully opposed to the shocking racism of apartheid, I savoured the opportunity to join the ritual of a debate for the first time in my life. I really engaged passionately, thinking of all the arguments that might be brought against apartheid, and figuring out how to contradict them.

The thrill lay in the novelty, not in any sense of justice. I visited the International Bookshop in the city to buy a printed copy of the *United Nations Charter*, wherein I found clauses to assist my cause: as I waved it vigorously in the air, I quoted Article 2.4, which prohibited one sovereign state from interfering in the internal affairs of another sovereign state. The Chinese foreign minister and his wolf warrior henchmen of today would be proud of me. As adjudicator, jumpy Joe Rich reluctantly awarded my team a win, based on the harsh logic of presented arguments rather than their moral worth, as he explained.

A person whom I admired as a great oracular strategist was the criminal barrister Frank Galbally, lanky and statuesque. He pulled his suit jacket tight when cross-examining a witness. While my parents tried to decide if my observations of court practices conformed to Brethren rules or not – not a lot of Brethren dogma mentioned criminal law explicitly – in my teens I spent many a gripping hour in the public gallery of the Supreme Court of Victoria, when Frank Galbally was staunchly defending a client against a murder charge. I loved his eighty per cent success rate of winning cases against the odds; the underdog found a true ally in him. I knew all about underdogs. I cheered when he went beyond his barrister brief and strongly criticised Exclusive Brethren practices publicly: he declared that they were 'a threat to public morals and a denial of fundamental human rights'. Frank was bold enough to criticise Brethren head on, to my delight, and his brother Jack Galbally campaigned in the Victorian Legislative Council for a Royal Commission, mentioned in the next chapter.

Their attitudes were widely publicised in print media, at the time that Mother enquired hesitantly of me, 'Is it a good idea to go to the courts, dear?' An eyebrow raised.

'I learn a lot,' I replied, keeping my head down.

'Would you say that it is educational?'

'Ooooh, definitely,' I assured with a sly sideways glance in the direction of her frown.

A potential landmine was left to rest there, no more being said.

Empathy

The empathy shown by the Galbally brothers, committed Catholics, was not to be found in my Brethren community at that time. I do not know how to determine whether empathy is learnt or innate; Brethren showed none of it towards any outside the tribe. Plymouth Brethren as a *bruderbund* were outcasts from the World and glued to seclusion. For me, empathy as an ability to understand and respond to another's perspective was absorbed and/or learnt at home, and school furnished extra opportunities to pick it up.

At primary school, the Home girls concerned me. They invited empathy. They were named from their residence, a Salvation Army home for girls, but mysteriously no one knew anything about them at the time, and teachers were not giving out any hints at all. The lonely behaviour of the Aboriginal girls suggested social segregation – as though they had leprosy. Brethren harboured no Aborigines, probably because they were never sufficiently extraverted to establish missions one hundred years back. At school, we were not encouraged to connect with the Aboriginal girls who arrived as a group in a van in the mornings, and who were collected straight after the final bell.

Striking features were their unfashionable basin haircuts and uniform gingham dresses, inviting ridicule. In my classes, they sat in the back corner and teachers never made any effort to engage them in discussion or class activities. They were excellent at running and playing with a ball at recess times, so that at full flight at top speed, they looked stunning, resembling dark sylphs with supernatural powers.

'Who are the dark girls in my class?' I was stirred to ask at home when aged ten.

'What do you mean?' asked Father, hardly interested.

'They have dark skin, come together on a bus and sit at the back, and go very quietly,' I said.

'I have no idea, I'm sure,' said Mother.

No adult knew anything about them. Enquiries began and ended there; the Aboriginal girls did not exist.

But I had reason to want to know more. Eleanor, a blonde girl who always sat in the front of class, was the apple of my roving eye. Somehow, I knew that her family belonged to the Salvation Army. I was also attracted to the lovely faces of the home girls, and their distinctive smiles, and wanted to get to know them, but boys and girls sat on opposite sides of the room and even our outdoor playgrounds were segregated.

At home, my young sister asked me a surprise question. 'Who will you marry when you grow up?'

'An Aboriginal girl,' was my instant reply. I required no time to ponder.

'Oh, no. How awful.' Bettina was deeply shocked, covering her face with her hands in horror. 'How could you think like that?'

'Why not?' I asked innocently.

'Well, that would not be right. I'm going to tell Mother.' And she hurried off.

I heard nothing more about my way-out thoughts from Bettina or Mother. Prejudice against Aborigines was very widespread, and because we had rarely seen an Aborigine, it was easier not to get to know any: out of sight, out of mind was the prevailing attitude. Racism ran very deep in the Australian psyche: in 1966, my friend from secondary school, hesitant but loveable Theo, took his Ukrainian girlfriend home to meet his parents for the first time. His miserable father commented, 'Well, she may be a wog, but at least she's not an abo.'

All that mattered to me in grade three was that Eleanor had a pretty pout, a charming smile and long blonde curls, and sat at the front of the class where I could watch her dreamily. Her precise way of speaking was contagious. I was well supplied with other objects of adoration also: I stared impolitely at the dark, translucent, burgundy skin of the home girls. What made their black hair glisten in the slanting sunlight? Where had they been? Where were they going? I wanted to travel with them on a mystery journey. Did they know of a different heaven from the one that I was promised? I was surprised that they were never included in group school photos and sad that they disappeared after grade six, never to be seen at secondary school.

I was unaware at the time that Eleanor lived in the William Booth Memorial Salvation Army Girls' Home in Brinsley Road, East Camberwell, run by the Salvation Army, where the home girls lived. Eleanor's parents managed the facility – effectively an orphanage – although the girls had been stolen from their Indigenous parents from around the country. A sinister government policy of assimilation aimed to eliminate the dark-skinned non-citizens altogether; few people knew about it. The awful aim was to breed out the darkness of the skin and of the innate culture (more than 60,000 years of satanic, pantheistic beliefs). Eleanor avoided talking about her home as a child, but explained to me later in life how much she detested the gaol-like atmosphere there and her father's severe depression as superintendent.

My concern revived about fifty years later (in 2005) when I co-managed a research project at Monash University called Trust and Technology, with the aim of designing digital systems to capture oral Koori knowledge before it was lost to posterity. At that time, I read the sad stories of the stolen girls (and boys) in a government report of 2004 titled *Forgotten Australians; A report on Australians who experienced institutional or out-of-home care as children*. It contained reams of testimony of shocking abuse. The girls' home imprisoned girls aged between four and fourteen from whom we could have learnt a lot if permitted. A wasted resource, Ruby Hunter, the well-known singer-songwriter, was among them. My research project may have been late on the scene but it managed to facilitate capture of considerable Aboriginal genealogy, know-how, environmental expertise and virtuous beliefs.

To Australia's permanent shame, the report of the Senate Community Affairs References Committee contained shocking testimony:

> My Mum [said one witness] spent years in Psychiatric Institutions due to the atrocious physical and mental abuse that herself and [her] sister endured for many years at the cruel hands of the 'so-called carers' at the Salvation Army children's home at Camberwell.

Mum told me of many cruel and inhumane things that happened to herself and her sister.

Ironically, Eleanor also suffered a mental breakdown after her training as a psychiatrist at university and in hospitals, and she was forced to abandon her career, and retire into care by Catholic nuns. Her childhood caused her unbearable distress.

The damage to the home girls was dreadfully destructive, making them feel utterly helpless, like nobodies. In addition to being ignored at school, they were sexually abused at the home and forced to do menial work in return for food and simple clothes. Ridicule and discrimination – the punishments that produced the desired result for a racist society – kept Aboriginal girls well beyond public recognition.

A very different view was shown at secondary school, where Mrs Hyrell Waten taught me history in 1959 with great confidence. She balanced the learning ledger by explaining that Aborigines lived in an idyllic communal society with no poverty, no violence and no inequalities. I marvelled at the news that they were healthy, contented and self-contained before the white invasion. She took us on an instructive excursion to explain Aboriginal artefacts in the city museum. Her husband was the author Judah Waten (*Alien Son*), who wrote about being a newly arrived Russian Jew in Australia in 1914; he no doubt empathised about Aboriginal alienation. I loved Hyrell's energetic approach to Australian history, and read Judah's novels enthusiastically later on in life.

My brother David alerted me to the fact that the Watens were Communists, a group whom I knew very little about, but he aroused my interest. It made sense that Hyrell was the first teacher who depicted Aboriginal ways of life in a positive, cooperative light. She explained ideas in a concrete and sensible way. As explained by David, communitarianism – with its advocacy of devotion of the individual to the whole community – was not unlike some of our Brethren practices. It was heretical to think that Aborigines, Communists, and Brethren clearly shared some common ways of thinking, but I did.

At the time of Hyrell's history classes, there were still many reds under Australian beds and she had Australian friends who were accused of spying. It did not inhibit her in any apparent way, nor limit her friendships with creative stars (like Noel Counihan the painter, or Christina Stead the writer), nor prevent her from campaigning for human rights for Aborigines, nor prevent her from being promoted to principal of Richmond Girls High School and Springvale High School. I followed her progress over time with deep admiration, but had no awareness (until the late 1960s) of the greater parallels between the undesirable features of the absolutist dogma of Brethren and Stalinism.

Formats

One of the reasons that I placed so much emphasis on the value of school learning and oral instruction – and their contributions to my daily life – was that as a child I did not benefit from having a wide variety of surrogate stories of human experiences to fall back on – no theatre, art, film, TV, radio or music. I was starved of back-up. Newspapers and books were my routine forms of imaginative representation of life and events outside my sheltered home refuge. As long as content was on the educational curriculum, then Mother (bless her) allowed me to gain from it, school thus delineating the moral boundaries of my knowing, viewing and listening, with Brethren removed from the equation. I made sure never to reveal Mother's liberating attitudes nor my sinful indulgences to other Plymouth Brethren, who seemed to find out nothing about them ever.

I vividly remember my mystification at my first experience of a feature film. I was taken with all the pupils of form four in 1962 – because we studied *A Tale of Two Cities* – to watch the story on black-and-white film at the Maling Road cinema. To my amazement, some girls put their heads in their hands and cried afterwards about Sydney Carton (acted by Dirk Bogarde), who delivered his final monologue at the end of the film, before his execution by guillotine:

> It is a far, far better thing that I do, than I have ever done. It is a far, far better rest that I go to than I have ever known.

I could see no realism in the film whatsoever, nor did I enjoy the plot, because I had no understanding of the genre of film. I cringed at the dreadfully contrived and over-sentimental characters in the film, at the fake film sets of Paris, and at the sobbing girls from my class on the pavement outside after the event: I only felt anger about what seemed to me like an excess of superficiality. Unsure whether the film was intended to be lifelike, or symbolic, I hurried away up Cross Street that afternoon when the class was freed to leave for home, feeling very alone and quite disoriented. My understanding failed me in that the film motifs and metaphors did not register with my thinking, and the purpose of the music soundtrack remained a deep mystery. Children who are brought up with film and TV absorb the tropes over time without need for explanation, but for me the experience was like an exotic culture, and I struggled to get the meanings. Who would teach me the language and interpret emotions? I could not read them in a book – they were buried in a quagmire of a mystery. In books, there were no keys to be found.

I did not welcome further consequences of my cultural cocooning, but I experienced similar emotions when I attended my first play two years later anyway, at the Emerald Hill Theatre, South Melbourne, where I saw *Death of a Salesman* by Arthur Miller. It was on the syllabus for English literature for form six and was staged as a money-spinner, that theatre always struggling on a shoestring. As a novice theatregoer, I was demure and nervous, and, in spite of being invited backstage to chat with the actors, left timidly as soon as the play finished, to be collected in the car by my anxious father outside. I was afraid of being tainted with sin, or of not knowing how to behave, if my truth were known. I had never sat in a darkened theatre and seen actors pretending so cleverly. In a court of law – in broad daylight – I had picked up some of the rules of interaction. In the theatre, light and sound were manipulated unaccountably. I was even more surprised when I read a printed report that said that in 'one performance…the students were so unruly that George Whaley [the producer] stopped the show and asked for the auditorium lights to be switched on so he could berate the hecklers'.

I had no idea that an audience could express an opinion openly. I reserved my final judgement of the play for the matriculation exam paper in English literature at the end of the year, in which I boldly criticised the play for its posturing and glorification of American values, in spite of never having been to another play in my life before. At that time, I was more censorious of the playwright than the performance, and even in later life, Arthur Miller plays never attracted me.

My proudest achievement in English literature was to research and write an essay, requested by my teacher Bob Ewins, whom I thoroughly admired, on the real-life experiences of Charles Dickens that shaped the characters and places in his 1861 novel *Great Expectations*. Pip, the narrator of the novel, was an orphan and Dickens took a special interest in 1857 in the establishment of orphanages by Plymouth Brethren in the UK. Ewins told my class that mine was the best essay that he had ever read – probably what he told others in other classes as well!

Storytelling

Films and plays were completely foreign forms of storytelling for me, because my access to stimulating and dramatic stories had been restricted to the Bible and permissible books. But what I lacked in other cultural entertainment and visual literacy, I made up for in affirming literature and home discussions. Some limits were imposed on my reading matter, for example, comics never being permitted, and certainly no glossy picture books were allowed. But because Aunt lavished lots of spare dollars on us as teenagers, we four children opened accounts at Cheshire's bookshop in a basement in the city, where we could buy any textbook that we wanted, and at the university bookshop also. It was amazing how easy it was for me to reclassify novels as textbooks if I tried.

Fiction was censored cursorily when brought home, but so long as the book title and cover looked innocuous, no questions were asked. Father expressed concern that my purchase of *Down and Out in London and Paris* by George Orwell might indicate that I intended to live rough when I went to London for three months to research in 1966–1967;

he took it to be a guidebook, not looking beyond the cover. As it happened, I was being funded by Aunt to live in a comfortable, small hotel in Bedford Square while I undertook my strategically chosen research (enabling exciting overseas travel). I wrote about the introduction of civil registration in England and Wales in 1837. Although the topic seemed boring when I was asked about it, it was actually a remarkably innovative public health initiative by the British government, with wide ramifications. It represented the beginning of government interest anywhere in the world in true statistical analysis of public health.

On that excursion, I spent four days a week in London libraries, and then on three non-work days visited historical sites listed in *The Blue Guide to London*, and avoided contact with Brethren in London effectively because there were none in the city. I was entreated to read my Bible all day on the Lord's Days, but Speakers' Corner in the expansive Hyde Park, the vast Maritime Museum in Greenwich, the denizens of Soho and their ilk held much greater appeal. I learnt how to have a good time on my own.

In the British Library I was befriended by a US literature professor and his wife who were doing research while on sabbatical. He alerted me to Stead's *The Man Who Loved Children*, a very rewarding discovery. Less worthwhile, they tried to set me up with their granddaughter – of my age – who lived in London. I was so naïve and fearful when I went walking with her along the Thames Embankment that I felt as cold and unappealing as the turgid river water surging beside the path. I wrapped my winter coat tightly around me for protection. Hobnobbing with non-Brethren was exposing.

Freedom to purchase reading matter had the result that I built up a personal library – of fiction and non-fiction – as did my siblings, and we shared good reads with each other with a total pool of about 30,000 books. The parental objective was to limit use of libraries, where we might brush up against undesirables, and having one's own resources meant less contact (or contamination) with fellow students at school or university. But the drawback was that study at home was often a lonely experience. Curiosity led me to read well beyond the boundaries of set curriculum.

My parents harboured very naïve views about the World on the other side of their fence. Separation was absolute. They viewed libraries as marginal spaces where potential terror lurked. Mother used to sing me an awfully sad children's song about a 'little Alabama coon' who was advised by his black mama to 'stay in your own backyard' to avoid bullying by white boys. Mother learnt it from my great-great-grandmother (Mary Eliza Price, born in 1863) and it moved me to tears; I remember standing alone in my own backyard and weeping copiously for the coon. The saying 'your own backyard' became part of our family lingo. I can still sing most of the verses, in a sad voice, but never inflict it on others any longer.

I doubt that Father ever ventured beyond his own backyard to enter a library. With some justification, as a girl Mother thought old men controlled the library at her Kyneton Mechanics' Institute, with its ageing book stock and expensive subscriptions, and believed (wrongly) that she was not permitted to enter to browse. In any case, it was used for boxing matches, dances, sporting events and cinema, all of which were prohibited to Plymouth Brethren. Mother was willing to accompany me gingerly only once to my local public library in Canterbury; I was banned from going on my own.

For an assignment for my history class in 1962, about the evolution of the town of Kyneton, I scoured the Public Library of Victoria in Swanston Street in the city on a Saturday – for the first time. I was lucky to collect a huge quantity of relevant data, and was unaware that the trip provoked a family crisis. I should have been aware. By quoting a letter of Saint Patrick's Day which Mother wrote to David, who was in Oxford, the home atmosphere is re-created; it is very telling in the way that it describes Mother's attitudes to libraries and to me as a person:

> When it got to 3 p.m. and [Graeme] was not home, when he had been told to be home by 1 p.m., we were very worried. Dad and Auntie Bett both thought of all the horrible people who frequent Public Libraries, and Auntie Bett also reminded me of the man

who spoke to you [David] once, while you were in there, and said he could help you and invited you home to his flat. Do you [David] remember? She [Aunt] had visions of Graeme being seduced. However, home he came, at 3.30 p.m., quite unconcerned – he was able to collect quite a lot of detail, and I think he was so interested in his work, that he forgot the time and did not have his watch with him. So we were most thankful to see him come in … He is such a friendly child that one hardly likes to think of him being abroad in the wicked, wide world on his own.

It is hard to believe that the child of fifteen years old was incapable of coping with the World! I deliberately left my watch at home so that I had no record of time passing. I was well aware that the home-dwellers regularly worked themselves up into a lather of panic about dreadful risks that their boys took, but I knew that I had to get my research done, in spite of pressure to never leave the overprotective home or Brethren surveillance.

Restraining independent learning was like giving a child a skipping rope but simultaneously banning its use. I believe that Mother never really understood the liberating power of education fully, no matter how much it tickled her curiosity. Very slowly, she realised that learning was transformative in every way – of people's identity, breadth of understanding, self-satisfaction, attitude formation and achievement. Late in life – in her late eighties, after Father died – she joined a women's writing group, where she gave herself permission to explore her own creative abilities in depth. She wrote creatively and furiously for workshops every week. But before that, when I was at school and university, she debated issues with us very apprehensively, petrified that her children's minds were being corrupted. Exclusive Brethren had no taste for education, nor any professed aim to extend themselves. We were 'born in iniquity, and in sin my mother conceive[d] me' (Psalm 51:5) and we stayed that way until we reached heaven for our transformation.

Before I could read to myself, Mother taught the appeal of stories. She would recite the lines of many children's books without looking at the page; she knew the words by heart because she had read them many times. She laid the opened book beside her, then she would tell me to turn over the page while she kept her eyes fixed on her ironing or cooking. She never made mistakes, never ironing the cooking, or vice versa. She had learnt all of the page breaks by heart.

As a young child, I shared a bedroom with my two older brothers. By the time that I started at school, David was already thirteen years old, and regularly immersed in reading anything and everything that he could lay his hands on. He was the fastest reader I have ever known. He was studying drama at secondary school and brought home his book of plays to perform at the foot of my bed and Peter's bed before sleep, acting out all of the individual characters himself, bouncing around and throwing his arms in the air. It seemed like magic when he changed his voice appropriately, in contrast to the boring recitation of the night-time prayer by rote –'May my sins be all forgiven' – so that I was enthralled by the play's storyline (a robbery) and very proud of David's talents. It was my first realisation that creative expression could transport me into realms of satisfying fantasy.

Listening to storytelling was funny too – like sharing jokes while sitting around a warm campfire. David was fond of telling shaggy dog stories. I remember his serious, furrowed brow as he told about a family of turtles having a picnic and a baby turtle sent back home to fetch lemonade. The stories were very drawn-out, full of diversions and irrelevant details, with a denouement of a boring anticlimax or a completely predictable punchline. We sat around him. As a young listener, I expected a clever or surprise resolution, but it never came, and a groan of disappointment was commonplace, especially when David managed to maintain the suspense to the end. These retold stories completely absorbed me when I was little – I pretended that I did not remember their endings so that I could hear them again.

War stories

Brethren lacked the narrative spark, and by overworking the material that they had to hand – the Bible – their stories lost their gloss. Learning too much of the detail of the Bible by heart obscured the attraction of grand sagas. As professional communicators, good teachers were champion storytellers, first-hand accounts proving intensely gripping.

I hung on every word of the secondary school expert, Ken Robertson, who (I was told later in life) was traumatised and needed heavy doses of tranquillisers to keep him going in class. His jowls drooped like a bulldog's but he had a glint in his eye. His tales remain everlastingly etched on my memory. He was a wing commander of bombers over Europe in World War II. He had bailed out of plunging planes on a parachute three times over enemy territory and managed to get back to the UK each time. I puzzled over how the crew coped; the chances of survival in the air in the war were slim, with more than half of them killed in action.

All students in our English class in form three were more spellbound by his reminiscences than we were by the cupidity of characters in *The Merchant of Venice* (set for the syllabus). We much preferred the former, about sheer survival against all odds. Robertson spoke with a quiet sibilance that evoked an ethereal image in my mind of a parachutist floating peacefully to earth from billowing storm clouds.

Two of his stories in particular were as absorbing as any adventure thriller. He told how eggs were rationed for airmen – and for all Brits, in fact. At an airbase before a bombing mission, crew would gently pencil their own name on a fresh egg, as well as the name of the person to whom they bequeathed their egg if they did not return from a sortie. Eventually, the egg would be used by someone for breakfast – it was too precious to waste – based on the wishes written on the eggshell! It made me ponder the extreme fragility of life and of fresh eggs seriously.

The second story concerned the printing of secret codes on rice paper. Before sorties, several wads of code were handed to the pilot before take-off, and secreted on every flight. If an aerial bomber had to be abandoned, crew were required to eat the pages of code from the books before leaping out, to keep them from enemy hands.

'We did not have time to worry about the flavour of the typewriter ink,' observed Robertson.

On one of his abandonments, a crew member with a small build could not manage to eat all the rice paper entirely on his own, before the crash. He hastily handed bits around to other crew to help with consumption as the plane disintegrated, and before they all bailed out successfully. As I sat in the classroom, I could smell the burning plane.

I felt that I owned Robertson's stories myself, they were so real, and I held them very close to my heart. Robertson must have sensed my wonderment, because a couple of years later he lent me his book of the watercolours of William Blake, the poet and painter. I pored over them with reverence, noting their original treatment of mystical spirituality, far more inspiring and creative than any Brethren artefact that I ever witnessed in word or print. I never really knew Robertson's motives, but I suspected that he was smitten by Blake's aesthetic sensitivity.

Dinner, deceit and dissent

A less fabricated framework for my learning was based on our dinner-table conversations, riddled with family politics, after David returned home from work at the University of Melbourne, Father returned from his printery, and Aunt from her pathologists' offices. Father invariably argued with David over many a controversial topic, as put forward by David – who delighted in posing confounding questions. I pitched in at any available opportunity, practising at giving my point of view, however half-baked it might be. I was the shrill barracker.

On a weeknight when Father arrived home a little late from work, the family waited for him to wash his hands before dinner. This habit meant that he shut his bedroom door and took a swig of sweet sherry from a two-litre glass flagon which was stashed on the floor of his wardrobe, beneath a pile of shoes. Accidentally, I discovered the flagon when aged about eleven. His secret Worldly tipple, a brave departure from Brethren orthodoxy, was well worth it from our perspective, because he would emerge for the meal without a care, full of good cheer, exuding a slight whiff of alcohol – a relief to one and all. It opened up the welcome prospect that any discussion at dinner might be both lively and civil at the same time.

Unintentionally, I was tutored as diminutive advocate on these occasions. An intellectual armoury was at hand. David was a very talented performer, and whilst my short-tempered father sighed in desperation, David would blithely guide our discussions over euthanasia, vivisection, psychological archetypes, interracial marriage, the monarchy, loyal public holidays, brain surgery, overpopulation, racism, exotic travel, savants, non-Christian religions, and much else besides. Because his leading questions were effectively about the fundamentals of the nature of the World beyond Brethren, the home discussions provided me with good grounding in logical thinking, mustering facts, memorising, detecting fallacies, and self-expression.

'Can a human act unconsciously without intent?' David asked.
'Is it possible for a pacifist to exercise self-defence?'
'What should be the rules of inheritance?'
'What is the most equitable form of a universal tax system?'
'Do animals have feelings?'
'Do humans need anthropomorphic pets?'
'Can animals have premonitions of death?'
'Can they commit suicide?'
'Can instant coffee be used to make a cappuccino?'
'Do we ever dream in colour?'
'What language will be spoken in heaven?'
'What is a soul?'
'Should Adventists be forced to take blood transfusions and vaccines?'

The questions stimulated entertaining goose chases, while Mother struggled hard to keep a lid on the muscularity of debates.

'Oh dear, do you think this food is properly cooked?' was typical of her heroic efforts at rhetorical diversion.

'Mrs Spence says that the tomatoes are doing well this year.'

It all else failed, the doctrinal vagaries of other religions and sects aroused our curiosity well. There was a lot to discuss. Outsiders were the most threatening groups of evil deviants in the World, so we asserted superiority with the sole purpose of reaffirming the self-evident – the innate correctness of Brethren doctrines. No shade of grey ever obscured our dazzling self-righteousness. As a consequence, I could describe the distinguishing features of the beliefs of a Congregationalist, Pentecostalist, Theosophist or Anabaptist, although it was not the most practical knowledge to assist in navigating the World of the future, nor to share with playmates in the schoolyard. For me, Predestination presented no greater a challenge to explain than Transubstantiation or Dispensationalism, but needless to say, such explanations were not in high demand in everyday conversations. Nevertheless, David cleverly managed to drag the entire family into ruminating on his original ideas.

David introduced me to a deception which excited me and set me on the path to letter-writing to editors of newspapers for years, to express opinions on controversial issues. He loved intellectual contests, and we always read 'Letters to the Editor' daily and tore apart their arguments. By no means literary masterpieces, writing 'Letters to the Editor' could stimulate instant gratification if accepted by the editor, and they flouted the Brethren requirements to avoid politics and to be self-effacing, yet fed my need to express bottled-up feelings of rebellious experimentation.

David's game was to get the letters editor of *The Age* newspaper to accept as many letters as possible in one prescribed week of five weekday issues, written by us from false addresses and under pseudonyms. We made it a rule to only write one letter per weekday. David was the winner, with three published, followed by me with two in one week. The letters all dealt with current events and political issues; we expressed fictitious and far-out points of view in order to capture the attention of the editor – rather like shock jocks do on radio. One missive by me dealt with teenage moral standards and another with commercialisation of football. Because we adopted a cover, Brethren could not track us down, and I was stimulated with a shudder of skullduggery, similar to that impetuous instant of showing off at school. I dared to confide my clever ruse only to close friends at high school; there were few of them.

I did not have many close friends at school because we were encouraged to socialise with Brethren children primarily, however boring they might be. My memories of Brethren teenage friends are sparse. I shared bike-riding and a tree house with Gordon Stephens in Surrey Hills, who was brash and handsome. He had an endless supply of quality chocolates, because he worked after school in a chocolate factory. He got his way.

Meetings were the reason for visiting Stawell, where I was attracted to Ronny Barker (of my age). His appearance amused me; he looked as though he was dressed awkwardly in a diving bell, swimming in an oversized suit which was probably handed down from one of his numerous older brothers. Extremely dirty glasses were his goggles. He moved sinuously as though he was submerged under water. His laid-back attitude to most things indicated a distinct lack of verve.

After prolonged meetings, his older brothers drove out of Stawell at dusk in their ute to shoot rabbits with spotlights and .22 rifles, and I was mad keen to join them. Their long-suffering mother pleaded with them to eat dinner before they left. My older brothers went, but even if I had been allowed to chase rabbits with them, which I was not, I doubt that Ronny would have been able to spot the prey because of his thick and grimy lenses in his glasses. Instead of potshots with bullets, Ronny and I would fill in time by walking together along gravel roads in Stawell at night, chucking smooth rocks aimlessly – we called them 'yonnies'. Our excitement consisted of making as many iron roofs to rattle as we could in the dark. I reached the limits of Brethren entertainment.

Sex chat

When they stayed for holidays, especially if Brethren boys had sisters, my brother Peter and I lay awake in bed listening excitedly to gossip about (among other topics) female sexual development. This scuttlebutt was exceptionally exciting. Sexual knowledge was never imparted by adults; we never had sleepovers with non-Brethren. I had no older sisters, and did not know at the time that the Brethren girl gossip was mostly quite incorrect. Thus Ken Clarke – aged about fourteen – informed Peter and me, reclining in our flannel pyjamas in our bunk beds, that his sisters developed a red lump in the centre of their sternums at pubescence. I impulsively checked my own sternum. Then mixed-up Peter Unwin – with four younger sisters and many breeding animals on his Scottsdale farm – described the process of reproduction in a way that completely confused me. What bit went where and when? I was utterly befuddled.

My internal chemistry was in flux. From a distance, I admired Heather, a Brethren teenager whom I watched leaving the school gate at Canterbury Girls' High School often in 1960. I arrived there breathless on my bike just as her classes ended. My own classes finished fifteen minutes earlier than hers. She was a rosy-cheeked girl, with dark plaits and well-developed physique, as beautiful as Venus in my eyes. I could not bring myself to speak to her; I simply did not know how to say that I liked her. The chasms between chemical yearning, religious reticence and meaningful conversation were too vast for me to bridge. Instead, I never got beyond melting into a red-hot blush, then riding home in the breeze to cool down.

All things considered, sharing misleading knowledge and confronting nerves were possibly better than finding out about human bodies from underhand means. An offensive man named Higgins owned a shoe repair business in Ocean Grove, then a sleepy town where my family holidayed regularly from 1950 onwards. Higgins was the closest resemblance in a human being I have ever seen to the Michelin tyre man – an expanding pile of pumped-up tyres. He wore heavy glasses, in black frames, that just managed to balance on the tip of his fat red nose, and his bulbous hands were permanently blackened with shoe polish and glue. He grunted.

Once, Mother visited his small shop at the front of his tiny house, and declared him a character. Little did she know. On every other visit, he compulsively showed Peter and me (and presumably other boys) indecent rubber figurines that he kept hidden beneath his grubby counter. I can still see the smirk on his face as he slowly lifted the figurines out, in order to attract attention, and pressed the stomach of a female figurine, for example, so that bulging breasts popped over the top of her red rubber bathing suit. Similarly, he hoarded rubber men who exposed themselves, and dogs that peed. The sly smile on his balloon face caused me to back out of the shop in fright; he was an ogre. As he followed me out backwards, Peter dared to ask how much money Higgins charged for them. I do not remember the exact price, but it was exorbitant.

On my last venture, I took my treasured football to him to mend because the pink bladder was peeping out from holes in the broken leather seams. He sewed them with leather thongs so that the seams stuck out and made the football fly through the air lopsided, as though it had ailerons attached. After that disaster, I never trusted him again; I judged the football destruction as far worse than any frippery with rubber figurines.

In form one at Camberwell High School, I encountered greater embarrassment – live touching at the end of an English class by the teacher, David Collins, a lot more threatening than the ogre. I was innocent and did not associate Collins's touching with sex at the time, but felt invaded nevertheless. In class time, he sent me to the tuck shop (by the swimming pool) to buy him Anticols when he had a bad throat, which seemed to be often, and I was more than happy with this chore in order to escape the tedium of the classroom for a few minutes into the open air. I suspected that the sugar in the throat lozenges was what he craved.

But he craved more than sugar: Collins was loose with his hands, and I avoided him assiduously after he stuck his hand down the back of my summer shorts on one occasion, after he asked me to wait until all the other students had left the classroom. His sly tentacles made me very uncomfortable instinctively. From then on, I took a circular route around him – as far away from his exploring fingers as I could. I expect that his wayward behaviour was never reported, because he went on to be appointed principal of the school from 1977 to 1986.

Perversity and pleasure

Much of the discussion of education and learning in this chapter could be summarised as the results of perverse problems that I encountered in orthodox teaching approaches and systems themselves. Perhaps this contradiction could be observed in the reuse of official Hansards, in the reversal of some applications of Biblical exegesis to expose weaknesses in Brethren doctrines, in adopting dogmatic attitudes towards imponderable suffering in order to win debates, in siding with Aboriginal minorities in their battles against mainstream racism, in supporting ideologies espousing improved egalitarianism, in battling as a novice to try to comprehend the cultural importance of film and theatre, in suffering embarrassment with non-Brethren women, in playing tricks on letters editors of newspapers, or in being frightened off sexual knowledge by adult sexual perverts. Such themes formed part of my story, but not the whole.

Many additional positive processes led to practices that advanced my understanding and know-how. Home culture is a vastly underrated learning resource generally, and its impact on my own learning was enormous. It was the place where I could explore the implications of a discovery, where I could ask dumb questions, where I could explore new impulses. In 1962, for example, from my limited knowledge of science from school, and with the help of an issue of the magazine *Popular Mechanics*, borrowed from my brother Peter, I constructed a functional anemometer, and fixed it to the roof outside my attic window. It cooperated by flying around in the breezes frantically.

Mother was my constant guide, holding me back whilst enabling me to push forwards, and withholding controversial knowledge while allowing my peers to fill essential gaps furtively. My brothers and my teachers helped me to enjoy the pleasures of taking in information, of making a case in an argument, of displaying genuine empathy, of encouraging true scholarship, and of using fiction and face-to-face storytelling to excite and to teach.

Nine

Ruptures

Breakdown

There is nothing more discombobulating than a mental breakdown. It hits its victim smack bang in the solar plexus, the centre of self-esteem – emotionally as well as physically – and it disrupts relationships. In the middle of 1972, at the age of twenty-six, I went into mental and emotional collapse, and, although not fully aware of it at the time, I attribute this to a Brethren upbringing and my subsequent confusion and loss of direction. The powerful feelings of guilt, fear, anxiety and paranoia that I internalised in my years among Brethren up to 1968, and then the disorienting escape into an untried, unfamiliar landscape, left me bereft of the equilibrium and necessary life skills to cope with my new freedoms and responsibilities. I was stuck in a jet-black tunnel, lost and fearful. During the breakdown, my mind raced as fast as if I had to deal with a catastrophic emergency, or run in an Olympic sprint, and I could not calm my brain even at night. I hesitated, floundered and muddled along until the mid-1970s, in what I call my fluky phase, when trial and terror drove my behaviour, sometimes for good, and sometimes around the twist.

How I left Brethren is tied intimately to why I left; the two are inseparable. In this chapter, I describe in an aggregated form the four main reasons why I left Plymouth Brethren, because I do not want to repeat the many details that have already been mentioned. The methods with which I arranged my flight from Brethren required me to identify means of escape, then maximise the benefits from them. Some presented themselves as surprise opportunities, others had to be mulled over and moulded for use.

The obvious reason for leaving was the emotional impact of Brethren on me, resulting in a breakdown. The second consisted of the internal conflicts and inconsistencies in Brethren philosophies and behaviours. The third reason for leaving was the awful effects of their insistence on the evil doctrine of Separation, and the final bundle of reasons was the multiple attractions afforded by the World beyond Brethren. The fragments of the jigsaw of my impending freedom were scattered across the table of life in my twenties.

Shelter in Ormond College

A brief summary of some of my activities from 1968 to 1975 (the fluky phase) helps to explain my collapse. My permanent exit from home heralded my first roll of the dice, when I chose to spend the year of 1969 in Ormond College at the University of Melbourne, in order to find my feet, test the waters and make new worldly-wise friends and acquaintances. Supported by a bursary, it was an absolutely liberating and stimulating experiment – but I was in a sheltered environment where pre-existing structures cosseted me.

In college, I was able to try out choir, act in the college play, learn billiards, ride a motorbike, hold parties until all hours, drink too much alcohol, play soccer and poker (I performed poorly in both), and chat with others at any hour – by an open fire in winter. I did not have to think about shopping, cooking or cleaning. College was a pleasant mix of light-hearted exploration of other people's natures and serious learning.

Around midwinter, the college performed *Ubu Roi (King Ubu)* as its annual play in the Union Theatre. It was raucous and bizarre. The actor and director Graeme Blundell – later to achieve fame in theatre and film – encouraged us as volunteer actors to devote our pent-up energies to improvisation in rehearsal and on stage. As well as encouraging exploration of the physique, this style allowed me to disguise my awkwardness in the limelight. I had the role of a palace guard, called a Palotin. I mumbled too much and got tangled up in other actors rushing around the stage. Improvisation lent itself to bouts of mayhem.

The play's characters and plot by Alfred Jarry perfectly suited my chaotic frame of mind. Although written in 1896, the script was relevant to the 1960s in that it was anarchically absurd, politically revolutionary, and appropriately scatological. I was very willing to cock a snoot at any authority, especially established religion, and was not surprised to learn that the play caused riots when it premiered in Paris. In Melbourne, the rehearsals and performances amused us as college actors much more than they could possibly have amused an audience. I had lots of riotous fun, but quickly learnt that I would not make the grade as an actor in an absurdist play or any other. I did not know enough about character.

Eating dinner in the dusky Ormond Hall with a hundred and fifty others was just as cordial, but much more decorous. At the start of a meal, Grace was said together in Latin (*Benedictus, Benedicat...*). At the end, we often ate a dessert known as sinker (heavy fruit pudding with custard). Food was served and cleared away by maids, who mostly were impecunious female students trying to pay their way through their studies. Then after dinner we triggled, that is, strolled around the block in academic gowns, chatting about our day with each other, ignoring derisive shouts from cars revving past in Royal Parade. Being in company made me feel that I was not alone in looking odd. I so desperately needed to belong.

Biking away

In late 1969, the burden of the future pressed in on me and I felt the need to flee Australia altogether. I was inside a pressure cooker that had to be released before it exploded uncontrollably. Travel had always rewarded me as a means of escape. Although I finished my Arts (Hons) degree in 1968, my parents were upset that I abandoned my law degree altogether at the end of 1969, after my social year in Ormond. Connecting with the World was more urgent for me than completing Law.

'I want to travel. I have an urge,' I told my brother. By moving on, I avoided hard decisions.

'But you've co-signed a lease on this terrace house with me,' he protested.

It was two storeys of a renovation in Drummond Street in North Carlton.

'Is it possible to wriggle out of the lease?' I begged.

David had just moved from Canberra to take up a lectureship at the new La Trobe University, and we rented together. He had left his wife and children. I was restless and rudderless, searching desperately.

After my law exams in November, I spent too much time on a mattress near the bay windows, which opened onto a glorious balcony decorated with cast-iron lace. I was devouring a book by Irish travel writer Dervla Murphy (*Full tilt: Ireland to India with a bicycle*). Murphy rode a bike overland on her own from Dublin to Delhi.

'How exciting would it be to ride a bike from Sri Lanka to London?' I pleaded with David. To show that I could be both exotic and bohemian at the same time, I lit up a Sobranie Black Russian cigarette.

'What about the cost?' David pointed out. He could have pointed to the cost of the cigarettes too.

'I could travel cheaply and eat locally,' I replied.

I was convinced of the thrill of such a pilgrimage well before devoting any real thought to the expense, and I sought no advice from an experienced bike rider about the road conditions on the long trip. I felt invincible, urgently needing to distance myself from my past. I was beginning to wonder whether I relied too heavily for inspiration on books – they had been another escape hatch for a long time – but they were not reality.

I found a like-minded companion to join me, and soon on board a ship, the *Chusan*, we lived a week in luxurious conditions, scoffing Roquefort dressing with our salads at mealtimes, crossing tropical waters in the Arafura Sea. I was mesmerised by the flying fish skimming the surface of the ocean like thin silver rockets. Several other young passengers – including a film-maker and fashion models – were taking flight on the grand tour to London to seek their fortunes.

As I lay on the top bunk in our little cabin below decks, calmed by the vibrations of the ship's engine, my thinking was far removed from the here and now. I stretched out to absorb *Thus Spake Zarathustra*, wherein Nietzsche presented a mystical representation of the meaninglessness of human reliance on the supernatural and emphasised the power of free thought to replace it. I was striving for self-direction and the book confirmed my understanding of the dead-end beliefs of Brethren. But what did it recommend in their place? My choice of reading matter indicated my state of mind well – I was not relaxed. I could have read *My family and other animals* or *Picnic at Hanging Rock* or another book made for unwinding.

With little practical thought, in Singapore we bought two sturdy Chinese bikes, and started riding north from Colombo with our cumbersome backpacks. Murphy, the inspiration for this trek, rode in the opposite direction from us. Her appeal to me lay in her determination to experience exotic places through a local community lens, without expensive Western accommodation or fancy foods. My fanciful dreams of imitating her ideals proved fatefully unrealistic.

We rode hundreds of humid kilometres in very high temperatures, slept on floors of wood and concrete and on the deck of a ferry, and fought off bed bugs and dysentery. But still we could not equal Murphy's resilience, or her gritty chutzpah, or her brash reliance on local hospitality. She was unique, fearless as an elephant, strong as an ox. She despised foreigners who

> always hold…aloof from the [local] people – not through hostility or superiority but through a strange unawareness of [their] own identity.

We were definitely more aware of our own cultural baggage than her stereotype, although in the poorest villages, we were repeatedly harangued by the new stereotype of 'Hippies, Hippies' – whose reputation had obviously preceded us.

Generally locals along the roadside in Sri Lanka were welcoming. Near Nalanda I laid a dropsheet on the ground for a rest in the middle of the day.

'Where are you going?' I had been asked a thousand times.

'To India, I replied.

'Yes, but where after that?'

'Oh, to Europe.'

'What is your country?' The enquirer rolled the name 'Australia' over and over several times, syllable by syllable, trying to understand where it was. To relieve his puzzlement, I decided to say that we were English.

'Are these bikes English?'

'No, they're Chinese.'

Another spanner in the works – very puzzled examination of the bikes ensued.

'How much did they cost?' was to be expected, a question asked shamelessly about any foreign object.

I roughly converted Singapore dollars to Ceylonese rupees – essentially a rapid calculation.

'Why do you ride by bicycle?' To the enquirer, a Westerner who could afford a bike could certainly afford a bus fare. 'It is easier to ride by bus.' From a purely economic perspective, his central proposition could not be denied.

I was rescued from the impeccable interrogation by a girl aged about ten, with thick kohl plastered around her dark eyes, who handed me an unfamiliar green nut, and showed me how to open it with her teeth. Fortunately, it was not a narcotic. My efforts to chew the woody seeds from inside, and not to grimace at the sour taste, caused gleeful giggles among her gaggle of friends who surrounded me for a ringside view.

Bike-riding (with loads) was dangerous and utterly debilitating the further that we rode. Our knees suffered from weeks of pedalling and we had swollen arms and cheeks from the blazing sun. There were no bike helmets or bottled water in those days. We relied on fizzy soft drinks and mountain streams when available for drinking. My diary records that on arrival at one Government Guest House – the best cheap accommodation – I drank nine litres of water from a gigantic ceramic urn in the hallway. This ingenious device – made by Doulton in England – kept the water cool by slight evaporation through the clay walls and filtered it through charcoal at its base.

A roaming sacred cow or straddled donkey was no hazard, nor bullock carts, water buffalo, wandering elephants, stray dogs, fluffy chickens, or naked toddlers defecating by the roadside. However, battling loaded lorries that resembled Disneyland on wheels, with their lurid decorations and piles of precarious freight, belching exhausts of noxious black, were asphyxiating to the riders in their wake. Normally, more passengers perched on top of the cargo than fitted inside those big lorry cabins. Roads were commonly narrow and potholed, and dreadfully hazardous in the dark; we often rode in the very early dawn or after dusk to avoid the heat. En route to Talaimannar in the north of Sri Lanka, the tracks were sandier and more slippery than when I had crossed the sandy Nullarbor Plain in a van, two years before. Slewing sideways required nimble footwork to prevent toppling.

In India, mobs overwhelmed as we cycled. They jeered and cheered, shouted and touted, pushed and pummelled, as we struggled to break through human barriers. So we sold the bikes. In Delhi, we boarded an old bus parked in Connaught Place – owned by two brothers from Lancaster (surnamed Baynham), who claimed to be mechanics and who promised to take us to London for a fare which we paid upfront in full. The Baynhams seemed sincere. But they were naïve.

The twisting road up the stony Khyber Pass wrapped snugly around the gullies and ridges, no safety fence preventing a tumble over the cliffs. Near the top, the bus steamed badly from the radiator, like a steam engine, and it was necessary to stop to find running water to refill it. And so our problems began.

No border post existed at the peak, where the yellow bus was stopped by hirsute tribesmen with decorated rifles and churras (local daggers). At that point, an Australian teacher travelling with us, named Franko, jumped off the bus and became embroiled in a very animated argument in Urdu or Arabic with the armed men. Franko was slight in build and sly in character. From body language, it was clear that the hostile horde did not want to allow us to go on. Their shouting at each other was bedlam.

After a tense half hour, watched by anxious passengers through the encrusted windows, our linguist returned to the yellow bus and waved the drivers on in haste, while trying to keep out of sight of the spectators. As we progressed, he told us that the guards wanted money, but he impressed on them that we were all pilgrims with no money, on the hajj bound for Mecca. Most of the twenty passengers were beardless, men wore slouch hats and colourful baseball caps, and women had brief shorts and sleeveless tops – the most unlikely mob of pilgrims ever to enter Afghanistan. In those days, there were few Muslims in Australia, and it proved a miracle that Australia was not well-known in tribal territory.

With the passengers concealing themselves as much as possible, Franko's ruse worked and, once free, the bus picked its way between potholes on the flat plains in larger and yet larger clouds of dust. Steam still poured from the engine under the driver's seat of the Bedford bus. Our mouths were gritty. Near Jalalabad, we bumped past neat villages with the only green vegetation in sight peeping over three-metre-high mud walls. The walled gardens grew limes, tangerines, oranges, grapefruit, lemons, pomegranates and grapes, all sold in the local markets. Against a backdrop of barren snow-capped mountains, some of the most spectacular, desolate landscapes in the world are in Afghanistan, the Hindu Kush mountains, rising to 7,400 metres. Humans look superfluous in the foreground of the peaks.

Near Tehran, our decrepit bus broke down altogether. It would move no further and was impounded by transport authorities because the Baynhams had neglected to insure it. It sparked off Franko's shocking temper. I found it hard to believe that he had really been a teacher in Australia. He yelled at the top of his voice and threatened to cut John Baynham's throat (brandishing his knife) if he did not refund US$100 on the spot. The threat was real, but in fact it was impossible to see any throat beneath John's huge black beard. Metaphorically, Franko obtained his pound of flesh, with the result that none of the rest of the passengers received any compensation at all. We were pathetic, impotent witnesses in the face of the worst in human nature. I pondered on how a teacher like Franko might confront misbehaving kids at school. Did he flash his knife at them often?

While we, with the sad remnant, waited in a cheap hotel for a week in Tehran, hoping for a fix, I suffered a migraine, and the wily brothers from Lancaster disappeared with whatever money was left. The rest of us – including Liz, Bob, Tony, Yvonne and Bill – struggled to find local buses to transport us to Istanbul. We passed through acres of glorious red opium poppies that stretched to the horizon. Afghanistan and Iran supplied most of the world's opium requirements, and about eight per cent of their local populations were fully addicted. In Istanbul, my companion and I gladly escaped onto the famous Orient Express, bound for Victoria Station in Westminster. Although it was a relief to arrive after seven long weeks since Colombo, I made it to London with only $50 in my wallet. Fortunately at that time, temporary jobs were very easy to come by in western Europe.

Part-time solutions

In Holland, I found paid work immediately. I stayed in a house in Gouda, right on the edge of a pretty, slow-flowing canal, called Karnemelksloot, complete with cute ducklings and decorated drawbridges. In the murky water of the canal, I noticed dumped bikes peeping, just as much an eyesore as shopping trolleys are today. I felt a pang of nostalgia for the abandoned bikes in Delhi.

A temporary job picking almost-ripe tomatoes inside snaking greenhouses near Gouda was on offer. It required a four a.m. start each day with a sleepy ride on a borrowed bike along dykes in the foggy gloom.

At the end of a nine-hour shift, the sun was up at full height. I drank deeply and was covered in verdant green inside my nostrils and ears, on eyebrows and beard. Green phlegm from the tomato plants filled my mouth and green covered my clothes. At the end of work shifts, I resembled a green praying mantis pedalling back to town. The green only washed off after several ablutions with copious soaping.

Enjoyable part-time manual labour aplenty was obtained easily on return to London – packing semi-trailers in a warehouse all night so that they could deliver goods to supermarkets in the morning; painting picture frames for the National Portrait Gallery in Charing Cross; shifting furniture down three storeys of posh Mayfair houses to double-parked removal trucks below. I transported 120 bottles of wine from the cellar. More exhausting was a job beside the Thames, at the Chelsea Flour Mills, where I lugged bags of flour weighing thirty-two kilos each from lorries into storage sheds for nine hours straight. The pay was 7/6d per hour, which would buy one London pub meal today.

Professional jobs were harder to come by. While in London, I tried unsuccessfully for the Australian diplomatic corps, being rejected (I suspected) because I was totally unaccustomed to 'doing small talk' at a cocktail party for applicants and local diplomats, which was set up in Australia House on the Strand.

And so I returned to Melbourne by plane to try to find secure paid employment for the first time. Although still in my fluky phase on return to Australia, I obtained a scholarship to research for my Master of Arts degree, but the 'income' was dismal. In my thesis, I wrote about the efforts of Prime Minister Billy Hughes to conscript Australian men into the overseas expeditionary forces in 1916. He failed to gain sufficient supporting votes in two plebiscites.

In Australia, by 1972 contemporary politics were changing with a dynamic new Labor leader in the person of Gough Whitlam, about to become prime minister, who opposed conscription for service in Vietnam himself. My political antennae were sensitised. For the first time on (black-and-white) television, I was able to watch policy speeches by political leaders. Gough Whitlam was a master performer, his voice full of authority and wit. In Victoria, Peter Ross-Edwards, leader of the Country Party, had greater difficulty. He found it hard to pronounce any words; at school he had been persecuted for a speech impediment. I collapsed in hysterical laughter when at election time, he announced on television that 'I promise to improve all your wives at the forthcoming erections.' I could hardly believe my ears. Our lives were definitely improved by those elections.

I supplemented the MA scholarship with other Melbourne jobs, while always feeling unsettled and impermanent. Exam invigilation of tertiary students at the Exhibition Buildings at the end of the year was a doddle, and well-paid. I remember one crazy examinee, Caz Smith, mounting a protest against all exams one afternoon, in the vast mock-Renaissance hall. Right in the middle of long rows of thousands of students, she stood up and undressed completely, which was easy because she loved kaftans. She was no Venus de Milo. She climbed majestically onto her own desk in the nude, shouting 'Down with exams', 'Exams are a health hazard', 'Exams are unfair'. Her voice was strident. I hesitated to intervene, because I knew of her oddness from encounters in Ormond College, and it took a couple of minutes before a female invigilator was able to find a blanket, rush at Caz, forcibly wrap her up and escort her to the toilets. Since that disruptive protest, I have not set eyes on her – not any part of her!

Work experiments

My next job was teaching at Altona North High School. There the branch of the teachers' union was extremely aggressive towards graduates who had no Diploma of Education, which I had not acquired. Apart from the head-in-the-clouds principal who was close to retirement, and a young French teacher who was strongly opposed to trade unions, I had no allies whatsoever, only sour faces. I felt isolated and victimised in the corridors, and even when just trying to supervise soccer outdoors on Wednesday afternoons, I felt as offside as the student players who attempted goals by evading strict enforcement of the rules. After six weeks, I abandoned trying to teach French to obstinate twelve-year-olds, and stumbling around the pitted soccer pitch.

With my new wife, I had a baby son. Though full of doubt and worry about the politics of my next attempt at work, I was desperate enough for income and tenure to join the Australian Security and Intelligence Organisation (ASIO) in Saint Kilda Road – late in 1971 – soon after our chubby baby arrived. The decision was more than fluky – it was bound to fail. The enticements of the job lay in the promises of interesting 'research' and a high salary – higher than any other available. I knew that I was good at research, but little else. I did not anticipate the paranoid work culture, the need for scrupulous secrecy about all my work activities, inside and outside ASIO, and the ultra-suspicious attitude of old hands in the spy agency, many of whom had worked there since their grounding in intelligence in World War II. I never encountered a workplace that was so silent. The only sound that I can describe was the faint buzzing of the harsh fluorescent tubes on the office ceiling. No casual office chit-chat disturbed the buzz. If asked about my new job, I was told to say that I worked for the Attorney-General's Department, which was strictly true – if misleading and uninformative.

What finally caused my departure after the standard trial period of six weeks was the monotony and shallowness of the research. I was required to spend all day scanning the daily newspapers and magazines looking for articles or cartoons that might show any influence of the Australian Communist Party. They were few and far between: how a cartoon would show Communist influence, I could not fathom. Bruce Petty and fellow cartoonists aimed to satirise and amuse, not indoctrinate. Should I be searching in cartoons for covert hammers and sickles in bushes that the artist might hide? The instructions certainly highlighted the absurdity of the bias of the work objectives. Every late afternoon when knocking off, all three of us in the office – with the solemnest of faces – locked our precious papers into our own drawer of a filing cabinet, as though they were gold ingots at Fort Knox. For an unknown reason I was required to lock first. I tried to bulk mine out to make my finds look as impressive as possible, but they never were.

On the face of it, the three of us were the desk Communist-watchers, processing intelligence from public sources. We met with my boss devotedly on Monday mornings in a locked office next to ours with soundproof doors, to report our findings. How he came to look nuggety and weather-beaten, I could not say; nothing personal was ever shared between staff. Spies are worse than engineers at socialising. Hesitantly, I confessed to my meagre discoveries and, smiling, my elfin boss asked me to read two booklets – *Communist Training and Indoctrination* and *Long-range Trends on the World Political Scene* – published by the CIA in the USA, which I still have. Whether they were intended as encouragement for my deficiencies, or essential information, I shall never know; in either case, they did not work. They made no mention of cartoons. Although I had read Karl Marx's *Capital* and *The Communist Manifesto* long before, the booklets adopted the naïve angle of informing me that

> Bolshevik thought and action…is not a spontaneous phenomenon; but the result of unrelenting indoctrination… The Communist [believes that he] possesses the only true theory of society and of the laws governing its transformation… Since there is no God, there are no absolute values.

At that point in my searching, I had absorbed enough dogma to last several lifetimes – I had no desire for any ideological publications whatsoever, nor of any further involvement with indoctrination in any shape or form. After my standardised span of testing my tolerance for a job (six weeks), I announced one morning in the office that I wanted to leave ASIO. I have never been removed from any organisation or event so fast in my life. It was as though I suddenly manifested threatening symptoms of the bubonic plague. The return of my security tag was required within a few seconds of my departing comments, and I was escorted instantly out the front door into the early morning mist.

But I was delighted that I was still paid for that 'day' of duty, never expecting the gold watch. My ejection had been thoroughly rehearsed by ASIO operatives: no exit interview or debriefing was ever contemplated. I was shut out by a wall of total rejection – rather akin to Exclusive Brethren's walls of silence for outcasts. Later, I saw one of the men from my ASIO office – with his stubby nose – at a trash and treasure Market in Camberwell. He ignored me assiduously. His tense wife, who was the officious ASIO librarian, never admitted where she worked when she was at professional librarianship meetings, which I also attended later. When I recently requested my 'work' record from the Commonwealth Archives, none existed.

It concerned me deeply – especially in view of my growing family – that the number of my job failures was mounting up. So I was relieved to be rescued by a welcome encounter with the delightful Margery Ramsay, deputy state librarian, then aged forty-eight, who visited universities looking for new recruits. At a friendly meeting at the Careers and Appointments office at the University of Melbourne, she had a broad smile, intelligent conversation, and listened attentively to my personal expectations. Foam formed in the corners of her lips as she spoke.

'You are finishing your Master's research?' asked Ms Ramsay.

'I hope to soon,' I replied.

'Have you researched in the State Library before?' wiping her lip, removing some lipstick as well as foam.

'I've spent hours reading old newspapers and conscription leaflets in the Merrifield Collection there.'

'Is it a good collection?'

'Amazing. The library must have been very open-minded in keeping political ephemera from so long ago.'

'We help many researchers in history – which is my own background too. The number of our patrons is growing rapidly all the time. The recent popularity of local and family history has increased enormously.'

'Can I ask some questions about tenure?'

'Normal public service conditions apply.'

I was relieved that we quickly proceeded to discuss the formalities, which assumed great importance to me because job satisfaction had continued to slip through my hands.

I was not ambitious, just seeking to fluke a fulfilling job, and the attraction of belonging to a group of research librarians with diverse interests was strong. The State Library of Victoria found funds for many new staff in 1972, so I joined on 4 January, along with eight other novices. In an encouraging spirit of collegiality, we all underwent in-house training together, and were given time off to enrol in a course in librarianship at the Royal Melbourne Institute of Technology (RMIT), situated conveniently across the road and the first of its kind at an Australian tertiary institution. Although expecting a far higher standard of teaching in a postgraduate degree than that offered by RMIT, we felt a valued part of the inevitable professionalisation and expansion of librarianship in Australia at that time. Sadly, funding of libraries always lagged behind professional advocacy. Librarianship never had high status.

I had the pleasure of learning an enormous amount about the sources for and application of knowledge about Australia, from Patricia Reynolds, the first La Trobe librarian. As the well-educated daughter of a Melbourne barrister and politician, she had studied history and literature herself. Despite her pompous façade, which many found off-putting, she was a pioneer in communicating the value of her services in Australian history and literature effectively to a broad public, liaising with influential researchers, ferreting out obscure sources of facts and opinions, managing to solicit invaluable historical texts and artefacts from potential donors, all the while overseeing bright-eyed new university graduates who had strongly divergent independent convictions. I do not recall meeting another person who was more effective at networking strategically.

I remember helping Pat Reynolds find copies of the original Batman Deed to give free to Burnum Burnum, a very handsome Aboriginal agitator, when he visited the Library. She had a strong moral compass, comparable to Burnum Burnum's. He had arranged for the return of Truganini's remains from the Hobart Museum to her people for burial.

In 1835, the Batman Deed 'ceded' the land of the local Aborigines, who supposedly 'sold' 500,000 acres of the Melbourne area to the white invader – a despicable settler from Van Diemen's Land, John Batman. He had massacred Tasmanian Aborigines before he arrived, and died four years afterwards of syphilis.

The humanity of Pat Reynolds was well demonstrated when I brought my baby boy to meet her in her office. She held him to her shoulder, and he took a liking to one of her diamond earrings, popped it off her ear and dropped it cleanly down her cleavage before any of us had taken notice of his swift movements. Only after we left in haste could she retrieve the lost treasure.

The library research was stimulating and the visitors entertaining. One Nancye Perry, an entomologist, insisted on the importance of me remembering the 'e' at the end of 'Nancye'. Try as I might, I failed to see how it affected the pronunciation of her name in any way. Nancye spoke fast in a series of clipped, tense sentences. She was intent on making you listen to her. She related a wartime yarn about dating a Plymouth Brother from the British navy in Sydney in 1945:

> He took me out to dinner one night. At…a restaurant in Kings Cross…he ordered a bottle of wine… When we'd finished our dinner, they charged him a [second time] for the wine. He and I made a terrible fuss about it…

I very much doubt that an alcohol-shy Plymouth Brother would have ordered wine. In any case, it seemed an utterly unremarkable event – but was imparted with pomp nevertheless.

In 1951, she was relieved to find her first job as entomologist and in a team to help find the cause of Murray Valley encephalitis (a particular mosquito). She invited me to her home for a wineless dinner. I would have been very grateful for a little moisture to help to wash down the fried Spam which was served as the main course of the meal. She showed me her tiny old snapshots of the Murray River work, for donation to the library. Later, she wrote her own obituary for posthumous publication in newspapers, emphasising that she was 'highly skilled' in puppy obedience training. To the very end, she was dying for recognition and renown.

Another notable character was a co-editor of *The Guinness Book of Records* (Ross McWhirter), in search of confirmation of the rumour that the tallest tree in the world was in Victoria. Pat Reynolds assigned me the task of finding out. Ross was urbane and imposing, but was mown down by bullets a few months after returning to England by a group from the Provisional Irish Republican Army (IRA). He had been a Conservative politician and openly advocated more British controls over the Irish.

I was delighted that, for several decades, results of my research about mountain ash were printed up in editions of the *Book of Records* as a world record, in spite of the slaughter of the editor. In my investigation of tall trees, after eliminating other states, I searched many Victorian forestry reports, narrowing the probable location to the Healesville area near Watts River. Many government reports about forests in the nineteenth century had been published. In colonial times, the tallest known mountain ash fell down in 1872 and measured a length of 152 metres. Since then, widespread logging rarely allows other trees to grow beyond a hundred metres, and so many potential tall trees are still not up to record height. Californian redwoods are in constant competition.

Fiction in the making

The combination of the onerous baggage of childhood traumas, coming to terms with a new marriage, caring about a new baby son, and a new job, took their toll around 1972. As my firstborn grew in his second year, and I settled into regular work as librarian, I found a cooperative childcare centre in North Carlton where the toddler stayed during the day for a few hours. In keeping with the spirit of alternative ideals of the time, a system was set up whereby parents 'paid' other parents in the group by serving as carers themselves for an equivalent length of time, on a rotating roster, without the exchange of any money, or supervision. The agreement was entirely oral. About fifteen children were involved and none of the parents had childcare qualifications, but we believed that we had struck on an original community-driven enterprise.

The unauthorised crèche filled most of the lower level of a two-storey terrace house in North Carlton, owned by a wealthy friend of the author Helen Garner, whose only daughter, Alice, a little older than my son, also enjoyed the day care. On visits to the crèche, I could not avoid noting the object of main romantic interest in Helen's first novel, *Monkey Grip* (1977). Javo spent his days snoring through his heroin fantasies in a bedroom near the front entrance of the shared house. In the novel, he drifted in and out of a relationship with the main female character (Nora), and stole from housemates to support his habit. It was strange to have one foot in a counter-cultural novel and to speculate about whether other house occupants were part of the narrative.

A little of the mystery faded when parents were invited to a meditation evening at the house, in order to meet other parents in a mood of genial sharing. It was kooky. On the appointed night, we squatted in the gloom of candles on the ground floor in a circle, clinging onto the back of a random neighbour with our knees, while the group slid around and around on bums to the elusive rhythm of Indian sitar music, inhaling sweet incense and sharing marijuana joints. Not long afterwards, when I went to collect my son from childcare one afternoon, I searched and searched but there were no adults to be found anywhere in the house or garden. Although the little ones were playing happily without supervision in a sandpit, the system seemed to lack basic protection.

There is nothing that I can find in Helen Garner's writings about the crèche. But Plymouth Brethren do crop up. Helen deduced that her Brethren ancestry caused restrictions on her emotional freedom.

She wrote that members of her family were not able to express endearments to one another openly, because her great-grandfather was a dour Plymouth Brother named Jabez Gadsden, who began a packaging dynasty in Melbourne, later co-managed by his grandson, Allen Gadsden, mentioned below as a hard-nosed Exclusive Brother in the 1960s. Helen's mother was specified as a beneficiary of Jabez's immense wealth in his will (1936). Helen asserts that

> endearments were never used in our family [because of] Plymouth Brethren two generations back on our mother's side [and] grim-jawed Mallee stoicism on our father's… It has taken [my family] all our lives to say dear, darling, sweetheart, without irony.

As well as in her many books, Helen explored her family relationships in psychotherapy.

The psyche

Throughout the period from 1968 to 1972, I needed a counselling prop like Helen. A lot of my effort went into job searching, starting a family and testing out a professional role. In my fluky phase, I was driven to explore therapy for myself and the potential of psychiatry. I was still searching for elsewhere. I gave little thought to the costs of trying out transactional analysis, group therapy or private briefings, and expended much money and emotion accessing the best available therapists.

As with the job journey, I sampled here and sampled there, and was convinced that better mental health lay just around the corner, and all that I needed was to learn from books or others. Dr Stanley Gold assisted with *How to bring up your parents*. But I failed to find long-term satisfaction for my muddled brain cells – which confused me at least as much as they must have confused my counsellors.

It is distressing even now to read tortured self-commentary that I wrote in a diary over fifty years ago and have kept. I reached a point where I became so weighed down by my sadder emotions that I could not concentrate on work, study or normal family interactions. I was in the grip of the black dog. The Brethren prophecy must be true, I thought; because I was outcast from their faith, inevitably I had become incapable and hollow. I was an oddity by being in Brethren, and I could not escape being an impotent renegade when out of Brethren.

Unbeknown to me at the time, I was not alone in my suffering of breaking down because of the burdens of Brethren. In Canada, Roy Daniells had collapsed emotionally in 1914 at the age of fifteen. The immediate cause of his pain was the Brethren advocacy that World War I was a premonition of Armageddon – the Biblical fight between good and evil, the catastrophic conflict when all non-Christian humanity is annihilated. As a Brethren child, Roy could not study or keep down a job because of fearful anxiety and depression. His English cousins went to war and returned damaged. Roy's breakdown lasted more than ten years.

As for me, I beat a miserable path to Kahlyn Private Hospital in Caulfield for serious treatment. I signed a form to agree to electro-convulsive therapy (ECT) to break the burden of my grim depression, and endured the first of three shocks without delay on a Monday morning. I well recall the awful lingering smell of the anaesthetic deep in the back of my throat, the straps on the gurney to hold me immobile, the positioning of the electrodes on my temples above my ears, and the terrible headache when I awoke later in a ward on my own. I did not know where I was.

The treatment worked on the principle that the patterns in my brain were deliberately disrupted by the shocks, and (with luck) they would rearrange in more wholesome ways afterwards. Any old habits were electrocuted, giving me the chance to put myself together again in fresh ways. Kahlyn hosted me for three weeks, during which time I thought that the TV in the lounge room was speaking directly to me, with a personal message controlled by an unknown force, and I found it hard to hold a conversation with any of the other mumbling inmates, who seemed far more comatose than me. Physically, I was fine. Emotionally, I was in pieces in a strange netherworld where everything was fluid and unreal; I felt desperately like a robot in need of reassembly.

After hospital, I recuperated for another three weeks in our little rented Carlton cottage of bluestone, getting stronger by the day, regaining my memory, proud to walk my growing boy in the nearby Exhibition Gardens with its ancient elms. Rediscovering all my sensory cues took time.

Then I was welcomed back to the State Library of Victoria to work for several more years. I never met the dangerous deviants that Mother feared in the library and – to my immense relief – after the Kahlyn treatment, a locum psychiatrist assured me that I was not mentally ill, just overanxious. I hardly believed my luck. Because I had worried about insanity for years, and some family members implied that I was off the beam permanently, I was immensely relieved to be assured that my derangement was a temporary aberration. As it proved to be.

I had found a work niche where the most interesting characters were the staff and users in the La Trobe Library section of the State Library. There were odd bods. For several mornings, a woman in a red shower cap positioned herself in the middle of the reading room, never conversing with staff. A retired schoolteacher shuffled in old desert boots and a gaberdine coat, in winter or summer, all the way from Kew, a two-hour walk, checking rubbish bins along the way and collecting leftover food scraps in her capacious bag. The smell was hard to tolerate; the cloakroom attendants found a special smell-proof repository for the bag. She had known better days and Miss Reynolds in her heyday. She shuffled to queue up at the pay window on Thursdays for a pay packet, under the delusion that she belonged to the staff.

The La Trobe Library was a remarkably stimulating meeting place for diverse interests. Many authors and academics sat in quiet corners making notes or writing novels (including Helen Garner), poems, plays and histories. Members of the American Civil War Roundtable of Australia gathered regularly, as did the Playing Card Collectors' Society of Victoria. A group of adoptees met beside the electoral rolls every Tuesday night to whisper noisily about the best ways to search for their real parents in published and archival records. A farmer wandered in with a piece of rusted barbed wire, asking to know about its manufacture. Architectural historians sifted through old drawings and photographs to determine the best ways to resurrect historic monuments. The State Artist searched for any pictures he could find of horse transport in Melbourne to help with a mural that the state government funded him to paint. An old sea pilot (even with a whiff of rum on his breath) spent months and years annotating old photographs of ships with their names – that he knew by heart from his time working on Port Phillip Bay. Keen mechanics came looking for old car manuals and pictures of vintage cars. Eager family historians showed off their collections of postcards in the desperate hope that they could be valued. I was glad to help the niece of Alfred Deakin, Australia's second prime minister, when I enabled her to refute media rumours that he had secretly taken Ned Kelly's scrotum, for use as a purse soon after Ned's execution in 1888. He had not. The library was a cornucopia of shared knowledge; it rescued trees, adoptees and reputations. Any day could spring a surprise enquiry.

In addition to finding obscure and macabre answers, all staff had the task of indexing published information that might be useful to others in future. Predicting usefulness was more of a gamble than an art. Laconically, my friend Chris noted in a subject index of magazine pictures that 'Women' could also be located among images of 'Household Appliances'. Foreseeing the future was hazardous.

Incoherence

The second bundle of my reasons for leaving Brethren related to the internal contradictions and inconsistencies in Brethren philosophies and behaviours. I set myself the impossible task of trying to make sense of illogical beliefs and deviant behaviours. Brethren were slow to change, leaving themselves open to takeover by the dictatorship of edgy Bruce Hales around 1960 to 1962. The sheen of Brylcreem on his flattened black hair matched his slippery, smooth manner.

The arrogance and ruthlessness of his dictatorship was paralleled by the earlier vice-like grip exercised by John Nelson Darby, up until his death in 1882, but no living member of my cult thought back that far. In my day, he was revered as 'beloved JND' without any further qualification, and Bruce Hales became 'the elect vessel'. My family's prevarication about military service, their reliance on non-scientific health remedies, their adherence to irreconcilable world views, and their lack of concern for the internal illogicalities or irrelevance of their narrow methods of biblical interpretation, led me to the inevitable conclusion that their dogma was atrophied, impenetrable and lacking consistency. Few others saw the conundrum in quite the same way.

The vagueness of dogma permeated many aspects of life. The morality of joining a credit union was discussed ad nauseam, as was contributing to superannuation, but doctrine on neither was settled in my time. Taking out life insurance was regarded as a failure of faith in God's personal support – and many an insurance policy had to be cancelled – but accepting a donation from any deceased estate, whether from Brethren or not, was a contradictory act that was strongly encouraged. For my own peace of mind, I felt an obligation to identify what wreckage I needed to leave behind me. I could not fade away silently like my brother Peter, nor play endless games with rules and personalities like brother David. I wanted clear reasons for acting.

Separation

The doctrine of Separation, the third cause of my own split from Brethren, manifested itself much earlier than was ever acknowledged in Brethren hagiographies; the worst of it is assumed to date from around 1960. Looking to the Rapture, depending on biased hagiographies, Brethren had no real knowledge of or interest on their true past.

I found evidence of the sad effects of Separation in handwritten letters from 1840 from Charlotte Cookworthy to her friend and sister-in-law, Fanny Bowker, stored in the Battye Library in Perth. Ample early evidence of disturbing family ruptures existed about adherence to Brethren bigotry, though it has never been publicised. In brief, Charlotte had three children from her first marriage, but the husband died.

She then joined Plymouth Brethren along with Fanny. In 1838, she upset Brethren in Plymouth by leaving them in order to marry John Garrett Bussell, son of an Anglican minister. The Brethren tried to kidnap the three children to keep them in their fold.

With the help of a sympathiser, the children were smuggled onto a boat to Calais, from where (in 1839) Charlotte and John sailed to the Swan River Colony on the *Montreal* as a melded family, along with sixty packages. John was already a veteran pioneer on the white frontier, before his marriage, first migrating to the colonial backblocks from England in 1830, employing Aborigines at his emerging farm on the one hand, slaughtering them on the other. Strangely, wanton murder struggled to exist side by side with goodness and mercy. Within a year of his second arrival, John, with Charlotte and Fanny, organised a massacre, which was dismissed far too glibly afterwards:

> The black men were killed by dozens, and their corpses lined the route of the march of the [white] avengers.

It is disturbing to think what the young children experienced in the wake of the executions. Celebrations of the pioneering families for eventually founding Busselton, in the Margaret River region of Western Australia, were far more magnanimous than the coincidental mentions of clearing out the indigenous locals by mass killings.

In the 1840s in *Father and Son*, comparable consequences of Separation were described, perpetuated in the 1960s with fresh emphasis on irrational new diktats, leaving no room for individual flexibility in belief. Pressing contemporary concerns in the 1960s – such as the spread of information technology, or nuclear war, or feminism – were regarded as works of the Devil. Shutting genocide out of the Brethren mind in the nineteenth century was comparable to pretending that modern change was not worthy of serious attention.

Black-and-white doctrine, ostentatious eccentricity and apartheid-like attitudes were advocated in a series of new edicts which controlled our activities with freshly invented sins. Even though we wore our doctrinal dancing shoes conscientiously, any effort to keep up was devoid of reward because one change was followed within a month by another in 1960.

Facial hair on men was evil. Eating with strangers, even a sandwich, or being in the presence of others who were eating, was evil. Allowing children to play at home with non-Brethren children was evil. Living far away from a Brethren meeting hall was evil. Living in a house which shared a common wall with another non-Brethren household was evil. Keeping pets was evil. Indoor plants and floral arrangements were evil, because tending them took time away from Bible study. Adopting a non-Brethren child was evil. Associating with non-Brethren in any way – even chatting in the street – was evil. Women's slacks were evil and dress hems above the knee were evil. Men wearing shorts was evil.

Remaining a single person was evil; marriage was strongly advised. If a Brother proposed to a Sister, she was bound to marry him, regardless of her feelings. So, in 1927 Horace Blake announced to Grace Benson at the Ealing railway station – on their way to work – that God had told him to marry her. They were both aged thirty, worked in the London Post Office, and attended Brethren Meetings. Their son observed that 'she didn't love Horace, in fact she didn't much like him, and she thought that her well-spoken family would probably not like him much either'. They did not. From then on, she was banned by Brethren from playing her violin – she had been a talented concert performer. In the 1960s, arranging a wedding on any day other than a Tuesday was evil, to keep it from interfering with all other meetings (which did not happen on a Tuesday). Marriages were legalised in a registry office, never in a Brethren hall or church.

Computers were evil, until Hales realised that they were becoming essential for running small businesses, which many of them relied on. Indeed, his own Sydney business sold office equipment, including computers. Not buying from Brethren businesses was evil. The mass media was evil because it misreported Brethren's honourable intent and had no interest in God. Automatic door openers for cars on garages were evil, because they used radio waves. Fax machines were evil. Singing any songs other than hymns was evil. Universities were evil because they encouraged students to think for themselves, promoting 'the mind' over 'the heart'. Supporting relations (such as an elderly parent) who were not Brethren was evil. In the workplace, Brethren could not join any trade union. Jury service was evil because jurors were locked up as a group – whether wicked or not – in a room together. Brethren farmers could not sell their wheat to the Australian Wheat Board, an evil association. Rural Brethren could not join a volunteer fire brigade because it was an evil alliance.

Extrusion

Thus not only did deliberate dysfunction become part of many of the trivialities of daily life, but the accumulative principles of Separation were exploited as a public spectacle and deterrent on a large scale. A typical implementation of Separation was found in my family's exclusion, which I took the trouble to record at the time, sensing it as a turning point.

The meeting hall in Prospect Hill Road, Camberwell, became the amphitheatre for public decapitations by the Exclusive Brethren. I kept detailed notes of the ejection of my family, of the words spoken in the hall, and sent them in letters to my brother David on 11 and 18 February 1962. My family's offence was supporting David on his scholarship trip to Oxford. The main victims lined up for executions were my uncle (Maurice) and aunt (Gertie) and my parents (Rowland and Marion).

The prosecution was led by Allen Gadsden, arrogant co-owner (with his non-Brethren brothers) of the biggest packaging company in Australia. His importance as uncle of Helen Garner has been mentioned. At weekly meetings in Canterbury, Allen would pat me on the head, as if to say 'Just remember who is boss cocky, lad.' Even when I grew tall I never felt comfortable around him. Twenty years hence, his company would be sold for a mere $60,000,000. He was ostentatiously arrogant and aggressive.

Two of his bouncy young acolytes, Ronald Young and Norman Grace, like hyperactive Squealer in George Orwell's *Animal Farm*, were keen to impress anyone who was impressionable. The third, ponderous Eustace A. Kelsey, was like Benjamin the old donkey, hoping to look full of wisdom, but who in actual fact presented as doddery – with one foot in the knackery.

My aunt concealed a little Grundig tape recorder in her handbag to make a recording of the conversation in the hall to check on later. Exclusive Brothers (with microphones) had a habit of lying about what was actually said after the event. (Later, Aunt discovered that the recorder had not turned on.)

The scene was set. My family and others had arrived at the hall. This care meeting was devoted entirely to executions.

My uncle was asked to stand. He rose gingerly to his feet. He had the audacity to open this tense conversation with 'I am concerned that the truth is not being spread about my nephew, David.'

Allen Gadsden crossed his legs fast in the front row and declared quickly, 'We are not concerned with untruthfulness. All we want to know is whether you support David in going to Oxford.'

Maurice: 'Yes.'

Allen had prepared his next move long before. The traditional Brethren practice was to administer the last rites by quotation. He quoted from the Bible to avoid discussion, bringing down the hatchet as fast as possible: '1 Samuel 15:2–3 says, To heed is better than the fat of rams. For rebellion is like the sin of divination.'

I remember wondering how that was supposed to apply to our case exactly.

Undeterred, Allen continued, quoting Mathew 18:17: 'If they still refuse to listen, tell it to the church; and if they refuse to listen even to the church, treat them as you would a pagan or a tax collector.'

My uncle did not resemble a pagan or a tax collector in any way, no matter from which angle you looked at him. He was slightly nondescript, and more than a little browbeaten, standing alone in the tenth row of seats. He took a deep breath before shamelessly exiting the hall, and thus exiting the Exclusive Brethren, with his wife.

Uncle Maurice was a salesman of textiles at work, a devoted husband to his pianist wife, and father to two children (my cousins) who were at home in sleepy Surrey Hills at the time. The Exclusive Brethren dumped them all as a job lot, in bulk, no further questions asked.

Now immediately it was my parents' turn. On that humid night, the heat in the hall generated by power-addled cerebrums was almost palpable. While braced for the end, my father tried hard to turn the tables, wiping his brow with a clean handkerchief. He was instructed to walk to the front row of senior executioners for processing.

Ronald Young puffed out his chest. 'Rowland, have you anything to say by way of repentance?'

Rowland Johanson: 'I repeat that David offered to remain here in Melbourne. I was governed by what the Brethren did by giving David a letter of commendation to go to Oxford.'

Flaunting his prowess, Allen Gadsden was desperate to sidestep my father's points, but tempered his coldness with a simper. 'You can see that the Brethren genuinely love the truth, genuinely love you. Why don't you change your mind and be with the Brethren?'

The appeal to love was hypocritical, blatant manipulation. Allen loved Father as much as a shark loves its prey.

Rowland: 'No.'

Norman Grace wanted to be part of the drama: 'David went against the counsel of the Brethren. He is compromising his position by living in the University at Oxford. Would you counsel David to come home to Melbourne now?'

Rowland: 'No.'

Eustace A. Kelsey chimed in with the official sentence, nebulous rhetorical questions from the Bible, that could be interpreted in any way you chose. Eustace read Amos 3:3–4 aloud in a solemn ramble, 'Can two walk together, except they be agreed? Will a lion roar in the forest, when he has no prey?' Matthew 18:8 followed: 'Therefore if your hand or your foot cause you to fall, cut them off and cast them from you…'

Not pretending to want to fraternise with lions, nor willing to amputate their limbs, Mother and Father stood and hastened from the circus together.

They were followed speedily by Aunt (without a recording), brother Peter and me. We last three were mere extras in the show trial, not asked for our views; we were expelled in absentia soon afterwards.

All the lingo of *Nineteen Eighty-Four* floated through my mind at that moment, if not actually spoken in the rapid glint of the guillotine: Big Brother, cult of personality, doublethink, counter-revolutionary activities, thought crime, obliteration of the self. We had all expected to be thrown out, and I breathed a sigh of relief that it was finally over, although the parental generation seemed surprised and shocked by their maltreatment and dismayed about their future. We all needed a breath of fresh air.

I am sometimes asked: in view of such sad and chaotic beliefs, why did people ever bother to join Plymouth Brethren at all? In my recollection, from about 1960 no one came from outside the breeding flock to taint the Exclusive bloodline. The early nineteenth-century British society was very different.

In Europe, society was still class-bound. Scientific and secular rationales for life on earth hardly existed in the 1840s, and certainly affected very few. *On the origin of species by means of natural selection* was not published until 1859; Friedrich Nietzsche began to publish his anti-religious philosophies in the 1870s; and Marx's *Capital* did not appear in English translation until 1887. Only late in the century were Sigmund Freud's analyses disseminated widely. By then, massive ructions were caused by their fresh world views, especially to theologies.

Up to the 1950s, most people in Australia practised a pretence of faith of some sort, even if they hopped about from local church to local church, as suggested in this memoir. Shopping around among Christians grew more and more acceptable with the growth of consumerism, and of more secular minds, but the enforcement of Separation stymied it totally on the part of Plymouth Brethren. Brethren could only link up with other identical Brethren, and they failed in that objective often.

Self-abnegation and avoidance of ostentation were commonplace. In the early days, wealthy Plymouth Brethren dispensed their largesse in dribs and drabs among the needy faithful, demonstrating that they were better than 'the World'. The poor were expected to feel rich and secure inside themselves in spite of having little or no bling to show. The dazzling aftermath to life – as promised – was as glitzy as any television extravaganza.

Most Brethren were middle-class, many small-business people, contented with the prospect of deferred gratification. In the case of Edward Petter of Barnstaple, Devon, business as a salesman for British biscuits provided opportunities to promote Brethren faith as he travelled around the globe. Commerce and worship were reciprocal, feeding off each other. In January 1891 from Cape Town, he wrote home,

> God had been good indeed in connection with the business in South Africa – merchants here are well pleased with their goods and several have sent further indents already… I have prayed continually that God would graciously give the goods favour with the merchants and with the people, and He has done both and the labour has not been in vain.

God and goods were inseparable for many Brethren. Once established in functional numbers by missionaries and merchants in the nineteenth century, bringing waves of new conversions, Brethren community breeding and family tradition took over around the start of the twentieth century – when my ancestors became hooked. The longer that converts stayed in the cult, the more they treasured their supportive communities, because they were guaranteed a social life, a job, spouse, extended family and later, in the 1960s, a house. There was nothing to lose but free choices.

Clear-cut rules demarcated the self-righteous and dependent souls, cunningly enforced by surveillance. Separation overwhelmed all other beliefs and practices, locking followers into a virtual world, with no pleasures, but with the promise of a fantastic future beyond. God was already waiting for them in heaven, and life was nothing more than a monotonous, laborious struggle to scramble there – life was never meant to be a search, a mystery, a game, a discovery, a liberation path, and certainly never a gamble.

Ten

Mould-breaking

Defiance

A game of cricket by twelve-year-olds in 1958 at Surrey Hills Primary School may seem forgettable, but it was the location for one of my bold blows against Brethren oppression. Smashing a cricket ball replaced my submissiveness on that day. I was all brawn and no finesse. The school cricket team needed an extra member to play in a scheduled competition in Surrey Hills, and my teacher asked me to substitute hurriedly. I had never played in a team before, nor had training, but I regularly played vigorous hit and miss in the schoolyard and in the street next to home.

Not telling my parents, I walked to Surrey Hills with other team members from my school on a Wednesday afternoon to launch my sporting career. I sat patiently in the shade on a bench for much of the afternoon, because the selected experts on my side had the right to bat first, reinforcing their prowess, and when we were ten runs short of a victory, and time was running out, my teacher finally chose me to go in to bat. He told me to 'just smash it'. I needed no encouragement.

I had a reputation for whacking the ball long distances as though playing baseball. The repetitive *thwack thwack thwack* on my bat took care of the deficit of runs. Within a few minutes, I managed to lift sufficient fours over the boundary to exceed the Surrey Hills total score, making my team clear winners. I remember being congratulated by my teacher's smiles and peers whooping, and feeling on top of the world; I was a saviour and (b)elated champion.

Back at school, another sneaky boy who belonged to Plymouth Brethren heard about my victory and told his father of my sin – wickedly playing sport in a team with unbelievers. Behind the scenes, his father told my Father, and I was banned from sinning at sporting competitions thereafter. But they were too late – I had caught the winner bug – and I proceeded to secretly win the triple jump for my school athletics group soon after, telling no family member, followed by a victory in a yo-yo competition, mentioned earlier. I never spoke again to that son of a Brother who dobbed me in. Conforming pressure encouraged kids to turn informer in order to attract adult praise, and enlivened long-term suspicion and bitterness.

Defiance was a dramatic method for resisting the encroachment of Brethren on my emerging arena. Most of this chapter is devoted to summarising how I escaped Brethren. There were four other means in addition to defiance, which I label as pacification, self-help, subversion, and escape by travel. They all help to explain *how* I escaped to my search for elsewhere. I describe each of the five means in the first part of this chapter, giving examples to indicate how they functioned. The bulk of this memoir so far has described what I left behind with Brethren, and focused on *why* I left it.

One additional answer to the how question describes a key event in 1968 in Canberra that sparked my final act of defiance. This is described in the last chapter, which also deals with my welcome discovery of four faithful elixirs that helped me to learn and understand significant means of support for my escape and rebirth.

The narrow-minded Brethren repression of competitive sport was exclusionary, intended to discourage growth of basic social interactions and physical enjoyment. It invited infraction. A black cloud of Brethren duress hung as a punishment over all of my natural impulses. Much of my light-heartedness and vitality was sucked out, as though by a monstrous vacuum cleaner.

The Brethren law against playing with non-Brethren boys was to prevent being tainted by evil. But it became impossible for my parents to enforce once I gained added independence at school. My brother Peter – at the same school – ignored me; I was free to make my own choices much of the time, including at home time, when I found my way from school. Temptation beckoned at the age of seven.

The New Zealand novelist Noel Virtue, trapped in a Brethren family at the same age as me, recounted his own disobedience:

> Despite being told, almost every day, that I must not play with anyone whose parents were not Brethren, as they would lead me into backsliding, I usually managed, with little-boy deceit, to mix with all the sinners after school… What was a boy supposed to do?

For certain, I was not supposed to play with David Manders, who lived at the top of the hill. He befriended me in spite of Mother's warnings against fraternising. His father was a merchant sea captain, rarely at home. David's mother bustled to and fro with portentous determination. I visited their house after school.

David decided that he had outgrown his big teddy bear and he invited me to help him to get rid of it. My own teddy was just a worn-out hand-me-down from brothers, ignored and neglected by me; I was not attached. We stuffed David's big teddy down the bowl of the outside dunny at the back of his house. I pulled the chain multiple times to flush big teddy away. But disaster struck. Teddy stuck fast in the bottom of the toilet bowl. We poked it with a stick, which only made it more secure.

To help solve the unhygienic impasse, in the end David was forced to call in his red-hot mother. She blew her top and sent me home pronto, so that I never had the chance to discover how big teddy finally emerged. I left him in a real jam. Could the toilet be used at all? I still felt bright red in the face from guilt when I reached the bottom of the hill. I was compelled to confess to Mother. David never spoke to me again – I never found out about big teddy's ultimate fate. Our imaginative play was choked off as fast as big teddy's water torture. In my head, the oft-quoted Biblical saying kept swirling around and around, like a whirlpool: '…be sure your sin will find you out' (Numbers 32:23). It was drummed into me time and time again at home, and experiences proved it to be true.

For most of 1956, fresh adventure in the classroom and schoolyard revolved around the Olympic Games in Melbourne. The frantic commotion was inescapable. In our flimsy exercise books, we drew the Olympic rings, the Olympic torch, and the Olympic medals until our coloured Derwent pencils went blunt beneath our chewed fingernails. We recited the Olympic oath.

Television arrived a few days before the games started. In a shop in Maling Road, Canterbury, the window was packed with new black-and-white television sets for sale. I could not help noticing that every afternoon a crowd gathered on the footpath outside the shop to watch Olympic events through the window (without the benefit of sound). While standing secretly in the crowd on the footpath, I witnessed the clash between the Russian and Hungarian water polo teams, where bloodied competitors hobbled from the pool. A mini-war broke out in the very pool where our school swimming sports were held annually. In Europe, Russia had just suppressed a democratic uprising in Hungary with tanks. What a hot conversation topic that water fight became in the schoolyard next day! My excitement was hardly contained.

After school one day, I told Mother that I was going to a shop to buy some sweets. In fact, I planned to watch as much of the Olympics as I could jam into the average time spent on an errand, while gawking from the footpath.

My bike was broken. I borrowed my sister's little purple bike – which was far too small – and set off in haste down the hill in Bryson Street in thongs and shorts. Halfway down, I was travelling too fast. One thong caught on the gravel on the road, my foot was dragged under the pedal, and I flew over the handlebars. I felt dreadfully injured, and still have scars on both elbows to show for it. Blood ran down my arms and legs as I limped home on foot.

I had never felt so deeply guilty. God's vengeance had caused the fall because I was sinning by going to watch television. Clearly it was a very evil attractant with extraordinarily enticing tentacles. I did not see any more Olympics in 1956, but neither did I confess to my enthralling escapades to the television shop. As I nursed my throbbing scars and dragged myself gingerly about the house in my bandages, the thrill of the memory was well worth the suffering.

Reaching the age of twelve marked a turning point in my physical confidence. Before that age, I was defiant in thoughts often, but rarely expressed them in action. As well as the winning streak in my final year competitions at primary school, I went up against my forty-nine-year-old father. Physical punishment by a father was not unusual in most families of my time, but mine was additional to the Brethren burden on my spirit. All the while, Father burst with empathy and overwhelming enthusiasm for needy Brothers and Sisters of an older generation. I feared his mood swings, ever alert to his contradictions.

One more anecdote shows how I confronted his aggression in kind head on. Every year, the fecund apricot tree at the very back of our home garden yielded a crop of delicious squelchy fruit which we as children consumed to our limits – until we were sick. Fights with overripe fruit which had dropped to the ground, were a sticky distraction when adults were out of sight. It was the best tree in the garden for climbing, because its branches were broad enough to squat on, to hide in and to keep watch over the distant house. I could keep an eye on my garden kingdom from my exalted eyrie – at least two metres above the ground! The garden had many happy hideaways where I escaped all scrutiny and control. One place that Brethren expectations never reached was my much-loved back garden. There, I felt untrammelled.

Each autumn after leaf-raking, Father laboriously pruned the ancient apricot tree, as old as Methuselah. After a pruning, Father expected me to help to collect the dropped cuttings for burning in the incinerator. My older brothers would mysteriously disappear at pruning time, but I was slower to wake up than them. The threat was that Father kept a few twigs in a cupboard for use as canes for thrashings. Mother turned a blind eye, Aunt cautioned avoidance. If you have ever handled an apricot twig, you will know how flexible and tough it is. It has small protrusions all along its length. It left too many nasty welts on my gluteus maximus. 'As the twig is bent, so grows the tree' is a very twisted saying.

When I was about ten, Peter and I found the twig hiding place in the cupboard under the stairs, and we grabbed and destroyed all the whips silently. We never saw any more of them after that, and I abandoned pruning. No mention was ever made of them by anyone again, not even by Father. They were wiped from family folklore completely.

But I continued to be belted with a leather strop – as I had since the age of six – for my sporadic sins, such as backchatting Mother or ignoring a command from Father. I took a stance by facing Father's tyranny head on at the age of twelve. I stood patiently waiting for punishment, which always occurred in the little bathroom. Being told to go to the bathroom meant only thing in our household; punishment by whipping was in the offing. But it suddenly dawned on me that it was time to stand up to the tyranny. When he entered, I raised my fists and threatened to punch Father on the nose if he dared to hit me, and he retreated without protest or comment, out of the room, never to harass me again. I was impulsively aggressive as I had never been before, fully intending to act, and was very pleased with my defiance. I told myself that it was time to challenge the oft-quoted furphy, that if a parent 'spared the rod' then a child was spoilt (Proverbs 13:24). Grandfather repeated the saying over and over again within my hearing. Ultimately, my self-talk was more effective than the biblical saying. As with the twigs, the thrashings were never alluded to ever.

Another son of a Plymouth Brother, the Harvard psychiatrist, John Money, wrote of similar thrashings by his father:

> The abusive interrogation and whipping that my father gave me when I was four had the serendipitous effect of…demonstrating the brutality of manhood and the moral self-righteousness of authority… My father died [when I was eight] without my being able to forget or forgive his unfair cruelty.

I have always wanted to confront over-aggressive people throughout my life, and have done so fearlessly, but whether my childhood beltings contributed to that urge, I cannot tell.

Helping

As well as defiance, my second device for resistance involved pacification, whereby I instinctively met an irritant with a special effort to defuse any negative connotations of a potentially volatile situation by offering to help. In spite of frequent whippings, generally I was a willing helper around home, needing recognition, and I volunteered successfully at school for every job as a monitor that was on offer.

For example, I collected wood for the classroom fireplace at primary school. I filled the ceramic ink wells in every wooden desktop twice a week, cleaned the blackboards of dusty chalk, mowed the front lawns of the school with Father's borrowed Victa, and lugged heavy wire crates of glass bottles of milk to classrooms before morning recess, then returned the empties to a shelter shed after children had drunk them all. The escape from classroom routine appealed and I felt responsible. Adults at home and in school seemed to appreciate offers of help, and it tended to impress on them a generous aspect of my nature. For better or for worse, I held the view that I was less likely to get into trouble if I helped. Helping was the means to engage with others without actually mixing with non-Brethren. Helping opened up opportunities.

As well as keeping Mr Baddeley onside in grade four, where I suffered from strappings most, firewood duty led to a stunning surprise. Every day, H.L.R. Baddeley rolled up his white shirt sleeves at the start of class. He wore knitted sleeveless jumpers and brushed his wavy hair back. He meant business; he had been principal in a country school. He spoke with a guttural burr and, as a chain-smoker in class, spat phlegm into the fireplace and threw his finished roll-your-own butts in as well. He may have been brash, but he was not prepared for what I revealed on the woodpile.

At the end of autumn, large trucks dropped split wood into a large shed next to the basketball courts, near fresh-smelling ancient pine trees. On one of my trips to resupply the classroom with fuel, I found Andrew Markus, son of Hungarian refugees, hiding in the woodpile, trying to avoid the cruel and incessant teasing from Anglo kids. I knew him because he lived near my house. He was an outcast, speaking no English, and (worse still) his parents sent him to school in thick leather lederhosen, which only made him more conspicuous. When he saw me, he hid below the pile.

Teachers had no idea that he was holed up in the woodshed. I remember feeling intensely sorry for him, but powerless to do much to help. I told Baddeley about him, but I doubt that he took the truancy news in. Andrew retired recently as Professor of Jewish Civilisation at Monash University. For decades, he researched marginalised social groups, including migrants. He told me that he spent two years at Canterbury State School avoiding contact with any people, mostly behind the woodpile. We were very ignorant of migrant cultures in 1956 – as we were of the taste of spicy pakoras or the sweet-and-bitter of expressos – and no special support was offered them. Eventually one of my kindly teachers, Mrs Le Couteur, then aged sixty-three, who had worked at the school for twenty years, took pity on Andrew and gave him special protection and instruction. I was relieved to see him squatting cosily by the class fire.

As well as uncovering surprises, helping was a means for me to interact with a wide audience on a casual basis, without actually socialising within a tight-knit formal group. Helping bypassed the Brethren rule against close interactions. Helping prised opened doors that would otherwise remain shut, neutralising potential threats. Helping drew attention to me.

But I failed to meet Father's exacting standards, intensely focused on me often. Every Sunday morning, he lined up all of the family leather shoes outdoors on the patio to impress with his devotion to cleaning and polishing. Spick and span was an essential sheen on the Lord's Day. Twice I volunteered to clean the entire collection – of fourteen shoes – only to be scolded at the end for insufficient polishing. In anger, I threw up my hands and ceased to help altogether, and instinctively I decided that chronic self-pity and grumbling was a necessary component of Father's frame of mind. No amount of effort at pacification on my part could change him. In an entry in my diary for 5 July 1965, I noted that Father presented a sermon at a graveside about 'happiness and joy in suffering', a theme which encapsulated many of his warped attitudes.

Self-help

My third device for escape is clearly related to the other devices, and I call it self-help, taking the initiative for pushing beyond constraints on my own. I realised that being noticed as an individual could be a boost for making an escape from drudgery. I learnt to harness emotional pressure to succeed – in Brethren ways and beyond.

Escaping deep boredom motivated my desire to serve a congregation and elicit its peripheral approval. At the start of the three-day meetings in the late 1950s, I managed to see some stardust.

The dull background scene was set by elderly Brothers slowly processing up wooden steps, onto the high stage in the Hawthorn Town Hall. They resembled would-be phantoms clad in black suits and stiff starched shirts, silent and solemn. They did not want to be seen as promoting themselves too brazenly, because ostentatious humility was a Brethren prerequisite for holiness. Partly due to their typical British reticence, and their unhurried manner, leading Brethren from England were assumed to be closer to God than cruder Australian Brothers. Besides, the genesis of Brethren itself enhanced reverence for the home country.

As I watched from my hard bench on the floor of the hall, I recalled only one occasion when Father ventured onstage uninvited, and that was during a visit by the plump octogenarian Percy Lyon from London. Father was an excellent practitioner but not on a par with the grandees of doctrinal orthodoxy, such as Percy, who no doubt used his good looks and charm as an estate agent (before retirement), just as he did during extensive international travel for the promotion of imperial sanctimoniousness. He had no family commitments.

My chance to shine at the age of twelve came at afternoon tea breaks between these drawn-out meetings, when the drone of moralising pieties from Percy paused for refreshments. Tea break was the only chance for a child like me to offer zealous community service. I yearned to show my independence. In a large anteroom to the main hall, I leapt at the opportunity to help to serve drinks and snacks to the motley mass of urban Bible-bashers and travel-weary visitors from the country.

First up, in the kitchen, I indulged in a delicious foretaste of fresh buttered favouries (now known as pikelets), supplied by McAlpin's Flour, and buttered by enslaved Sisters. I stuffed as many as I could fit in my mouth at once, as the singing of the final hymn could be heard fading next door in the main hall.

Then (unable to speak with a bulging mouth of favouries) I filled a huge aluminium teapot, and proceeded to pour boiling hot tea into wobbling china cups, balanced on matching white saucers by knobbly arthritic hands of older Brothers and Sisters, seated expectantly in long rows of creaking bentwood chairs.

'My, you've got lots of cups to fill.'

I nod and chew.

'You are such a good boy to help.'

'Will there be some sugar, do you think?'

I mumble and nod.

'How lovely that you are helping.'

I chew.

'Shall I lean further forwards?' asked an elder, stooping for the ritual pouring. If she stooped much further, I could have poured the tea down her nose.

'No need, thanks.' At last my mouth is freed of masticated favourie.

'I s'pose you'll be back with refills?'

'Oh, certainly,' I promised, although others were serving too.

'What's your name, dear? Your parents must be so proud.'

When my teapot was hot and full, the chances of losing control were great. Others flinched, but not me; I was aroused by the activity after the soporific inaction next door. Hot tea assisted oldies to wash down their anchovy paste sandwiches, or curling Kraft cheese and shredded lettuce sandwiches on white bread. The respite between the sessions next door lasted for half an hour, just enough time for a cuppa and visit to the polished toilets down the corridor. The same strained regimen was repeated on each of the next two days.

Looking beyond hundreds of cups of tea, I was driven at the end of secondary school, by dint of disciplined work, to achieve dux of school in 1964. Self-discipline in study felt virtuous, and I applied myself harder than ever before in that year – and Brethren knew nothing of it. At the end-of-year presentation at Speech Night in the Hawthorn Town Hall – the same hired earlier for meetings – I was determined to enjoy my moment in the spotlight on the stage. In front of eight hundred or more half-applauding students and parents, my chest swelled with pride. I floated on air across the stage – like a throbbing hovercraft – to collect my prize of books. Now I could put to rest the months of anxiety about completing the exams successfully. At the end of school, I had the pleasure of realising how far I had come since those lifeless three-day meetings, how much positive change had occurred in the space of five or so years, from wobbling a teapot to top shelf. Self-help progressed my search markedly.

Subversion

The fourth means of escape I call subversive. Subversion functioned beneath an appearance of acquiescence to a line of acceptable behaviour – for example, professing sincere beliefs – while at the same time pursuing an end that undermined the orthodoxy. For much longer than me, my brother David – a mobile encyclopaedia – was more expert at finding ways around rules than me. For years, he managed to walk both sides of the street. Given a chance, I followed doggedly. The narrow

Plymouth Brethren catechism allowed little scope for imaginative action within it, although excitement was generated by pushing the limits with David.

As already mentioned, late in 1962 when David was studying at Oxford University, my aunt and I met him in Jordan to travel to Israel to explore old Christian sites; we were still in the rump of the cult, but keen to stretch our wings whenever possible. David decided that he and I should try to find some of the caves at Wadi Qumran, where the Dead Sea scrolls of Bible manuscripts had been discovered fifteen years before. It was exhilarating and revealing.

From geography lessons at school, I knew that a wadi was a deep, dry ravine worn down by flooding in times of heavy rain. Leaving Aunt in a tent café at the shore of the sweltering Dead Sea, David and I scrambled up cliffs at the side of the wadi to a small cave peeping like the eye of Cyclops from the heights. On the slopes where the ochre rubble was rough and slippery, we were covered in dust, but reaching the shade of a dry, barren cave, we were rewarded with the view back across the vast valley cradling the Dead Sea. Even from the cliffs, I could smell the sea's sulphur, and see the murky turquoise of the flat water and the misty sky of deep azure beyond.

The scrolls had been removed to museums, of course, but I was full of excitement from the strenuous climb and intimate archaeological connection. I could hardly wait to get my hands on the Penguin book (1961) about the discovery which David described – *The Dead Sea Scrolls*, by John Marco Allegro, an English archaeologist – where he recounted the discovery of the oldest known versions of the Bible.

David had stirred me by telling about the book, so on arrival in Oxford soon afterwards, I hurried to Blackwell's Bookshop, near Balliol College, to buy it. The story of the surprise find was thrilling in itself, and Allegro's hypothesis that the scrolls proved the non-existence of Jesus was more fascinating, even if his hasty translation of the contents of some scrolls was pooh-poohed by other scholars later on. At least there was room for doubt, for the possibility of an alternative interpretation; scholars all agreed that some slabs of the 'Bible' had been omitted over centuries, some altered by scribes. The Bible text was not fixed; the scrolls showed that the religious communities which created the scripts relied not on one Divine Author, as Plymouth Brethren asserted, but on a caste of scribes who aimed to collectively transmit ancient traditions to future generations. The text of the Bible was not set in stone until mechanical printing began in Europe in the sixteenth century. Even then it perpetuated copying and translation errors.

It was instructive to me that a Jewish sect, the Essenes, who curated the scrolls in the desert, had several of the characteristics of Exclusive Brethren, and clearly, all sects were alike in their narrowness. The Essenes required a two-year initiation process for males before being admitted to their priesthood, and then newcomers handed over all possessions to the community. They purified by washing themselves daily, worshipped, studied and taught daily, and ate meals only with their own. Women were excluded because the Essenes lived celibate lives dedicated to God. God predestined them as 'Sons of Light' to fulfil His prophecies, so they believed that they lived in 'the last days' before the world would end suddenly. Fulfilling their premonitions, occupying Roman troops destroyed them and their settlement around AD 70, leaving the secret scrolls unattended, hidden in caves. To my young mind, the parallels with the Essenes, the New Testament versions of Jesus and the behaviour of Exclusive Brethren were uncanny.

My interest in archaeology continued. *The prehistory of Australia* by John Mulvaney absorbed me strongly when I found a vacation job at the end of a university year, helping the author dig at the Keilor Terrace excavation, where an exciting date for Aboriginal and megafauna remains of about 45,000 BP was unearthed. In the trenches, Mulvaney was agile and sure-footed, an excellent teacher and passionately committed to his discipline. I was rewarded by fossicking with a trowel, and sharing anecdotes with experienced diggers. With Mulvaney's 'petrol money', I rode my cantankerous Lambretta motor scooter to the excavation site on weekdays for five weeks, and back home, giving me plenty of time to ponder the absurdity of the Biblical 'Creation of the Earth' in 7,000 BP. The Bible was becoming more and more irrelevant. My well-meaning enthusiasm to find out about an ancient culture firsthand led me to further subversive doubts about the foundations of Brethren beliefs.

Travel escapades

From previous mentions of travel in this memoir, it will be obvious that travel was an opportunity for escape from burdensome Brethren, physically and emotionally. It was the same for other Brethren boys; Noel Virtue, zookeeper and novelist, escaped the emotional claustrophobia of New Zealand and Brethren by retreating to London in his twenties to wallow in the Swinging Sixties. When I include all the freedoms permitted on my beach holidays alongside those of overseas excursions, then time spent in travel was a truly blissful release valve. On top of the ten or so weeks spent each year at the beach during school and university holidays, before I left Brethren in 1968, I had spent a total of four months on a world tour (1962) and three months researching in London (1966–1967).

Any physical withdrawal from oppression was welcome, even as a temporary deliverance. Flight was as good as fight as far as I was concerned. Taking some young Brethren along with me added an air of fellowship. I never lost the urge to create my own adventures, and including Brethren in them gave them cachet. Thus at the end of the 1965 academic year, the university vacation allowed an opportunity for exploring in the wilds. Open spaces turned me on.

I organised a climb up Frenchmans Cap near the headwaters of the Franklin River in Tasmania with two younger Brethren, Kenneth and Graham. Graham promptly lost a heel when his cheap boot got stuck in black mud, and he had to hobble along unbalanced without it for three days. I was quietly pleased that I had spent money on good Austrian hiking boots – which lasted for years. In places, the mud on the track reached up to our knees. Kenneth complained about the discomfort of the bunk beds at the Lake Vera hut, made of split logs (the splinters got into his sleeping bag). In contrast, I was so exhausted each night that I could have slept on a bed of nails if necessary.

From the hut, we managed to scramble up the steep white granite to the peak of the Cap with difficulty, at 1,446 metres, from where the panorama was spectacular. It spanned across misty Macquarie Harbour in the west, unending green wilderness in the south, and row on row of other peaks (some under snow) in the north. Although fatigued, I felt that I was soaring like an eagle. We became so absorbed by the wonderful views as we rested on the peak, photographed the expanses and followed the path of a distant thunderstorm, that we lost track of the time.

As a result of our delay, half of our descent down the Cap track was in pitch black after sunset, feeling for the direction of the soaked path with our soggy toes, while clutching at each other's jackets to stay in touch. The little torch battery went flat, thick clouds covered the dark sky. Our only support was each other. I was terrified as we slipped and slid and plunged in unison.

Leeches always clung to me on bushwalks, as though they had a secretive entitlement to my succulent legs. The descent from Frenchmans Cap was no exception. Twice, doctors have needed to extract dead leeches from inside my infected middle toe, where they burrow in and die, after being carried away with enthusiasm for my juice. I was oblivious to the leeches bulging beneath my soggy gaiters at the end of the Cap descent in the dark. There was no method to exclude them. I have never been so relieved to arrive at a destination as when we located the primitive wooden Lake Vera hut again in the hollow, late that night.

Misty rain clung to us all next day as we trudged wearily out of the primeval forest. We continued to another national park at Cradle Mountain, in Kenneth's ute, where sleety snow descended on us, even in the middle of summer. Yet the beautiful vistas of shafts of sunlight on lush button grass, sharp peaks, contorted deciduous beech trees and lake-filled cirques more than compensated for any physical discomfort. The landscape embraced me.

At the end of each university year, during each exam time, I dreamed up an escape by means of a country trip while I swotted over my revisions. At the end of 1967, I organised a VW Kombi van holiday to Western Australia, with five other young Brothers. At the end of a day, when we tired of driving across the treeless plains, over vibrations like corrugated iron, over potholes of dust, dust, and more dust, with partly opened windows for air conditioning, we often camped exhausted near the main road. Ambitiously, I provided the team with a copy of the *Presbyterian Women's Missionary Union Cookbook* to stimulate variety in meals, and I remember making a delicious Veiled Country Lass on the camp stove for dessert, from one of its recipes. The fact that it originated from Presbyterians and not Brethren did not affect our enjoyment of the small treat at all.

To ensure that Aboriginal groups in South Australia could only experience a nomadic lifestyle, and not settle, our federal government had agreed to allow tests of nuclear weapons at Maralinga ten years before our arrival. The lethal British explosions forced many Aborigines to migrate south from the desert, to an area set aside as the Yalata Mission, near the highway, where we paused for a look-see. The part of the mission that we visited was managed by the Lutheran Church, deliberately separated from the other part, consisting of the United Aborigines' Mission of Australia (UAM) – ostensibly to avoid 'confusing' the Aborigines with their clashing theologies. Why any human would be incapable of understanding straightforward doctrinal differences was beyond my comprehension. The differences were insignificant. We were all too familiar with proselytising Christians who were unable to reconcile their divergences, blaming their congregations for ignorance of the Truth. Missions were about to disappear altogether, in fact, and our enlightened Lutheran host – a stocky pastor – reminded us that we were not to perve on local Aborigines as though they were museum exhibits. We stayed only a short time. I bought a decorated blue-tongue lizard carved from wood that I treasured, as did my children to come.

Leaving the Nullarbor Plains, we travelled to the bottom south-west corner of the continent, to Albany, where I souvenired a large whale tooth, found near the old whaling station that was also on the verge of closing. The sea air was redolent with the stink of rotting blubber. Whales were disappearing in dangerous quantities. More than 1,300 kilometres north at Carnarvon we saw a different kind of station altogether, a tracking station which just opened, built by NASA to follow Gemini, Apollo and Skylab satellites. The conglomerations of shiny steel buildings for processing whales and extraterrestrials in Albany and Carnarvon looked equally dull to us as outsiders.

We stretched our horizons for six weeks of hot touring rather than just limiting ourselves to being sedentary and holy. On the coast, we swam a lot. We contacted only one family which clung to the edge of Brethren respectability in Fremantle, soon to collapse into the arms of Open Brethren. Rigour in the Plymouth Brethren rumps was in decline everywhere, as numbers of adherents dwindled. When Philip Cossham visited Fremantle thirty years before us, on his migration to New Zealand, he met twenty-five Plymouth Brethren in Fremantle in one day. The diary of his journey – the source of this figure – was mentioned earlier. Although shrinkage was protracted, it was inexorable.

Last fling

Trying harder was the recommended antidote to my inner doubts. I felt an obligation to try as hard as I could to immerse myself, to follow Brethren precepts, to adhere to their lifestyle, to cut their attitudes to shape. I prayed for divine guidance but only got the engaged signal. No one answered. Earnestly and innocently, I did my best to conform to the mould, but that trial turned out badly, and I had ample reason to set out on a fresh search of my own. It beckoned.

Unthinkingly, when my family and I were thrown out of Exclusive Brethren, we all joined the small rump of Plymouth remnants in 1962. We fell quickly out of one toxic alliance into another, and it failed to adapt in any constructive way. In today's world of instant communication, we could have become aware of thousands of other cults, but as naive survivors in 1962, we buried our heads in the sand, pretending that there was no downside whatsoever to our departure from mainstream Exclusivism. The principle of Separation should not be allowed to derail the rest of our precepts, we asserted. Arrogantly, we saw ourselves as guardians of the *true* faith alone – ours was the only acceptable heritage. We still thought of ourselves as torch-bearers. No one was allowed to accuse us of abandoning the straight and narrow of the chosen few (Matthew 7:14). But serious trouble was about to arise – when some of the fuzzy-headed in our rump wanted to abandon rules other than Separation. Antiquarianism was under threat.

Unlike many, I was energised (at the age of fifteen) by liberation from the sallow faces of Exclusive Brethren. It presented opportunities. Father was troubled by the vacuum, glad to be free of the endless prying and invective of Exclusives, and anxious to explore the opportunity for managing in a new fiefdom. Mother grieved for her losses of lifelong friends; her loyalty and trust had been utterly shattered. Aunt seemed unmoved and preoccupied. I never regretted leaving Brethren, I never had any post-hoc yearning for their odd ways, and never felt any inclination to adopt another religion. From 1968, I was alienated in perpetuity.

Soon after my family's removal by Exclusive Brethren in 1962, the tyranny of Bruce Hales senior ended in 1965 with his violent overthrow – as savagely as the coup that brought him to power. His own aunt reported that he was a chronic alcoholic, dying in 2006. He was cast out like a filthy rag, stabbed in the back, because of his advocacy of a bad small business model for which he was blamed by his enemies as a financial disaster. Predictably, a like-minded henchman led a renewed dictatorship, devoid of any fresh Brethren theology – a pattern of serial replacements that soon became established. The events were as though I lived through ancient Greek mythological wars.

I have overlooked chronological order in this chapter in order to illustrate important themes about how I escaped. The crucial tests of Brethren ways and the impacts of my deviations at different times – as outlined – showed that their culture was not only evil, illogical, hypocritical and unsustainable, but that they were incapable of providing any long-lasting stimulus.

In the short period between 1960 and 1962, Brethren destroyed their own community, betrayed the dedication of thousands of their own followers, and turned traditional persuasion and acquiescence into hard-hearted harassment and antisocial persecution. They migrated from a porous ghetto to a self-inflicted concentration camp. There was no turning back for me.

The consequences of Exclusive Separation were far-reaching. In 1963, at the instigation of Jack Galbally, member of the Legislative Council and brother of the famous barrister, Frank, the government in Victoria funded a Royal Commission to enquire into Scientology because it was treating families badly. The commission report refused to accept the possibility that Scientology was a religion. It began with dangerously familiar observations:

> The evidence has shown its theories to be fantastic and impossible, its principles perverted and ill-founded, and its techniques debased and harmful.
>
> There are some features of scientology which are so ludicrous that there may be a tendency to regard scientology as silly and its practitioners as harmless cranks… [But] scientology is evil; its techniques evil; its practice a serious threat to community, medically, morally, and socially; and its adherents sadly deluded and often mentally ill.

Although not mentioned in the report, Brethren were very afraid; I recall furtive and whispered discussions about the possible consequences of the report. Rumours made the rump more paranoid. The chief secretary of Victoria, Arthur Rylah, was asked by thirty-seven recently excluded Brethren members to officially investigate family cruelty and separation of children from parents. He passed the buck to the police. In Brisbane, detectives established a task force to investigate Brethren behaviours, and newly excommunicated members called for a Queensland Royal Commission, which did not eventuate. These frozen investigations put us all on edge, even those of us on the verge of departure from the rump.

Eleven

Arrival

The last straw

It is appropriate that the Arabic saying 'the final straw that broke the camel's back' originated in a religious argument about good and bad morals back in 1684. As well as camels, the backs of horses, donkeys and monkeys have also featured in past usage of the saying. My own back could be included when I vividly recall the straw that ultimately broke my historical connection to Brethren – and my loyalty to my brother David. They were linked inextricably.

My final break occurred in Canberra in June 1968. Typically climactic, at the Australian National University, David formed a relationship with one of his students, eleven years younger, and left Turid and their two children, so that he could live with his new lover. Although cruelly he kept the liaison secret from his wife for months, and his Melbourne family for even more months, he continued to profess to adhere to Brethren tenets when he visited Melbourne, seriously conflicted. His need for subterfuge and adventure trumped all logic and human dignity. Although I was still attached to the Brethren rump, that June he determined that I needed a lover, and that he would provide her. I was dumbfounded.

David's inept experimentation pulled an emotional rug from under me – I had clung to him as a reliable mentor for far too long. It was common for me to holiday with his family in my mid-year break from university study. When I visited Canberra this time, David shocked me by taking me to a pub to meet his new conspirators. The atmosphere was utterly unfamiliar to me, never having socialised in a bar before. Brethren never went into bars.

On a walk with him in a pine forest the previous day, our habitual exercise from years back, he revealed how tense and muddle-headed he felt. He looked scrawny and unkempt, like a scarecrow on steroids. I became very wary of the change in him. I no longer trusted him.

At the Hotel Kurrajong, he plied me with glasses of beer and with a friend of his girlfriend, who he claimed was interested in me. She was probably his fantasy.

'This is Penny, Graeme,' said David with an introduction that I was expected to treat as significant.

'Oh, I'm so tired of working on an essay about morality and euthanasia,' Penny launched. 'I am so tired of reading about it. The arguments are endless.'

'That's a big topic.' I was tentative.

A full schooner appeared without invitation at the end of David's extended arm – looking insurmountable.

'There's much more to it than just ethics. I've been reading Peter Singer and others.' Penny swilled like a veteran in a manner that showed that the amber beverage was familiar to her.

'He's a talented man. I've heard him speak in Melbourne in public lectures on the ethics of the Vietnam War.'

'Now that's really interesting. What sort of person is he?' she rambled.

While the others knocked back schooners like tenpins in a bowling alley, I was distracted and wished that an earthquake would swallow me up. But Canberra has no large earthquakes. The chatting was the least of my memories. The sour smell of the pools of spilt beer on the circular Laminex tabletop in the bar stuck fast in my mind. I felt disoriented and repulsed and could only wish to slip off my uncomfortable stool and get far away in order to mull over David's crazy behaviour. Even though I was certain that the time for my escape had arrived, David still felt that he had a right to manage it himself. He planned to control me while he lost all control. I was taken aback and troubled.

On my dreary drive back to Melbourne in my maroon Morris Mini Minor soon after, I accepted that the time had finally come to take my destiny into my own hands. I had drained my existing lifestyle, now a place of anguish. I was running on empty. Schooners were not the answer. The Brethren rump was not the answer. David's advice was not the answer. David had failed me – just as much as Brethren – and I could rely on them no longer.

As he settled into his self-destructive groove, David wanted it all, convinced that he could maintain the religious and familial status quo alongside his uncontrolled deviation. I needed time and space to identify my own normative solutions, my own corrective counterbalances, my own map of the challenges that lay ahead of me.

I was so self-absorbed that I did not know how to support Turid properly. I felt vulnerable and inward-looking. It was clear that I could not rely on David or his search – that would only end at nowhere. My search would have to switch full-throttle to elsewhere. I was floundering in a maelstrom.

This chapter describes what immediate alternatives presented themselves to replace the worn-out Brethren rump. There were three primary processes involved in reaching my new path at last. Firstly, I found the many attractions of the World alluring. Secondly, my single source of long-term benefit – reading – continued to shed light on many mysteries along my journey, whilst also providing commentary on broad social and political changes which echoed my own emerging concerns. Lastly and importantly, I discovered four significant means for groping my way towards my preferred direction.

After Canberra, new horizons looked very inviting. In recent weeks, a university acquaintance had hosted me to evening dinners at his Queen's College in Melbourne, where Michael enjoyed study and friendships. I needed a gentle landing like his place. Nearby Ormond College was larger and appealed to me as a social hub and an alternative to my sterile mansion in North Balwyn; by then, university colleges were no longer virtual monasteries, nor were they obsessed with fagging and ragging, but they still retained a slight whiff of European traditions about them, which appealed. I had adhered so strictly to Separation from the World – it had isolated me so much from others – that I craved peer companionship. I applied to Ormond and was interviewed by the most gracious and urbane man in the form of the Master, Rev. Dr Davis McCaughey, and admitted with a bursary at the start of 1969. In his gentle Irish brogue, he allotted me a spacious upstairs room on the third floor, with its own fireplace, beneath the bell that I grew to ignore – it struck at six a.m. daily. Students in neighbouring rooms were compliant early risers, one studying engineering, the other political science. No influence of Presbyterianism was detectable in spite of Ormond's origins in religious donations.

After years of struggle, my long-awaited launch into the World was fully primed and ready to begin. In my mind, since first reading it in 1964, I retained Robert Browning's encouraging maxim: 'A man's reach should exceed his grasp, or what's a heaven for?' Experimentation – guided by a handful of known attractants – took over my life. I was relieved of the spectre of the Brethren rump for ever.

Just a Show?

Decades of compliance fell away quickly as the attractants of the World blossomed for my eager sampling. In Parkville and Carlton, I buzzed around the nearby theatres, cinemas, concert-halls, sports venues, cafés, clubs, pubs and societies. I felt like a bee let loose in a florist shop, savouring all the colours and aromas. I indulged in too many at once, causing cultural hay fever, and it took a while to sort the tasteful from the bizarre, but at least my movement away from the past was unwavering. My direction was fixed.

At university in 1969, I joined the Young Christians Club to find out if I had missed out on any aspect of Christianity by being Brethren. I imagined that there might be more to it than I knew, and it was the last chance to find out. The very first club event – replete with atmospherics of candlelight, comfy cushions and beanbags, and unopened

Bibles scattered on the floor of a meeting room in the Student Union – was as close to a Brethren Prayer Meeting as was possible. It was definitely not my scene.

I hung in for the first social gathering of the club to welcome the likes of me. It was a trip by van in February to picnic horse races at a Gisborne country meet. I had never been to a horse race before (nor since). Club members drank too much, availing themselves of the 'food' trucks on site. I asked one – an experienced punter – about which horse to place a bet on. On his advice, I selected a horse and placed all my money on it.

The race began when an official dropped a rope in front of the assembled horses at the starting point of the track. The dropping rope frightened my horse so much that it reared up and raced back clockwise in the wrong direction around the track. The symbolism of the horse's escape from the race was not lost on me. Everyone cheered enthusiastically. By the time that the jockey managed to turn my horse around, the rest of the horses, having run anticlockwise, came thundering towards it – and the finish.

After Gisborne, I abandoned involvement in horse racing altogether, in spite of other enticements to persist. The club did not need me, nor I it. I determined that it was actually a marriage exchange, though such a pedestrian purpose would be denied by its very proper members – all furrowed brows, short back-and-sides, forlorn frocks, impeccable politeness.

There was such a lot to learn and I wanted to accelerate my learning lickety-split. With my first adult date, Sue, from St Mary's College, I went to the Comedy Theatre to see *Just a Show* starring Barry Humphries. I knew Sue from school days. She was Catholic and criticised me for calling her a Roman Catholic, even while I was trying my hardest to be ecumenical. I was unfamiliar with the proprieties of Worldly nomenclature; I was just following the derogatory Brethren label of old.

The newspaper reviews of the show claimed that the comedian Humphries interacted with his audience, which seemed like the chance for informal fun to me, but what I saw was Humphries waving gladioli and shouting at latecomers. Was that normal or interactive? It was certainly not impromptu. Dressing in drag and castigating late arrivals did not seem even vaguely amusing to me; clearly he expected applause by breaking some implicit rules of theatre behaviour. Was it satire? What were the rules? Was an audience expected to remain passive at all costs? Was abuse interactive? What should I say at interval to Sue? All the doubts made me wet with sweat from anxiety. As my granddaughter now says, I was over-thinking the situation then.

I had more success with music and another woman friend. I needed to understand cultural protocols urgently. Folk music proved easier to relax with; in many ways, that creative form was close to familiar hymns and to the negro spirituals that I had the pleasure of hearing in music classes at school. Our teacher played us LP records which demonstrated the history of music, so I welcomed an introduction to the origins of blues and jazz, and gospel, and sang memorised lyrics out loudly at every opportunity. I empathised with Louis Armstrong when he reiterated in his matchless bass, 'Nobody knows the trouble I've seen…'

Unbeknown to me at school, I had the best music teacher in Australia at the time, Miss Alexandra Cameron, from 1959 to 1962. I am still embarrassed to record that I did not appreciate her talents; she wrote the only Australian school textbook on music, conducted the entire school in singing at speech nights, and also formed a small school orchestra. To our detriment, most boys of my generation thought that appreciating music or choir was downright effeminate.

Alexandra Cameron was a little lady, about the size of Edith Piaf, the French singer nicknamed the 'Sparrow'. At a concert at speech night in the body of the Hawthorn Town Hall, hard-working Miss Cameron slipped off her chair part-way through conducting the entire school in song, falling to the parquet floor, causing gasps of horror. After a short silence, she quickly scrambled back onto the chair, apparently unharmed, and continued to lead us in the 'Hallelujah Chorus' to its very exultant finish. With gusto we sang, 'Forever and ever. Hallelujah! Hallelujah!' My admiration for her swelled.

I made friends with a music fan, Sylvia, in 1968. She seemed extraordinarily mature, studying social work, and having been immersed in the World all of her life. She shared a flat with other students in Saint Kilda. Her father was a dairy farmer in Korumburra, her sister a doctor in Brighton, her brother a scientist in Canberra, and her uncle an aviation journalist everywhere. Could she possibly be more Worldly? It was an immense relief that she regarded my religious genesis as neither here nor there, when I confessed it, and she went on to become a committed Jungian therapist at the Tavistock Institute in London. I greatly admired her single-mindedness and persistence with her dreams. When it came to work, I had neither.

She and I spent many happy nights inhaling smoke from Benson & Hedges and imbibing black Nescafé in rough basement caverns in Little Lonsdale Street, listening to guitars and songs by 'Dutch' Tilders and Margaret Roadknight – my special local favourites. On LPs on my new record player in college, I followed the advice of in-house experts and bought records by John Lee Hooker, Ry Cooder, Joan Baez, Arlo Guthrie, Pete Seeger, and Simon and Garfunkel. They became my oft-replayed favourites. Then it made me feel strong and spartan to stand coatless in a torrential thunderstorm at the Myer Music Bowl on the sloping lawns, to hear Bob Dylan sing 'A Hard Rain's A-Gonna Fall'. I connected with Dylan. The screaming of the audience still rings in my ears.

Never having seen much cinema, I had a backlog to catch up on. Instead of attending lectures during the day, I would spoil myself with an old film such as *Ben Hur*, which I had only heard of and not seen, or *Gone with the Wind*, which seemed to never end. I mixed these viewings up with recent releases of films like *Elvira Madigan* and *Shame*, shown in the Carlton 'Bughouse'. Smoking was still permitted in that little cinema, and it was relaxing to recline on an op-shop sofa in the back row, peering at the movie through an ever-thickening smokescreen.

On one of my visits to the Bughouse, Annie shrieked unexpectedly from the back of the cinema through the fog, and gave me an enormous fright. It sounded like a murder. At interval I realised that she was simply expressing excitement at the film plot, in her visceral way, from her wheelchair at the back, with her carers, Rosie and Chris.

Annie was born with cerebral palsy – she could not talk – and was left by her natural parents to fend for herself in Saint Nicholas' Hospital in Fitzroy at the age of three. Rosie worked there and believed that Annie had the maturity and intelligence to live with her and her partner, and fought a legal battle to obtain guardianship of Annie. The dramatic story of her escape and assisted communication was told powerfully in the book *Annie's Coming Out*, followed by a film. I knew Rosie and Chris via mutual friends. Rosie assisted Annie all the way in her search for elsewhere.

I craved exposure to cultural icons urgently, believing every one of my chosen films to be masterpieces, not knowing if they were. I grew to love film as great entertainment and visual stimulation – but never understood film theory.

The attractions of the World beyond Brethren, which I began to explore, catered for the full gamut of human emotions and behaviours, and not just a narrow spectrum around defensiveness, isolation, introversion, surveillance and subservience. Life outside the corral – outside 'your own backyard', or the tribe of predestined saints – was very exciting. I was impressed by the many original forms of self-expression. Outside Brethren lay cultural stimulation, and enormous thrills, scope for a variety of human relationships, creative passions, self-directed learning, self-development, free thinking, political experimentation, travel mobility, alternative lifestyles, and so on. While the potential seemed endless, my challenge was which adventure to tackle first.

Titled

The single continuous evidentiary thread that stitched together my Brethren past and my liberated life lay in books. They reflected my interests and answered my urgent questions. If I had not encountered something in books, it made me all the more curious. As can be seen in earlier parts of this memoir, books provided me with a dependable patchwork of great significance. Reading was my habitual window onto the World, thrown wide open by Mother, which began with her early storytelling. Books on any topic whatsoever contained all the wisdom of the universe, I thought. They wanted to be revealed to me. They were my faith surrogate, perhaps substituting for real-life experiences also.

Books were friends and my trusted filters. Book after book, fiction and non-fiction, focused my attention on changing values and social mores, and provided insights into situations and experiences that were far removed from my own confined home paddock. Books were companions during my searching in happy and sad times, during my confident and uncomfortable states of mind, and when dealing with the familiar and unknown. They enlightened and filtered and broadened, all at the same time. A feeling of getting to know a little of the character of the authors was usually rewarding. Curious natures like mine expect knowledge to be searchable, endless and free. I knew how to read cautiously between the lines, to search for hidden meanings.

As well as indicating my reading preferences, and my urge to know, the titles reflected some of the global concerns of the day and potentially affirmed the directions of my new world views. I had no training in political science, Brethren avoided politics altogether, so books helped fill voids. I never could find enough time to catch up.

My tastes were often directionless, driven by accessibility rather than informed choice based on review. David could always be relied on to recommend a title for me to read. Or for anyone else. He consumed books incredibly fast, in the time taken to eat a meal. Or he could read an entire novel in a single visit to the porcelain throne. Encouragingly, he was always keen to know what I thought of his recommendations and accepted criticism.

Reacting to Stalinism, *Nineteen Eighty-Four* and *Animal Farm* by George Orwell – suffering tuberculosis – enabled me to realise that I was not unusual in wanting to rebel against the tyranny of Brethren.

As well as sex, the government censor also banned Chairman Mao Tse-Tung's *Little Red Book* from schools, but when I got my hands on a copy, the aphorisms were remarkably trite, and I gave it away to a friend at school immediately. I was repelled by the Vietnam War, in 1967 reading *The Report from Iron Mountain*, which professed to be propaganda from a US think-tank, but may have been a hoax meant to convey a strong anti-war message. Its ambiguity was attractive; scholars still argue about how genuine it was.

The beginnings of a climate crisis were outlined distressingly in Rachel Carson's *Silent Spring* and led me to judge pesticides disapprovingly for ever; I have made every effort to eat only organic or biodynamic food for more than fifty years. In *The Feminine Mystique* by Betty Friedan, well before Germaine Greer found her place in the sun, the demeaning controls by patriarchy over the female body, lifestyle and opportunities opened my eyes wide to the abhorrent treatment of women by Brethren, and the rest.

While some may have experimented with sex physically, I resorted to *Lady Chatterley's Lover* (D.H. Lawrence) and *The Group* (Mary McCarthy), where access to terse references to sexual exuberance were restricted by censors. Sexual exploration did not happen at all for the bulk of my adolescent peers, in spite of what the mass media of today may assert in relation to liberation in the 'Sixties'. *Private Eye* and *Mad* magazine provided some titillation in magazine form.

Confused by the civil rights movement in the USA, and deeply shocked by the assassination of Martin Luther King, the complex fates of North American minorities were explained somewhat by the *Autobiography of Malcolm X* (black Muslims) and the autobiography of David Suzuki (interned Japanese in Canada).

At university, I was tempted (but failed) to join Abschol, a non-government organisation to assist in education of Australian Aborigines. Tom Roper tried to encourage me to participate but I hesitated to commit to any political causes, however deserving. Ideology still frightened me. I absorbed some passive resistance techniques from the evocative autobiography of Charles Perkins – the first Aboriginal graduate in Australia – published in 1975. But due respect for Aboriginal culture was very tardy and limited in scope. Geoffrey Blainey did not publish his academic study *Triumph of the Nomads* until the same year.

Penguin Books put out many magazine-like publications of confronting photographs. I regularly looked at *Magnum* and *Post* for the beginnings of my visual literacy and aesthetic education, anchored in documentary and street photography. Pictures from the Vietnam War could not avoid being shocking – in spite of being selected by political allies.

Politics gripped my imagination, seeping into much of my reading in the 1960s. It became unavoidable. Reflections on the ethics of the Israeli prosecution of an abducted Nazi tyrant – of special interest to a fresher law student like me, studying international law – were described in *Justice in Jerusalem* by the attorney-general of Israel. Leon Uris was paid by the young Israeli government to write *Exodus*; no novel at the time (to my knowledge) dealt with the inhumane displacement of Palestinians.

My understanding of European history came mostly from textbooks and academic journals. My knowledge of Asia was minimal. One English historian in particular stands out: Marion Gibbs in 1953 published *Feudal Order*, exploring the effects of mediaeval society in Europe on modern politics. At the age of sixty-six, she came from Cambridge University to teach us in Melbourne for a term. She was refreshing; I had never met anyone before who was so enlivened by her discipline, nor so committed to advocating for the current relevance of her favoured field of history. Every student bought her black-covered book, devoid of any design adornment. In it, she assumed a Marxist posture, though apparently many Marxist historians criticised her for not being Marxist enough. What is 'enough' when adopting (or rejecting) a systemic creed? Whether from a speech impediment or excessive saliva, I do not know, but she could not help spitting as she spoke moistly with great authority. As her students, we held her in great affection but learnt to give her a wide berth during conversations.

Political awareness grew. Continual access to all sorts of reading matter meant that I was able to keep track of global themes, connecting them to my own tiny spot in the universe of knowledge, sharing ideas informally with like-minded readers. Reading was a bridge, in the absence of all other media. I benefitted in that my brothers and I shared books, and opinions about them, pooling our vicarious engagement with the World beyond Brethren. It was very common for one of us to say, 'I reckon that you might like to read this.'

Four guides

I am glad that I was the third child in my unusual family, because I had the chance to observe the escapes of my two older brothers before taking my own plunge. I closely observed the departures of others too, of course. How did they do it? How did they cope? Did they suffer disadvantage? Could I learn from how they escaped? Watching others survive (and thrive) enervated my own strength to chart my course, independently from the rest.

As I grew into myself, clusters of constructive attitudes developed within me over the space of some years. They stirred glimmers of hope. They were abstract and are not quickly described, but it is important to understand how I found them.

It was not until I was well on my way to freedom that I began to fully replace archaic dogma and constraints, invented by others – which I threw overboard from my modus vivendi – with new corrective thinking. I relied on fresh ways to underpin and affirm my new behaviours from the early 1970s.

I name the mental supports as guides or elixirs or signposts or healing agents or scaffolding. The precise name does not matter. Their functions mattered. They were defensive shields and offensive weapons. They formed a mental checklist that I reviewed now and again. They were new aids to me, and I was delighted to discover them.

They helped me to find my way out of the emotional hole that I had fallen into. They showed me how to avoid conflict, or resolve it.

They gave me strength and a fresh sense of purpose. They proved to have long-term value. They were far better than prayers or rationalisations or tonics or homeopathic remedies, even if they were somewhat amorphous for a start. I identified them as four welcome clusters of needs for my survival and satisfaction – identifying them as physical needs, emotional needs, creative and aesthetic needs, and intellectual needs. If all the needs were satisfied, then life was sure to be fully functional and gratifying for me.

Strange as it may seem, after Brethren I had to find a comfortable, new identity. It did not just pop into existence automatically on a day in 1968. Most of all, it revolved around the growth of life-giving self-perception and development of restorative aspirations. Hence the importance of knowing needs.

I pondered on my motivations for making my way into the great unknown, the promised land – or was it a risky pie in the sky? In truth, the supports were not immediately to hand, but emerged as a result of fresh trials, risks, adventures, misjudgements, deductions, assumptions and mistakes. And reflecting on them in dialogue with others was invaluable. They taught me the essence of constructive ways of living today.

They determined what baggage to abandon without qualms. They were the means whereby my new self meshed comfortably with the new contexts, while at the same time permitting the survival of a handful of selected remnants of the old world. A few old features were redeemable. How much of the old should be kept, and how much new should be embraced? It was sometimes hard to judge, but the new certainly worked better than the old on its own.

I confirmed that the guidelines applied constructively in different situations.

Each of the four clusters of needs took from the past and modified legacies in fresh contexts with new knowledge and experience. The ability to merge them reduced tensions within me and with outsiders. Simplistic 'Omnipotence' collapsed by the wayside like floppy retreads from a flat tyre.

The guidelines – based on needs – structured, matured and consolidated, protecting my back, propelling me forwards, reassuring me of my ability to make safe decisions. The guidelines were simple and comprehensible, designed for avoiding the negative reservations that were entrenched in my psyche by a Brethren upbringing, for gauging the pressures on me as an independent adult, for building productive relationships, for expressing emotional expectations, for predicting emotional reactions and for discovering viable new ways of exploring.

My prolonged search expanded and still expands my horizons, relationships and experiences. By continuous reflection, I identified the key personal helpers to show me the way. I fully articulated them first – as in an epiphany – in the ambient rooms of a therapist, who midwived the discovery. His obituary correctly noted that

> he had the professional wisdom and the courage to recognise where theory was refuted by living circumstances. He knew about the healing properties of play, humour and gentle teasing: he was patient and gently persistent.

In addition to the four signposts, I learnt a lot from partners, especially from my second and third wives, and from other stable supporters in between. I feel very grateful to have enjoyed constructive relationships for long periods. My second wife and I had another boy, my third child, Tim, before she died of cancer much too young (aged forty-three in 1988). The two-year-old son was a diversion and mighty inspiration in my grief. My third wife, Turid, who was married to my brother David before he died (in 1985), is solidly behind me, still invaluable in every way in my life. Our long connection is a firm anchor; I first befriended Turid sixty years ago and we still travel side by side.

Physical needs

My list of four needs may seem less than prosaic, perhaps as mundane as a shopping list, but it amounts to a valued means of escape from my past and guide for my future. My first bundle – of physical needs – simply relates to lifestyle, to good health and diet and plenty of exercise. Since childhood, food was always nourishing and entertaining, usually eaten in company, especially when living at home. My fourth-grade teacher imparted an important lesson: make sure that you sweat from exercise at least once a day. Since then, I have sweated a lot by walking, riding bicycles, playing kick-to-kick football and amateur cricket, chopping firewood, fishing, playing tennis, table tennis and squash, climbing mountains, swimming, exercising at the gymnasium, and having sex. But not without pauses.

A random selection from my diary (for 16 November 1965) confirmed what an important part walking played in my leisure time. My university exams had just finished, and with David I released tension by clambering over twenty-four kilometres of the coast at Phillip Island, sighting penguins, koalas, seals, mutton birds, ibis nests and cormorants in one day. I identify very strongly with the directive poem by Robert Frost – written in 1915 – about 'The road not taken', and the freedoms that his choice of routes enabled:

> I shall be telling this with a sigh
> Somewhere ages and ages hence:
> Two roads diverged in a wood, and I —
> I took the one less travelled by,
> And that has made all the difference.

At the start, I had no option but to follow a less travelled path with Brethren. In the heyday of their control over me, Plymouth Brethren held back constructive physical activities by disallowing team sports or group activities (even choir) outside their community. When I visited Los Angeles with Aunt in 1962, I had my eyes opened by the son of Brethren being taken by parents to baseball coaching, as though it was completely compatible with Brethren mores; no such liberty ever crossed my childhood path in Melbourne. In reality, there was little standardisation of Brethren rules, and no means to achieve it.

Emotions

Emotional needs, my second group, were more shaped by my personality, than were my physical needs. The two cannot be entirely separated. My emotional needs revolved around self-expression and relationships with friends and my partners. Inevitably, I brought my own baggage to intimacy. Each of my three marriages yielded emotional lessons and permanent rewards. As well as close connections, including with friends and acquaintances, it was important for me to experience a gamut of feelings, whether positive or negative, as much as possible.

As I unpack my emotional story throughout this memoir, I have outlined responses to smothering and proscribing belief. Fittingly as I write this, I happen to hear a recording of Edith Piaf singing that she 'regrets nothing' about her struggles: *Non, je ne regrette rien*. Her highly emotional voice buoyed her up during her short, traumatic life. She inspired me.

Many times, I had the good luck to be able to call on the personal support of allies in navigating disasters – deaths, divorce, separations, a house-fire, displacement, emotional crises, confusion and indecision, loneliness, difficult confrontations with individuals. I endeavoured to reciprocate in kind where I could. I have lived in a melded family with Turid since 1995, and our eight children, seventeen grandchildren and two great-grandchildren teach inspirational lessons in emotional wisdom, and share deep affection. They all have their own vital commitments, of course, but I try to walk alongside them emotionally when asked, without depending on them vicariously.

The extraordinary power of love, and its associated emotions, I have found so infinitely variable that it never ceases to amaze me. Divine love, as articulated by Brethren, never appealed. It was always dumped on individuals in truckloads willy-nilly: because God loved me so much – sacrificing his only Son for me – I was expected to reciprocate, which I could never envisage achieving in a truly equal manner. It made me ungrateful, caused by feelings of insignificance and emasculation. I shook my head in despair. I groaned inside. It carried no meaning at all in practical terms, any more than in emotional terms.

Much more willingly, I embraced the 1969 poem of James McAuley where he captured some of the power and scope of genuinely-shared love:

> One thing at least I understood
> Practically from the start,
> That loving must be learnt by heart
> If it's to be any good.
> It isn't in the flash of thunder,
> But in the silent power to give –
> A habit into which we live
> Ourselves, and grow to be a wonder.
> Some like me are slow to learn:
> What's plain can be mysterious still.
> Feelings alter, fade, return,
> But love stands constant in the will:
> It's not alone the touching, seeing,
> It's how to mean the other's being.

Hidden emotional treasures can be found in most searches for genuine understanding.

Aesthetics

My third group of needs I call aesthetic needs, which is broad in scope. How long is a piece of string? Several of my experiences illustrate its elongated ambit.

Aesthetic is not a comprehensive descriptor, because it must encompass my yawning ignorance at the time of my departure from subjective faith, which was a narrow personal affair, and it demands a big role for creativity, which is not obviously part of aesthetics. Hope and creativity are to be found in many of my activities, and, as with the second bundle of needs (emotional), partly it is influenced by my optimism and other aspects of my personality. Sensuousness belongs here too. Storytelling is basic to creativity in my mind, and I include it in aesthetic needs. Some people call them spiritual needs or ritual needs instead.

The most demanding example of creativity in my experience was performing before an audience in a lecture or presentation or conference, requiring agile inventiveness and maximal expressiveness. Although I must have done it hundreds of times, the resulting satisfaction never ceased. A good presentation demands thorough homework, passion for the topic, careful projection of what the audience needs to know, conveying a memorable storyline, encouraging interaction along the way, and more than tokenistic feedback about whether the audience learnt something, to make their attendance worthwhile. If ever I heard a recording of my voice, I was shocked at how nasal I sounded.

One of my pleasures at university in the 1960s was attending lunchtime lectures by all manner of experts whom I was unlikely to ever get to know in real life. I watched their deliveries closely. I never tired of borrowing little tricks. I was also critical, picking too many holes in their efforts. Each day, a yellow sheet for collection from a wooden box in the Student Union advertised the day's presentations and meetings. The box was near the cheap barber shop, and always my first port of call when I arrived on campus.

As I munched away on odourful egg sandwiches, Sir Zelman Cowen, then dean of the Law Faculty, spoke in clipped sentences about the relationship between law and race. His thinning curly hair stayed firmly in place as much as his thoughts. On the yellow foolscap sheet, Jim Cairns, member of the House of Representatives for Lalor, soon to be Australian treasurer, was a crowd-puller. His voice was very nasal. He was a strong opponent of the US war in Vietnam, having recently visited Washington, and gently expressed the hopeful (but incorrect) view that the US was realigning its war policy. Brimming with soulful zeal, Judah Waten waved his arms about a lot and claimed that Russian society survived World War II 'unscathed' and that the Jews in Israel were waging a holy war against Arabs from racist motives. He courted controversy.

In September 1967, I was enthralled by little Professor Charles Birch, a Sydney ecologist, speaking on science and religion. In my diary, I recorded that he was as 'lively as a ballet dancer' in his delivery, moving and gesturing wildly as he spoke fast. He authored or co-authored eighteen books, and eighty-five articles related to science, philosophy and religion. In mid-career in the 1940s, he gave up pure science (agricultural science, biology, population growth) to investigate the role of emotions in the development of all life in the universe. It was a bold deviation, too vast for success. I was intrigued by his description of God as a type of life force, in an anti-materialist sense, and I believed that the professor was looking at me piercingly through his thick glasses, informing me personally that the Bible was so much 'mumbo jumbo' and that the Christian God was too interventionist, and certainly no better than Buddha or Muhammed. Was I sitting on a nest of theological bull ants in that lecture theatre? He had been an evangelical Anglican when young, which he regretted, and he was sorry that evangelicalism was dominating Christian philosophy globally. He wanted science to work harder to understand consciousness and the soul, if feasible, and he certainly challenged me to think creatively about the fundamentals of Brethren.

As well as being entranced by formal presentations – which may have originated with the appeal of some good preachers whom I heard among Brethren – aesthetic needs were satisfied in fresh ways once I abandoned Brethren. I learnt to appreciate and study photography as practice and as art.

Slowly, public galleries around the world were accepting photography as a legitimate art form. Dianne Arbus – in a ground-breaking style – was memorialised at the Museum of Modern Art in New York in 1967. My own humble public exposure began in 1968 when my aesthetic antennae were tickled by a competition of the Photographic Club at the University of Melbourne. I submitted a coloured photo of an apricot sunset over Lake Burley Griffin taken from beneath the Commonwealth Bridge in Canberra, and to my surprise it won the $25 first prize.

Fully enthused, I hurried to join the Hawthorn Photographic Club in order to improve my skills. The old male members warned me against the snobbishness of the nearby Camberwell Camera Club. But rather, I was deterred by the Hawthorn lot, because they stimulated each other monotonously by discussing their favourite luscious nude models. They did not even bother to review the techniques behind the black-and-white photos that they showed me of the models, whom they had hired in the past. With little more than smut to offer, I wasted my membership fee by leaving the club after a couple of visits. For me, aesthetic sensibility meant much more than lust. I found a better photography course at Prahran Tech where I learnt a lot.

In the Picture Collection at the State Library of Victoria was a cornucopia of photos by Johannes Wilhelm Lindt, the migrant German photographer (1845–1926). Little was known of him. Late in life, he built a large studio at the side of his mansion that he called 'The Hermitage', near Narbethong, for lantern slide shows, dancing, listening to Schubert live, and society parties. I visited the derelict studio to see the wooden buildings for myself. The dense, wet forest was reclaiming them.

Lindt sold thousands of photographs – both in documentary and in the pictorial style – printed individually from glass plate negatives and published in books. He was close friends with his compatriot, the botanist Ferdinand von Mueller, founder of the Melbourne Botanical Gardens, and commissioned him to design his favoured mountain garden on Black's Spur. I researched Lindt's life sufficiently to be invited to give a lecture about him by John Cato at the newly established Photography Studies College in South Melbourne.

In a more abstract sense, I was keen to find out what artists aim for when they present their unique views of reality and in different material forms, to value the thoughtfulness, energy and skills behind successful theatre performances, to explore new forms of music that were quite unknown in my past, and to write, to write anything, to try to make a message as clear as a bell. Always behind my writing was this challenge: did my interpretation adequately describe, entertain and make sense?

Not until I abandoned barren Brethren could I appreciate the generative virtues of a fuller range of aesthetic drives.

Intellect

The fourth and final set of needs I group as intellectual needs. I am happiest when my brain is busy, observing and enquiring about why it is, analysing it as it is. Evidence of the application of my grey matter in my development has popped up in this memoir a lot. At RMIT University, my boss called me a Renaissance Man, a scholar with an interest in many fields of knowledge, because she used me to interact with other schools of thought beyond her own. But I was never comfortable with tags or labels of that sort. It is possible that my restlessness with any single stereotype may be due to my abhorrence of the past straightjacket imposed by dogma.

Working as a professional research librarian for ten years (before university teaching) provided an introductory platform to explore different ways of thinking in many disciplines, to be found in a variety of forms and sources of knowledge. Then over twenty-five years at universities, I was keen to teach and research across more than one subject area – I immersed myself in librarianship, evaluative bibliography, research methods, editing and publishing, the sociology of information technology, research ethics, modern Australian history, the history of printing and the book, community informatics, migration studies and small business, and social disadvantage and cross-cultural relations. I was never content to settle within one subject area permanently. Every topic enabled me to plunge into fresh research projects and international projects. All strands could be related to one another if required. Along the way, my output included supervision of research students, paid consultancies, numerous conference papers, and writing books and articles.

Once I discovered them, the four needs became etched on my awareness and latched onto my passions. They continue to reap untold rewards for me. In contrast, Brethren had shown as much vitality as a soggy plastic bag. The four elixirs were faithful guides. They rebalanced the mouldy mediocrity of Brethren mindsets while at the same time reminding me that every day promises a sustaining new spark.

Glancing back

Occasionally in the street, I come across Exclusive Brethren, identifiable by their lowered heads, avoidance of eye contact, black Bibles and hymn books in hand, long skirts and dresses swishing, skimpy scarves perched on the women's heads, and long hair swirling down their backs. They proceed with the synchronicity of penguins. The familiar stern faces of more than fifty years ago become rarer and rarer, having changed irrevocably or gone to heaven. For a decade after my escape, my parents continued to hear gossip from a fifth column of ex-friends whom they knew before 1962. Although they pretended to remain secretive, Exclusive Brethren could not contain themselves. I lost interest in the leaked news of their strangulating dramas and the litany of suicides and distress, which never subsided. They shocked themselves unceasingly by contributing to disaster.

Fancifully, I sometimes wondered what I might have been if I was not brought up Brethren, but of course it is impossible to hazard a guess. The forces on my personality – whatever it was in its raw state – had multiple origins. I cannot tease them apart. No one was born into the cult as a *tabula rasa* and no single influence was overwhelming on me.

On this question, I am attracted by the reflections by Primo Levi, the Italian Jew who was one of a tiny minority to survive horrific Nazi concentration camps, escaping miraculously.

> I do not and cannot know what I would be today if I had not been in the Camp… It is almost impossible to foresee the behaviour of an individual… If a man sets out towards a crossroad and does not take the left-hand path, it is obvious that he will take the one on the right, but almost never are our choices between two alternatives. Then, every choice is followed by others, all multiple, and so on, *ad infinitum*. Last of all, our future depends heavily on external

factors... One does not know his future or that of his neighbour... No one can say what his past would have been like 'if'.

I can assert with confidence that my current way of life is far more attractive than the world that I was born into. I have tried to explain why and how I abandoned old ways, by contrasting the old with the new. Although I regretted missing out on a lot when young, and (at the same time) I am a little nostalgic for the simple (if controlled) childish lifestyle that I enjoyed at home, I have made the most of my search for transformative change. Boredom and constraint dissolved. At the beginning of my liberation, I wanted to immerse myself as fast as I could in as many non-Brethren activities as possible, and some early exposure was inevitably fleeting and foolhardy. Fully unfurling my wings took patience and external warmth. But by the time that I succeeded in harvesting an admirable bundle of pleasures, with the application of the four props, as many young adults do, I rested content that my search for elsewhere had proved productive and worthwhile, and I modified the pace of my odyssey.

Today, I ask myself whether the Brethren were of any benefit to me at all? Was there any silver lining? Many defectors settled their ongoing faith elsewhere after leaving, as though complete abandonment of God was a flimsy bridge too far. Scars remained with the Canadian ex-Brother Roy Daniells, who wrote in 1979,

> Let me admit that I have never completed my escape from them. They say that, in the old days, a released galley-slave could always in a seaport town be recognised because he walked with...his legs skewed as though still in irons. It is the same with me... The Plymouth Brother who is no longer in fellowship is still haunted by thoughts of the moral polarity of the universe, the imminence of final catastrophe, the scene of the Last Judgment. He still feels he may step casually into an abyss, as one might make one casual step off the sidewalk in the path of a ten-ton truck.

I am relieved that I do not harbour any such haunting fears myself. It is hard to identify any lasting largesse from Brethren. A sense of belonging and entertainment by interesting characters could be expected from any family or community, not just from a cultish clique such as my Brethren. Religious faith did not allow any secular logic as an acceptable component of thinking. My ratiocinations were not à la mode, but they were not unique to an evaluation of Brethren ethos as such. Other faiths also dismiss them as deviant. I became practised in the arts of struggle and escape, which – in some circumstances – may be understood as reactive benefits. The same reflections on rebound may relate to my cynical attitude to so-called comprehensive philosophies or panaceas for life. The Harvard psychiatrist John Money was brought up in a Plymouth Brethren family in the 1920s in New Zealand, and cut their dogma down to size when he wrote later in a professional journal,

> The fact is that all those who hold absolutist beliefs are in many ways similar to the paranoiacs with their delusionary beliefs.

In my early days, I defined 'elsewhere' negatively as anywhere beyond Brethren boundaries, physical and emotional, but later in life it came to mean more – the accumulation of selected experiences that enabled me to function with loving companionship, happiness in mind and body, and resolve to stay beyond the bounds of dogma. To me, belonging to place seems as visceral as breathing. Australian Aborigines speak of the comfort and rewards of being 'on country'. Theirs is an integrated physical, spiritual, emotional and personal heritage which I cannot expect to share. But by avoiding negativity in the early (fluky) days of escape – where I was not comfortable, not cared for fully, not understood, not supported, not respected, that is, when I had just escaped raw out of the cult – and adding layer upon layer of multiple positive rewards since – then I am convinced that I have settled in a far better territory. Unlike my parents, I never felt exiled from a comfortable space among Brethren, nor sensed any nostalgia for Brethren ways.

Writing this memoir has taught me to value self-recognition more deeply and to appreciate the fruits of drawing broad comparisons of disassociated observations and pieces of evidence. Living through fresh struggles and coming to terms with the results, my experience built up with the help of the four foundations, bringing calm, reassurance and renewal. For me, the emotional landscape changed from the need for eternal caution and interminable trouble, to enthusiastic and satisfying discovery.

As I come to the end of my journey, shared with other free-range adults, I feel an urge to sum up key concrete early impulses that inspired my search. Plenty of reading, openness, curiosity, adventure, membership of supportive communities, loyal friends, and the desire to know – which infuse this memoir – remained with me steadily throughout my quest for happiness. When I took the initiative to challenge barriers, to scrutinise fairness, to find acceptance, to assert my identity, to respect imagination and to weigh up the consequences of non-compliance, my repertoire expanded far beyond old-fashioned gospel truths. Liberating experiences became milestones in their moment, reassuring me, and assuming significance in posterity by illuminating this narrative. I have not tried to extend my story beyond the late 1970s, with the deliberate intention of concentrating on my sombre beginnings.

As salutary new patterns emerged, my greater age brought fewer threatening surprises. In his own memoir, Barak Obama, one-time president of the USA, has written,

> The act of writing is…a chance to be inquisitive with yourself, to observe the world, confront your limits, walk in the shoes of others, and try on new ideas…
>
> The young man you meet in these pages is flawed and full of yearning, asking questions of himself and the world around him, learning as he goes. I know now, of course, that it was just the beginning for him. If you're lucky, life provides you with a good long arc.

Like Obama, I have been lucky.

www.ingramcontent.com/pod-product-compliance
Lightning Source LLC
Chambersburg PA
CBHW070054110526
44587CB00013BB/1450